OpenCV 3 Computer Vision Application Programming Cookbook

Third Edition

Recipes to help you build computer vision applications that make the most of the popular C++ library OpenCV 3

Robert Laganiere

BIRMINGHAM - MUMBAI

OpenCV 3 Computer Vision Application Programming Cookbook

Third Edition

First published: May 2011

Second edition: August 2014

Third edition: February 2017

Production reference: 1070217

Published by Packt Publishing Ltd.
Livery Place
35 Livery Street
Birmingham
B3 2PB, UK.
ISBN 978-1-78646-971-7

www.packtpub.com

Credits

About the Author

Robert Laganiere is a professor at the School of Electrical Engineering and Computer Science of the University of Ottawa, Canada. He is also a faculty member of the VIVA research lab and is the co-author of several scientific publications and patents in content-based video analysis, visual surveillance, driver-assistance, object detection, and tracking. Robert authored the OpenCV2 Computer Vision Application Programming Cookbook in 2011 and co-authored Object Oriented Software Development published by McGraw Hill in 2001. He co-founded Visual Cortek in 2006, an Ottawa-based video analytics startup that was later acquired by `http://iwatchlife.com/` in 2009. He is also a consultant in computer vision and has assumed the role of Chief Scientist in a number of startups companies such as Cognivue Corp, iWatchlife, and Tempo Analytics. Robert has a Bachelor of Electrical Engineering degree from Ecole Polytechnique in Montreal (1987) and MSc and PhD degrees from INRS-Telecommunications, Montreal (1996). Visit the author's website at `http://www.laganiere.name/`.

I wish to thank all my students at the VIVA lab; I learn so much from them.

About the Reviewer

Luca Del Tongo is a computer engineer with a strong passion for algorithms, computer vision, and image processing techniques. He's the coauthor of a free e-book called Data Structures and Algorithms (DSA) with over 100k downloads so far and has published several image processing tutorials on his YouTube channel using Emgu CV. During his master's thesis, he developed an image forensic algorithm published in a scientific paper called Copy Move forgery detection and localization by means of robust clustering with J-Linkage. Currently, Luca works as a software engineer in the ophthalmology field developing corneal topography, processing algorithms, IOL calculation, and computerized chart projector. He loves to play sport and follow MOOC courses in his spare time.

You can contact him through his blog at `http://blogs.ugidotnet.org/wetblog`.

www.PacktPub.com

For support files and downloads related to your book, please visit www.PacktPub.com.

Did you know that Packt offers eBook versions of every book published, with PDF and ePub files available? You can upgrade to the eBook version at www.PacktPub.com and as a print book customer, you are entitled to a discount on the eBook copy. Get in touch with us at service@packtpub.com for more details.

At www.PacktPub.com, you can also read a collection of free technical articles, sign up for a range of free newsletters and receive exclusive discounts and offers on Packt books and eBooks.

https://www.packtpub.com/mapt

Get the most in-demand software skills with Mapt. Mapt gives you full access to all Packt books and video courses, as well as industry-leading tools to help you plan your personal development and advance your career.

Why subscribe?

- Fully searchable across every book published by Packt
- Copy and paste, print, and bookmark content
- On demand and accessible via a web browser

Customer Feedback

Thank you for purchasing this Packt book. We take our commitment to improving our content and products to meet your needs seriously—that's why your feedback is so valuable. Whatever your feelings about your purchase, please consider leaving a review on this book's Amazon page. Not only will this help us, more importantly it will also help others in the community to make an informed decision about the resources that they invest in to learn.

You can also review for us on a regular basis by joining our reviewers' club. **If you're interested in joining, or would like to learn more about the benefits we offer, please contact us**: customerreviews@packtpub.com.

Table of Contents

Preface

Augmented reality, driving assistance, video monitoring; more and more applications are now using computer vision and image analysis technologies, and yet we are still in the infancy of the development of new computerized systems capable of understanding our worlds through the sense of vision. And with the advent of powerful and affordable computing devices and visual sensors, it has never been easier to create sophisticated imaging applications. A multitude of software tools and libraries manipulating images and videos are available, but for anyone who wishes to develop smart vision-based applications, the OpenCV library is the tool to use. OpenCV (Open source Computer Vision) is an open source library containing more than 500 optimized algorithms for image and video analysis. Since its introduction in 1999, it has been largely adopted as the primary development tool by the community of researchers and developers in computer vision. OpenCV was originally developed at Intel by a team led by Gary Bradski as an initiative to advance research in vision and promote the development of rich vision-based, CPU-intensive applications. After a series of beta releases, version 1.0 was launched in 2006. A second major release occurred in 2009 with the launch of OpenCV 2 that proposed important changes, especially the new C++ interface, which we use in this book. In 2012, OpenCV reshaped itself as a non-profit foundation (http://opencv.org/) relying on crowdfunding for its future development. OpenCV3 was introduced in 2013; changes were made mainly to improve the usability of library. Its structure has been revised to remove the unnecessary dependencies, large modules have been split into smaller ones and the API has been refined. This book is the third edition of the *OpenCV Computer Vision Application Programming Cookbook* and the first one that covers OpenCV version 3. All the programming recipes of the previous editions have been reviewed and updated. We also have added new content and new chapters to provide readers with even better coverage of the essential functionalities of the library. This book covers many of the library's features and explains how to use them to accomplish specific tasks. Our objective is not to provide detailed coverage of every option offered by the OpenCV functions and classes but rather to give you the elements you need to build your applications from the ground up. We also explore, in this book, fundamental concepts in image analysis and we describe some of the important algorithms in computer vision. This book is an opportunity for you to get introduced to the world of image and video analysis. But this is just the beginning. The good news is that OpenCV continues to evolve and expand. Just consult the OpenCV online documentation at http://opencv.org/ to stay updated about what the library can do for you. You can also visit the author's website at http://www.laganiere.name/ for updated information about this cookbook.

What this book covers

Chapter 1, *Playing with Images,* introduces the OpenCV library and shows you how to build simple applications that can read and display images. It also introduces the basic OpenCV data structures.

Chapter 2, *Manipulating Pixels,* explains how an image can be read. It describes different methods for scanning an image in order to perform an operation on each of its pixels.

Chapter 3, *Processing the Colors of an Image,* consists of recipes presenting various object-oriented design patterns that can help you to build better computer vision applications. It also discusses the concept of colors in images.

Chapter 4, *Counting the Pixels with Histograms,* shows you how to compute image histograms and how they can be used to modify an image. Different applications based on histograms are presented that achieve image segmentation, object detection, and image retrieval.

Chapter 5, *Transforming Images with Morphological Operations,* explores the concept of mathematical morphology. It presents different operators and how they can be used to detect edges, corners, and segments in images.

Chapter 6, *Filtering the Images,* teaches you the principle of frequency analysis and image filtering. It shows how low-pass and high-pass filters can be applied to images and presents the concept of derivative operators.

Chapter 7, *Extracting Lines, Contours, and Components,* focuses on the detection of geometric image features. It explains how to extract contours, lines and connected components in an image.

Chapter 8, *Detecting Interest Points,* describes various feature point detector in images.

Chapter 9, *Describing and Matching Interest Points,* explains how descriptors of interest points can be computed and used to match points between images.

Chapter 10, *Estimating Projective Relations in Images,* explores the projective relations that exist between two images in the same scene. It also describes how to detect specific targets in an image.

Chapter 11, *Reconstructing 3D scenes,* allows you to reconstruct the 3D elements of a scene from multiple images and recover the camera pose. It also includes a description of the camera calibration process.

Chapter 12, *Processing Video Sequences*, provide a framework to read and write a video sequence and to process its frames. It shows you also how it is possible to extract the foreground objects moving in front of a camera.

Chapter 13, *Tracking Visual Motion*, addresses the visual tracking problem. It shows you how to compute the apparent motion in videos. It also explains how to track moving objects in an image sequence.

Chapter 14, *Learning from Examples*, introduces basic concepts in machine learning. It shows how object classifiers can be built from image samples.

What you need for this book

This cookbook is based on the C++ API of the OpenCV library. It is therefore assumed that you have some experience with the C++ language. In order to run the examples presented in the recipes and experiment with them, you need a good C++ development environment. Microsoft Visual Studio and Qt are two popular choices.

Who this book is for

This cookbook is appropriate for novice C++ programmers who want to learn how to use the OpenCV library to build computer vision applications. It is also suitable for professional software developers who wants to be introduced to the concepts of computer vision programming. It can be used as a companion book in university-level computer vision courses. It constitutes an excellent reference for graduate students and researchers in image processing and computer vision.

Sections

In this book, you will find several headings that appear frequently (Getting ready, How to do it, How it works, There's more, and See also). To give clear instructions on how to complete a recipe, we use these sections as follows:

Getting ready

This section tells you what to expect in the recipe, and describes how to set up any software or any preliminary settings required for the recipe.

How to do it...

This section contains the steps required to follow the recipe.

How it works...

This section usually consists of a detailed explanation of what happened in the previous section.

There's more...

This section consists of additional information about the recipe in order to make the reader more knowledgeable about the recipe.

See also

This section provides helpful links to other useful information for the recipe.

Conventions

In this book, you will find a number of text styles that distinguish between different kinds of information. Here are some examples of these styles and an explanation of their meaning.

Code words in text, database table names, folder names, filenames, file extensions, pathnames, dummy URLs, user input, and Twitter handles are shown as follows: "We can include other contexts through the use of the `include` directive."

A block of code is set as follows:

```
// Compute Laplacian using LaplacianZC class
LaplacianZC laplacian;
laplacian.setAperture(7); // 7x7 laplacian
cv::Mat flap= laplacian.computeLaplacian(image);
laplace= laplacian.getLaplacianImage();
```

When we wish to draw your attention to a particular part of a code block, the relevant lines or items are set in bold:

```
// Compute Laplacian using LaplacianZC class
LaplacianZC laplacian;
laplacian.setAperture(7); // 7x7 laplacian
cv::Mat flap= laplacian.computeLaplacian(image);
laplace= laplacian.getLaplacianImage();
```

New terms and **important words** are shown in bold. Words that you see on the screen, for example, in menus or dialog boxes, appear in the text like this: "Clicking the **Next** button moves you to the next screen."

Reader feedback

Feedback from our readers is always welcome. Let us know what you think about this book-what you liked or disliked. Reader feedback is important for us as it helps us develop titles that you will really get the most out of.

To send us general feedback, simply e-mail `feedback@packtpub.com`, and mention the book's title in the subject of your message.

If there is a topic that you have expertise in and you are interested in either writing or contributing to a book, see our author guide at `www.packtpub.com/authors`.

Customer support

Now that you are the proud owner of a Packt book, we have a number of things to help you to get the most from your purchase.

Downloading the example code

You can download the example code files for this book from your account at `http://www.packtpub.com`. If you purchased this book elsewhere, you can visit `http://www.packtpub.com/support`and register to have the files e-mailed directly to you.

You can download the code files by following these steps:

1. Log in or register to our website using your e-mail address and password.
2. Hover the mouse pointer on the **SUPPORT** tab at the top.
3. Click on **Code Downloads & Errata**.
4. Enter the name of the book in the **Search** box.
5. Select the book for which you're looking to download the code files.
6. Choose from the drop-down menu where you purchased this book from.
7. Click on **Code Download**.

You can also download the code files by clicking on the **Code Files** button on the book's webpage at the Packt Publishing website. This page can be accessed by entering the book's name in the **Search** box. Please note that you need to be logged in to your Packt account.

Once the file is downloaded, please make sure that you unzip or extract the folder using the latest version of:

- WinRAR / 7-Zip for Windows
- Zipeg / iZip / UnRarX for Mac
- 7-Zip / PeaZip for Linux

The code bundle for the book is also hosted on GitHub at `https://github.com/PacktPublishing/OpenCV3-Computer-Vision-Application-Programming-Cookbook-Third-Edition`. We also have other code bundles from our rich catalog of books and videos available at `https://github.com/PacktPublishing/`. Check them out!

The source code files of the examples presented in this cookbook are also hosted in the author's Github repository. You can visit the author's repository at `https://github.com/laganiere` to obtain the latest version of the code.

Downloading the color images of this book

We also provide you with a PDF file that has color images of the screenshots/diagrams used in this book. The color images will help you better understand the changes in the output. You can download this file from `https://www.packtpub.com/sites/default/files/downloads/OpenCV3ComputerVisionApplicationProgrammingCookbookThirdEdition_ColorImages.pdf`.

Errata

Although we have taken every care to ensure the accuracy of our content, mistakes do happen. If you find a mistake in one of our books-maybe a mistake in the text or the code-we would be grateful if you could report this to us. By doing so, you can save other readers from frustration and help us improve subsequent versions of this book. If you find any errata, please report them by visiting `http://www.packtpub.com/submit-errata`, selecting your book, clicking on the **Errata Submission Form** link, and entering the details of your errata. Once your errata are verified, your submission will be accepted and the errata will be uploaded to our website or added to any list of existing errata under the Errata section of that title.

To view the previously submitted errata, go to `https://www.packtpub.com/books/conten` `t/support`and enter the name of the book in the search field. The required information will appear under the **Errata** section.

Piracy

Piracy of copyrighted material on the Internet is an ongoing problem across all media. At Packt, we take the protection of our copyright and licenses very seriously. If you come across any illegal copies of our works in any form on the Internet, please provide us with the location address or website name immediately so that we can pursue a remedy.

Please contact us at `copyright@packtpub.com` with a link to the suspected pirated material.

We appreciate your help in protecting our authors and our ability to bring you valuable content.

Questions

If you have a problem with any aspect of this book, you can contact us at `questions@packtpub.com`, and we will do our best to address the problem.

1

Playing with Images

In this chapter, we will get you started with the **OpenCV** library. You will learn how to perform the following tasks:

- Installing the OpenCV library
- Loading, displaying, and saving images
- Exploring the `cv::Mat` data structure
- Defining regions of interest

Introduction

This chapter will teach you the basic elements of OpenCV and will show you how to accomplish the most fundamental image processing tasks: reading, displaying, and saving images. However, before you start with OpenCV, you need to install the library. This is a simple process that is explained in the first recipe of this chapter.

All your computer vision applications will involve the processing of images. This is why OpenCV offers you a data structure to handle images and matrices. It is a powerful data structure with many useful attributes and methods. It also incorporates an advanced memory management model that greatly facilitates the development of applications. The last two recipes of this chapter will teach you how to use this important data structure of OpenCV.

Installing the OpenCV library

OpenCV is an open source library for developing computer vision applications that can run on multiple platforms, such as Windows, Linux, Mac, Android, and iOS. It can be used in both academic and commercial applications under a BSD license that allows you to freely use, distribute, and adapt it. This recipe will show you how to install the library on your machine.

Getting ready

When you visit the OpenCV official website at `http://opencv.org/`, you will find the latest release of the library, the online documentation describing the **Application Programming Interface** (**API**), and many other useful resources on OpenCV.

How to do it...

From the OpenCV website, find the latest available downloads and select the one that corresponds to the platform of your choice (Windows, Linux/Mac, or iOS). Once the OpenCV package is downloaded, run the WinZip self-extractor and select the location of your choice. An `opencv` directory will be created; it is a good idea to rename it in a way that will show which version you are using (for example, in Windows, your final directory could be `C:\opencv-3.2`). This directory will contain a collection of files and directories that constitute the library. Notably, you will find the `sources` directory that will contain all the source files (yes, it is open source!).

In order to complete the installation of the library and have it ready for use, you need to take an important step: generate the binary files of the library for the environment of your choice. This is indeed the point where you have to make a decision on the target platform you wish to use to create your OpenCV applications. Which operating system do you prefer to use? Which compiler should you select? Which version? 32-bit or 64-bit? As you can see, there are many possible options, and this is why you have to build the library that fits your needs.

The **Integrated Development Environment** (IDE) you will use in your project development will also guide you to make these choices. Note that the library package also comes with precompiled binaries that you can directly use if they correspond to your situation (check the `build` directory adjacent to the `sources` directory). If one of the precompiled binaries satisfies your requirements, then you are ready to go.

One important remark, however. Since version 3, OpenCV has been split into two major components. The first one is the main OpenCV source repository that includes the mature algorithms. This is the one you have downloaded. A separate contribution repository also exists, and it contains the new computer vision algorithm, recently added by the OpenCV contributors. If your plan is to use only the core functions of OpenCV, you do not need the `contrib` package. But if you want to play with the latest state-of-the-art algorithms, then there is a good chance that you will need this extra module. As a matter of fact, this cookbook will show you how to use several of these advanced algorithms. You therefore need the `contrib` modules to follow the recipes of this book. So you have to go to `https://github.com/opencv/opencv_contrib` and download OpenCV's extra modules (download the ZIP file). You can unzip the extra modules into the directory of your choice; these modules should be found at `opencv_contrib-master/modules`. For simplicity, you can rename this directory as `contrib` and copy it directly inside the `sources` directory of the main package. Note that you can also pick the extra modules of your choice and only save them; however, you will probably find it easier, at this point, to simply keep everything.

You are now ready to proceed with the installation. To build the OpenCV binaries, it is highly suggested that you use the **CMake** tool, available at `http://cmake.org`. CMake is another open source software tool designed to control the compilation process of a software system using platform-independent configuration files. It generates the required `makefile` or `solution` files needed for compiling a software library in your environment. Therefore, you have to download and install CMake. Also see the *There's more...* section of this recipe for an additional software package, the **Visualization Toolkit** (**VTK**), that you may want to install before compiling the library.

You can run `cmake` using a command-line interface, but it is easier to use `CMake` with its graphical interface (**cmake-gui**). In the latter case, all you need to do is specify the folder containing the OpenCV library source and the one that will contain the binaries. Now click on **Configure** and select the compiler of your choice:

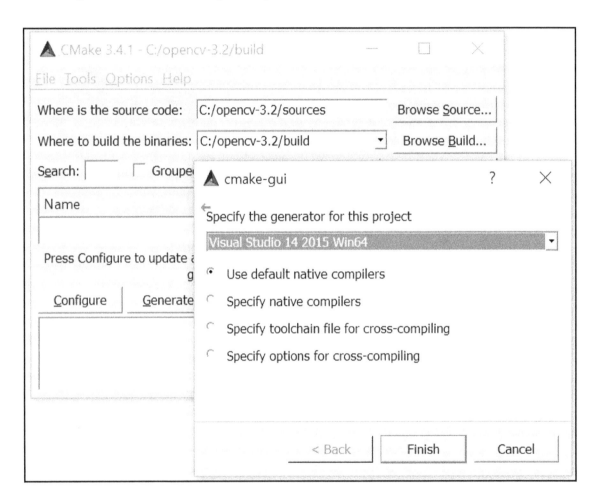

Once this initial configuration is completed, CMake will provide you with a number of configuration options. You have to decide, for example, whether you want to have the documentation installed or whether you wish to have some additional libraries installed. Unless you know what you are doing, it is probably better to leave the default options as they are. However, since we want to include the extra modules, we have to specify the directory where they can be found:

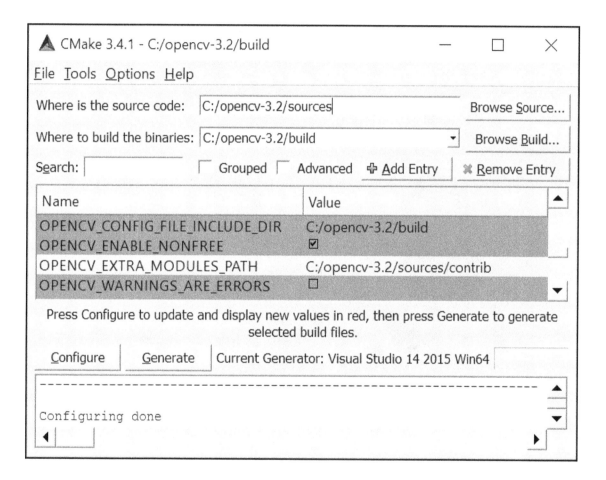

Once the extra module path is specified, click on **Configure** again. You are now ready to generate the project files by clicking on the **Generate** button. These files will allow you to compile the library. This is the last step of the installation process, which will make the library ready to be used in your development environment. For example, if you select MS Visual Studio, then all you need to do is open the top-level solution file that CMake has created for you (the `OpenCV.sln` file). You then select the **INSTALL** project (under **CMakeTargets**) and issue the **Build** command (use right-click).

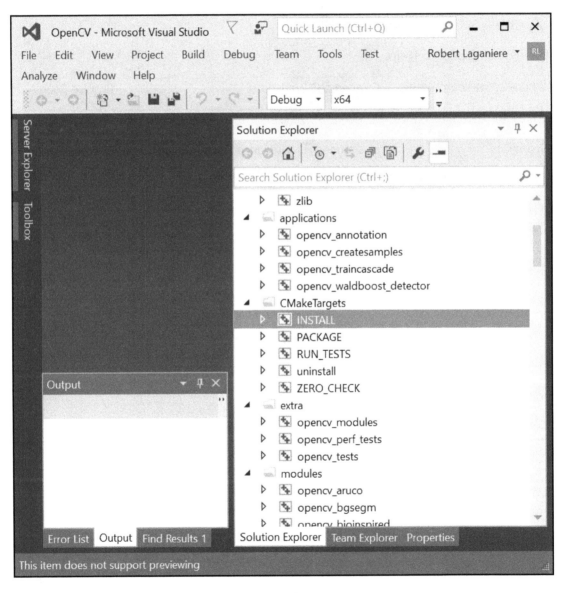

To get both a **Release** and **Debug** build, you will have to repeat the compilation process twice, one for each configuration. If everything goes well, you will have an `install` directory (under `build`) created. This directory will contain all the `binary` files of the OpenCV library to be linked with your application as well as the dynamic library files that your executables have to call at runtime. Make sure you set your system's `PATH` environment variable (from **Control Panel**) such that your operating system would be able to find the `.dll` files when you run your applications (for example, `C:\opencv-3.2\build \install\x64\vc14\bin`). You should also define the environment variable, `OPENCV_DIR` pointing to the `INSTALL` directory. This way, CMake will be able to find the library when configuring future projects.

In Linux environments, you can use Cmake to generate the required `Makefiles`; you then complete the installation by executing a `sudo make install` command. Alternatively, you could also use the packaging tool `apt-get` which can automatically perform a complete installation of the library. For Mac OS, you should use the `Homebrew` package manager. Once installed, you just have to type `brew install opencv3 --with-contrib` in order to have the complete library installed (run `brew info opencv3` to view all possible options).

How it works...

OpenCV is a library that is in constant evolution. With version 3, the library continues to expand offering a lot of new functionalities with enhanced performances. The move to having a full C++ API, which was initiated in version 2, is now almost complete, and more uniform interfaces have been implemented. One of the major changes introduced in this new version is the restructuring of the modules of the library in order to facilitate its distribution. In particular, a separate repository containing the most recent algorithms has been created. This `contrib` repository also contains non-free algorithms that are subject to specific licenses. The idea is for OpenCV to be able to offer state-of-the-art functionalities that developers and researchers want to share while still being able to offer a very stable and well-maintained core API. The main modules are therefore the ones you get when you download the library at `http://opencv.org/`. The extra modules must be downloaded directly from the development repository hosted on GitHub (`https://github.com/opencv/`). Since these extra modules are in constant development, you should expect more frequent changes to the algorithms they contain.

The OpenCV library is divided into several modules. For example, the `opencv_core` module contains the core functionalities of the library; the `opencv_imgproc` module includes the main image processing functions; the `opencv_highgui` module offers the image and video reading and writing functions along with some user interface functions; and so on. To use a particular module, you have to include the corresponding top-level header file. For instance, most applications that use OpenCV start with the following declarations:

```
#include <opencv2/core.hpp>
#include <opencv2/imgproc.hpp>
#include <opencv2/highgui.hpp>
```

As you learn to work with OpenCV, you will discover more and more functionalities available in its numerous modules.

There's more...

The OpenCV website at `http://opencv.org/` contains detailed instructions on how to install the library. It also contains complete online documentation that includes several tutorials on the different components of the library.

The Visualization Toolkit and the cv::viz module

In some applications, computer vision is used to reconstruct the 3D information of a scene from images. When working with 3D data, it is often useful to be able to visualize the results in some 3D virtual world. As you will learn in `Chapter 11`, *Reconstructing 3D Scenes*, the `cv::viz` module offers many useful functions that allow you to visualize scene objects and cameras in 3D. However, this module is built on top of another open source library: VTK. Therefore, if you want to use the `cv::viz` module, you need to install VTK on your machine before compiling OpenCV.

VTK is available at `http://www.vtk.org/`. All you have to do is download the library and use CMake in order to create the binaries for your development environment. In this book, we used version 6.3.0. In addition, you should define the `VTK_DIR` environment variable, pointing to the directory containing the built files. Also, in the configuration options proposed during the OpenCV installation process with CMake, make sure that the `WITH_VTK` option is checked.

The OpenCV developer site

OpenCV is an open source project that welcomes user contributions. The library is hosted on GitHub, a web service that offers version control and source code management tools based on Git. You can access the developer site at `https://github.com/opencv/opencv/wiki`. Among other things, you can access the currently developed version of OpenCV. The community uses Git as their version control system. Git is also a free open source software system; it is probably the best tool you can use to manage your own source code.

> Downloading the example source code of this book:
> The source code files of the examples presented in this cookbook are also hosted on GitHub. Please visit the author's repository at `https://github.com/laganiere` to obtain the latest version of the code. Note that you can download the example code files for all the Packt books you have purchased from your account at `http://www.packtpub.com`. If you have purchased this book elsewhere, you can visit `http://www.packtpub.com/support` and register yourselves there to have the files e-mailed directly to you.

See also

- The author's website (`http://www.laganiere.name/`) also presents step-by-step instructions on how to install the latest versions of the OpenCV library
- Visit `https://git-scm.com/` and `https://github.com/` to learn more about source code management.

Loading, displaying, and saving images

It is now time to run your first OpenCV application. Since OpenCV is about processing images, this task will show you how to perform the most fundamental operations needed in the development of imaging applications. These are loading an input image from a file, displaying an image on a window, applying a processing function, and saving the output image.

Getting ready

Using your favorite IDE (for example, MS Visual Studio or Qt), create a new console application with a `main` function that is ready to be filled.

How to do it...

The first thing to do is to include the header files, declaring the classes and functions you wish to use. Here, we simply want to display an image, so we need the `core` header that declares the image data structure and the `highgui` header file that contains all the graphical interface functions:

```
#include <opencv2/core.hpp>
#include <opencv2/highgui.hpp>
```

Our main function starts by declaring a variable that will hold the image. Under OpenCV, this is done by defining an object of the `cv::Mat` class:

```
cv::Mat image; // create an empty image
```

This definition creates an image of size 0x0. This can be confirmed by accessing the `cv::Mat` size attributes:

```
std::cout << "This image is " << image.rows << " x "
          << image.cols << std::endl;
```

Next, a simple call to the reading function will read an image from a file, decode it, and allocate the memory:

```
image= cv::imread("puppy.bmp"); // read an input image
```

You are now ready to use this image. However, you should first check whether the image has been correctly read (an error will occur if the file is not found, is corrupted, or is not in a recognizable format). The validity of the image is tested using the following code:

```
if (image.empty()) {  // error handling
  // no image has been created...
  // possibly display an error message
  // and quit the application
  ...
}
```

The `empty` method returns `true` if no image data has been allocated.

The first thing you might want to do with this image is display it. You can do this using the functions of the `highgui` module. Start by declaring the window on which you want to display the images, then specify the image to be shown on this special window:

```
// define the window (optional)
cv::namedWindow("Original Image");
// show the image
cv::imshow("Original Image", image);
```

As you can see, the window is identified by a name. You can reuse this window to display another image later, or you can create multiple windows with different names. When you run this application, you will see an image window, as follows:

Now, you would normally apply some processing to the image. OpenCV offers a wide selection of processing functions, and several of them are explored in this book. Let's start with a very simple one that flips an image horizontally. Several image transformations in OpenCV can be performed in-place, meaning the transformation is applied directly on the input image (no new image is created). This is the case for the flipping method. However, we can always create another matrix to hold the output result, and this is what we will do:

```
cv::Mat result; // we create another empty image
cv::flip(image,result,1); // positive for horizontal
                          // 0 for vertical,
                          // negative for both
```

The result is displayed on another window:

```
cv::namedWindow("Output Image");    // the output window
cv::imshow("Output Image", result);
```

Since it is a console window that will terminate when it reaches the end of the `main` function, we add an extra `highgui` function to wait for a user key before we end the program:

```
cv::waitKey(0); // 0 to indefinitely wait for a key pressed
               // specifying a positive value will wait for
               // the given amount of msec
```

You can then see that the output image is displayed in a distinct window, as shown in the following screenshot:

Finally, you will probably want to save the processed image on your disk. This is done using the following `highgui` function:

```
cv::imwrite("output.bmp", result); // save result
```

The file extension determines which codec will be used to save the image. Other popular supported image formats are JPG, TIFF, and PNG.

How it works...

All classes and functions in the C++ API of OpenCV are defined within the `cv` namespace. You have two ways to access them. First, precede the `main` function's definition with the following declaration:

```
using namespace cv;
```

Alternatively, prefix all OpenCV class and function names with the namespace specification, that is, `cv::`, as we will do in this book. The use of this prefix makes the OpenCV classes and functions easier to identify within your code.

The `highgui` module contains a set of functions that allow you to easily visualize and interact with your images. When you load an image with the `imread` function, you also have the option to read it as a gray-level image. This is very advantageous since several computer vision algorithms require gray-level images. Converting an input color image on the fly as you read it will save you time and minimize your memory usage. This can be done as follows:

```
// read the input image as a gray-scale image
image=  cv::imread("puppy.bmp", cv::IMREAD_GRAYSCALE);
```

This will produce an image made of unsigned bytes (`unsigned char` in C++) that OpenCV designates with the constant `CV_8U`. Alternatively, it is sometimes necessary to read an image as a three-channel color image even if it has been saved as a gray-level image. This can be achieved by calling the `imread` function with a positive second argument:

```
// read the input image as a 3-channel color image
image=  cv::imread("puppy.bmp", cv::IMREAD_COLOR);
```

This time, an image made of 3 bytes per pixel will be created and designated as `CV_8UC3` in OpenCV. Of course, if your input image has been saved as a gray-level image, all three channels will contain the same value. Finally, if you wish to read the image in the format in which it has been saved, then simply input a negative value as the second argument. The number of channels in an image can be checked using the `channels` method:

```
std::cout << "This image has "
          << image.channels() << " channel(s)";
```

Pay attention when you open an image with `imread` without specifying a full path (as we did here). In such a case, the default directory will be used. When you run your application from the console, this directory is obviously the current console's directory. However, if you run the application directly from your IDE, the default directory will most often be the one that contains your project file. Consequently, make sure that your input image file is located in the right directory.

When you use `imshow` to display an image made up of integers (designated as `CV_16U` for 16-bit unsigned integers or as `CV_32S` for 32-bit signed integers), the pixel values of this image will be divided by `256` first. This is done in an attempt to make it displayable with `256` gray shades. Similarly, an image made up of floating points will be displayed by assuming a range of possible values between `0.0` (displayed as black) and `1.0` (displayed as white). Values outside this defined range are displayed in white (for values above `1.0`) or black (for values below `0.0`).

The `highgui` module is very useful to build quick prototypal applications. When you are ready to produce a finalized version of your application, you will probably want to use the GUI module offered by your IDE in order to build an application with a more professional look.

Here, our application uses both input and output images. As an exercise, you should rewrite this simple program such that it takes advantage of the function's in-place processing, that is, by not declaring the output image and writing it instead:

```
cv::flip(image,image,1); // in-place processing
```

There's more...

The `highgui` module contains a rich set of functions that help you interact with your images. Using these, your applications can react to mouse or key events. You can also draw shapes and write text on images.

Clicking on images

You can program your mouse to perform specific operations when it is over one of the image windows you created. This is done by defining an appropriate **callback** function. A callback function is a function that you do not explicitly call but which is called by your application in response to specific events (here, the events that concern the mouse interacting with an image window). To be recognized by applications, callback functions need to have a specific signature and must be registered. In the case of a mouse event handler, the callback function must have the following signature:

```
void onMouse( int event, int x, int y, int flags, void* param);
```

The first parameter is an integer that is used to specify which type of mouse event has triggered the call to the callback function. The other two parameters are simply the pixel coordinates of the mouse location when the event has occurred. The flags are used to determine which button was pressed when the mouse event was triggered. Finally, the last parameter is used to send an extra parameter to the function in the form of a pointer to any object. This callback function can be registered in the application through the following call:

```
cv::setMouseCallback("Original Image", onMouse,
                     reinterpret_cast<void*>(&image));
```

In this example, the `onMouse` function is associated with the image window called **Original Image**, and the address of the displayed image is passed as an extra parameter to the function. Now, if we define the `onMouse` callback function as shown in the following code, then each time the mouse is clicked, the value of the corresponding pixel will be displayed on the console (here, we assume that it is a gray-level image):

```
void onMouse( int event, int x, int y, int flags, void* param)  {

  cv::Mat *im= reinterpret_cast<cv::Mat*>(param);

  switch (event) {  // dispatch the event

    case cv::EVENT_LBUTTONDOWN: // left mouse button down event

      // display pixel value at (x,y)
      std::cout << "at (" << x << "," << y << ") value is: "
              << static_cast<int>(
                      im->at<uchar>(cv::Point(x,y))) << std::endl;
      break;
  }
}
```

Note that in order to obtain the pixel value at (x, y), we used the at method of the cv::Mat object; this is discussed in Chapter 2, *Manipulating Pixels*. Other possible events that can be received by the mouse event callback function include cv::EVENT_MOUSEMOVE, cv::EVENT_LBUTTONUP, cv::EVENT_RBUTTONDOWN, and cv::EVENT_RBUTTONUP.

Drawing on images

OpenCV also offers a few functions to draw shapes and write text on images. The examples of basic shape-drawing functions are circle, ellipse, line, and rectangle. The following is an example of how to use the circle function:

```
cv::circle(image,                      // destination image
          cv::Point(155,110),          // center coordinate
          65,                          // radius
          0,                           // color (here black)
          3);                          // thickness
```

The cv::Point structure is often used in OpenCV methods and functions to specify a pixel coordinate. Note that here we assume that the drawing is done on a gray-level image; this is why the color is specified with a single integer. In the next recipe, you will learn how to specify a color value in the case of color images that use the cv::Scalar structure. It is also possible to write text on an image. This can be done as follows:

```
cv::putText(image,                     // destination image
          "This is a dog.",            // text
          cv::Point(40,200),           // text position
          cv::FONT_HERSHEY_PLAIN,      // font type
          2.0,                         // font scale
          255,                         // text color (here white)
          2);                          // text thickness
```

Calling these two functions on our test image will then result in the following screenshot:

Note that you have to include the top-level module header `opencv2/imgproc.hpp` for these examples to work.

See also

- The `cv::Mat` class is the data structure that is used to hold your images (and obviously, other matrix data). This data structure is at the core of all OpenCV classes and functions; the next recipe offers a detailed explanation of this data structure.

Exploring the cv::Mat data structure

In the previous recipe, you were introduced to the `cv::Mat` data structure. As mentioned, this is a key component of the library. It is used to manipulate images and matrices (in fact, an image is a matrix from a computational and mathematical point of view). Since you will be using this data structure extensively in your application development processes, it is imperative that you become familiar with it. Notably, in this recipe, you will learn that this data structure incorporates an elegant memory management mechanism.

How to do it...

Let's write the following test program that will allow us to test the different properties of the `cv::Mat` data structure:

```cpp
#include <iostream>
#include <opencv2/core.hpp>
#include <opencv2/highgui.hpp>

// test function that creates an image
cv::Mat function() {
   // create image
   cv::Mat ima(500,500,CV_8U,50);
   // return it
   return ima;
}

int main() {
   // create a new image made of 240 rows and 320 columns
   cv::Mat image1(240,320,CV_8U,100);
   cv::imshow("Image", image1); // show the image
   cv::waitKey(0); // wait for a key pressed

   // re-allocate a new image
   image1.create(200,200,CV_8U);
   image1= 200;

   cv::imshow("Image", image1); // show the image
   cv::waitKey(0); // wait for a key pressed

   // create a red color image
   // channel order is BGR
   cv::Mat image2(240,320,CV_8UC3,cv::Scalar(0,0,255));

   // or:
   // cv::Mat image2(cv::Size(320,240),CV_8UC3);
   // image2= cv::Scalar(0,0,255);

   cv::imshow("Image", image2); // show the image
   cv::waitKey(0); // wait for a key pressed

   // read an image
   cv::Mat image3=  cv::imread("puppy.bmp");

   // all these images point to the same data block
   cv::Mat image4(image3);
   image1= image3;
```

```
// these images are new copies of the source image
image3.copyTo(image2);
cv::Mat image5= image3.clone();

// transform the image for testing
cv::flip(image3,image3,1);

// check which images have been affected by the processing
cv::imshow("Image 3", image3);
cv::imshow("Image 1", image1);
cv::imshow("Image 2", image2);
cv::imshow("Image 4", image4);
cv::imshow("Image 5", image5);
cv::waitKey(0); // wait for a key pressed

// get a gray-level image from a function
cv::Mat gray= function();

cv::imshow("Image", gray); // show the image
cv::waitKey(0); // wait for a key pressed

// read the image in gray scale
image1= cv::imread("puppy.bmp", CV_LOAD_IMAGE_GRAYSCALE);
image1.convertTo(image2,CV_32F,1/255.0,0.0);

cv::imshow("Image", image2); // show the image
cv::waitKey(0); // wait for a key pressed

return 0;
}
```

Run this program and take a look at the images it produces:

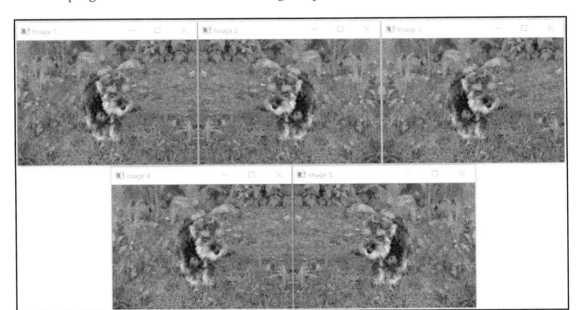

How it works...

The cv::Mat data structure is essentially made up of two parts: a header and a data block. The header contains all of the information associated with the matrix (size, number of channels, data type, and so on). The previous recipe showed you how to access some of the attributes of this structure contained in its header (for example, by using cols, rows, or channels). The data block holds all the pixel values of an image. The header contains a pointer variable that points to this data block; it is the data attribute. An important property of the cv::Mat data structure is the fact that the memory block is only copied when explicitly requested for. Indeed, most operations will simply copy the cv::Mat header such that multiple objects will point to the same data block. This memory management model makes your applications more efficient while avoiding memory leaks, but its consequences need to be understood. The examples of this recipe illustrate this fact.

By default, the cv::Mat objects have a zero size when they are created, but you can also specify an initial size as follows:

```
// create a new image made of 240 rows and 320 columns
cv::Mat image1(240,320,CV_8U,100);
```

In this case, you also need to specify the type of each matrix element-CV_8U here, which corresponds to 1-byte pixel (grayscale) images. The U letter here means it is unsigned. You can also declare signed numbers using S. For a color image, you would specify three channels (CV_8UC3). You can also declare integers (signed or unsigned) of size 16 and 32 (for example, CV_16SC3). You also have access to 32-bit and 64-bit floating-point numbers (for example, CV_32F).

Each element of an image (or a matrix) can be composed of more than one value (for example, the three channels of a color image); therefore, OpenCV has introduced a simple data structure that is used when pixel values are passed to functions. This is the cv::Scalar structure, which is generally used to hold one or three values. For example, to create a color image initialized with red pixels, write the following code:

```
// create a red color image
// channel order is BGR
cv::Mat image2(240,320,CV_8UC3,cv::Scalar(0,0,255));
```

Similarly, the initialization of the gray-level image could have also been done using this structure by writing cv::Scalar(100).

The image size often needs to be passed to functions as well. We have already mentioned that the cols and rows attributes can be used to get the dimensions of a cv::Mat instance. The size information can also be provided through the cv::Size structure that simply contains the height and width of the matrix. The size() method allows you to obtain the current matrix size. This is the format that is used in many methods where a matrix size must be specified.

For example, an image could be created as follows:

```
// create a non-initialized color image
cv::Mat image2(cv::Size(320,240),CV_8UC3);
```

The data block of an image can always be allocated or reallocated using the create method. When an image has already been previously allocated, its old content is deallocated first. For reasons of efficiency, if the new proposed size and type matches the already existing size and type, then no new memory allocation is performed:

```
// re-allocate a new image
// (only if size or type are different)
image1.create(200,200,CV_8U);
```

When no more references point to a given `cv::Mat` object, the allocated memory is automatically released. This is very convenient because it avoids the common memory leak problems often associated with dynamic memory allocation in C++. This is a key mechanism in OpenCV (introduced in version 2) that is accomplished by having the `cv::Mat` class implement reference counting and shallow copy. Therefore, when an image is assigned to another one, the image data (that is, the pixels) is not copied; both images will point to the same memory block. This also applies to images either passed or returned by a value. A reference count is kept such that the memory will be released only when all the references to the image are destructed or assigned to another image:

```
// all these images point to the same data block
cv::Mat image4(image3);
image1= image3;
```

Any transformation applied to one of the preceding images will also affect the other images. If you wish to create a deep copy of the content of an image, use the `copyTo` method. In this case, the `create` method is called on the destination image. Another method that produces a copy of an image is the `clone` method, which creates a new identical image as follows:

```
// these images are new copies of the source image
image3.copyTo(image2);
cv::Mat image5= image3.clone();
```

In the example of this recipe, we applied a transformation to `image3`. The other images also contain this image; some of them share the same image data, while others hold a copy of this image. Check the displayed images and find out which ones were affected by the `image3` transformation.

If you need to copy an image into another image that does not necessarily have the same data type, use the `convertTo` method:

```
// convert the image into a floating point image [0,1]
image1.convertTo(image2,CV_32F,1/255.0,0.0);
```

In this example, the source image is copied into a floating-point image. The method includes two optional parameters: a scaling factor and an offset. Note that both the images must, however, have the same number of channels.

The allocation model for the `cv::Mat` objects also allows you to safely write functions (or class methods) that return an image:

```
cv::Mat function() {

    // create image
    cv::Mat ima(240,320,CV_8U,cv::Scalar(100));
    // return it
    return ima;
}
```

We can also call this function from our `main` function as follows:

```
// get a gray-level image
cv::Mat gray= function();
```

If we do this, the `gray` variable will then hold the image created by the function without extra memory allocation. Indeed, as we explained, only a shallow copy of the image will be transferred from the returned `cv::Mat` instance to the gray image. When the `ima` local variable goes out of scope, this variable is deallocated. However, since the associated reference counter indicates that its internal image data is being referred to by another instance (that is, the `gray` variable), its memory block is not released.

It's worth noting that in the case of classes, you should be careful and not return image class attributes. Here is an example of an error-prone implementation:

```
class Test {
  // image attribute
  cv::Mat ima;
  public:
    // constructor creating a gray-level image
    Test() : ima(240,320,CV_8U,cv::Scalar(100)) {}

    // method return a class attribute, not a good idea...
    cv::Mat method() { return ima; }
};
```

Here, if a function calls the method of this class, it obtains a shallow copy of the image attributes. If this copy is modified later, the `class` attribute will also be surreptitiously modified, which can affect the subsequent behavior of the class (and vice versa). This is a violation of the important principle of encapsulation in object-oriented programming. To avoid these kinds of errors, you should instead return a clone of the attribute.

There's more...

When you are manipulating the `cv::Mat` class, you will discover that OpenCV also includes several other related classes. It will be important for you to become familiar with them.

The input and output arrays

If you look at the OpenCV documentation, you will see that many methods and functions accept parameters of the `cv::InputArray` type as an input. This type is a simple proxy class introduced to generalize the concept of arrays in OpenCV and thus avoid the duplication of several versions of the same method or function with different input parameter types. It basically means that you can supply either a `cv::Mat` object or other compatible types as an argument. Since it is declared as an input array, you have the guarantee that your data structure will not be modified by the function. It is interesting to know that `cv::InputArray` can also be constructed from the popular `std::vector` class. This means that such objects can be used as input parameters to OpenCV methods and functions (however, never use this class inside your classes and functions). Other compatible types are `cv::Scalar` and `cv::Vec`; the latter structure will be presented in the next chapter. There is also a `cv::OutputArray` proxy class that is used to designate parameters that correspond to an image that is returned by a function or method.

Manipulating small matrices

When writing your applications, you might have to manipulate small matrices. You can then use the `cv::Matx` template class and its subclasses. For example, the following code declares a 3x3 matrix of double-precision floating-point numbers and a 3-element vector. These two are then multiplied together:

```
// a 3x3 matrix of double
cv::Matx33d matrix(3.0, 2.0, 1.0,
                   2.0, 1.0, 3.0,
                   1.0, 2.0, 3.0);
// a 3x1 matrix (a vector)
cv::Matx31d vector(5.0, 1.0, 3.0);
// multiplication
cv::Matx31d result = matrix*vector;
```

As you can see, the usual math operators can be applied to these matrices.

See also

- The complete OpenCV documentation can be found at
  `http://docs.opencv.org/`
- `Chapter 2`, *Manipulating Pixels*, will show you how to efficiently access and modify the pixel values of an image represented by the `cv::Mat` class
- The next recipe, *Defining regions of interest* , will explain how to define a region of interest inside an image

Defining regions of interest

Sometimes, a processing function needs to be applied only to a portion of an image. OpenCV incorporates an elegant and simple mechanism to define a subregion in an image and manipulate it as a regular image. This recipe will teach you how to define a region of interest inside an image.

Getting ready

Suppose we want to copy a small image onto a larger one. For example, let's say we want to insert the following logo into our test image:

To do this, a **Region Of Interest** (**ROI**) can be defined over which the copy operation can be applied. As we will see, the position of the ROI will determine where the logo will be inserted in the image.

How to do it...

The first step consists of defining the ROI. Once defined, the ROI can be manipulated as a regular cv::Mat instance. The key is that the ROI is indeed a cv::Mat object that points to the same data buffer as its parent image and has a header that specifies the coordinates of the ROI. Inserting the logo is then accomplished as follows:

```
// define image ROI at image bottom-right
cv::Mat imageROI(image,
         cv::Rect(image.cols-logo.cols,     // ROI coordinates
                  image.rows-logo.rows,
                  logo.cols,logo.rows));     // ROI size

// insert logo
logo.copyTo(imageROI);
```

Here, image is the destination image and logo is the logo image (of a smaller size). The following image is then obtained by executing the previous code:

How it works...

One way to define an ROI is to use a `cv::Rect` instance. As the name indicates, it describes a rectangular region by specifying the position of the upper-left corner (the first two parameters of the constructor) and the size of the rectangle (the width and height are given in the last two parameters). In our example, we used the size of the image and the size of the logo in order to determine the position where the logo would cover the bottom-right corner of the image. Obviously, the ROI should always be completely inside the parent image.

The ROI can also be described using row and column ranges. A range is a continuous sequence from a start index to an end index (excluding both). The `cv::Range` structure is used to represent this concept. Therefore, an ROI can be defined from two ranges; in our example, the ROI could have been equivalently defined as follows:

```
imageROI= image(cv::Range(image.rows-logo.rows,image.rows),
                cv::Range(image.cols-logo.cols,image.cols));
```

In this case, the `operator()` function of `cv::Mat` returns another `cv::Mat` instance that can then be used in subsequent calls. Any transformation of the ROI will affect the original image in the corresponding area because the image and the ROI share the same image data. Since the definition of an ROI does not include the copying of data, it is executed in a constant amount of time, no matter the size of the ROI.

If you want to define an ROI made up of some lines of an image, the following call can be used:

```
cv::Mat imageROI= image.rowRange(start,end);
```

Similarly, for an ROI made up of some image columns, the following can be used:

```
cv::Mat imageROI= image.colRange(start,end);
```

There's more...

The OpenCV methods and functions include many optional parameters that are not discussed in the recipes of this book. When you wish to use a function for the first time, you should always take the time to look at the documentation to learn more about the possible options that the function offers. One very common option is the possibility to define image masks.

Using image masks

Some OpenCV operations allow you to define a mask that will limit the applicability of a given function or method, which is normally supposed to operate on all the image pixels. A mask is an 8-bit image that should be nonzero at all locations where you want an operation to be applied. At the pixel locations that correspond to the zero values of the mask, the image is untouched. For example, the copyTo method can be called with a mask. We can use it here to copy only the white portion of the logo shown previously, as follows:

```
// define image ROI at image bottom-right
imageROI= image(cv::Rect(image.cols-logo.cols,
                         image.rows-logo.rows,
                         logo.cols,logo.rows));
// use the logo as a mask (must be gray-level)
cv::Mat mask(logo);

// insert by copying only at locations of non-zero mask
logo.copyTo(imageROI,mask);
```

The following image is obtained by executing the previous code:

The background of our logo was black (therefore, it had the value 0); this is why it was easy to use it as both the copied image and the mask. Of course, you can define the mask of your choice in your application; most OpenCV pixel-based operations give you the opportunity to use masks.

See also

- The `row` and `col` methods will be used in the *Scanning an image with neighbor access* recipe of `Chapter 2`, *Manipulating Pixels*. These are a special case of the `rowRange` and `colRange` methods in which the start and end indexes are equal in order to define a single-line or single-column ROI.

2
Manipulating Pixels

In this chapter, we will cover the following recipes:

- Accessing pixel values
- Scanning an image with pointers
- Scanning an image with iterators
- Writing efficient image-scanning loops
- Scanning an image with neighbor access
- Performing simple image arithmetic
- Remapping an image

Introduction

In order to build computer vision applications, you need to be able to access the image content and eventually modify or create images. This chapter will teach you how to manipulate the picture elements (also known as **pixels**). You will learn how to scan an image and process each of its pixels. You will also learn how to do this efficiently, since even images of modest dimensions can contain hundreds of thousands of pixels.

Fundamentally, an image is a matrix of numerical values. This is why, as we learned in Chapter 1, *Playing with Images*, OpenCV manipulates them using the `cv::Mat` data structure. Each element of the matrix represents one pixel. For a gray-level image (a black-and-white image), pixels are unsigned 8-bit values (that is, of type `unsigned char`) where 0 corresponds to black and 255 corresponds to white.

In the case of color images, three primary color values are required in order to reproduce the different visible colors. This is a consequence of the fact that our human visual system is trichromatic; three types of cone cells on our retinae convey the color information to our brain. This means that for a color image, three values must be associated to each pixel. In photography and digital imaging, the commonly used primary color channels are red, green, and blue. A matrix element is, therefore, made of a triplet of 8-bit values in this case. Note that even if 8-bit channels are generally sufficient, there are specialized applications where 16-bit channels are required (medical imaging, for example).

As we saw in the previous chapter, OpenCV also allows you to create matrices (or images) with pixel values of other types, for example, integer (CV_32U or CV_32S) and floating point (CV_32F) numbers. These are very useful to store, for example, intermediate values in some image-processing tasks. Most operations can be applied on matrices of any type; others require a specific type or work only with a given number of channels. Therefore, a good understanding of a function's precondition is essential in order to avoid common programming errors.

Throughout this chapter, we use the following color image as the input (refer to the book's graphics PDF or to the book's website to view this image in color):

Accessing pixel values

In order to access each individual element of a matrix, you just need to specify its row and column numbers. The corresponding element, which can be a single numerical value or a vector of values in the case of a multi-channel image, will be returned.

Getting ready

To illustrate the direct access to pixel values, we will create a simple function that adds **salt-and-pepper** noise to an image. As the name suggests, salt-and-pepper noise is a particular type of noise in which some randomly selected pixels are replaced by a white or a black pixel. This type of noise can occur in faulty communications when the value of some pixels is lost during the transmission. In our case, we will simply randomly select a few pixels and assign them a white color.

How to do it...

We create a function that receives an input image. This is the image that will be modified by our function. The second parameter is the number of pixels on which we want to overwrite white values:

```cpp
void salt(cv::Mat image, int n) {

  // C++11 random number generator
  std::default_random_engine generator;
  std::uniform_int_distribution<int>
              randomRow(0, image.rows - 1);
  std::uniform_int_distribution<int>
              randomCol(0, image.cols - 1);

  int i,j;
  for (int k=0; k<n; k++) {

    // random image coordinate
    i= randomCol(generator);
    j= randomRow(generator);
    if (image.type() == CV_8UC1) { // gray-level image

      // single-channel 8-bit image
      image.at<uchar>(j,i)= 255;
    } else if (image.type() == CV_8UC3) { // color image

      // 3-channel image
      image.at<cv::Vec3b>(j,i)[0]= 255;
      image.at<cv::Vec3b>(j,i)[1]= 255;
      image.at<cv::Vec3b>(j,i)[2]= 255;
    }
  }
}
```

The preceding function is made of a single loop that assigns n times the value 255 to randomly selected pixels. Here, the pixel column i and row j are selected using a random number generator. Note that using the type method, we distinguish the two cases of gray-level and color images. In the case of a gray-level image, the number 255 is assigned to the single 8-bit value. For a color image, you need to assign 255 to the three primary color channels in order to obtain a white pixel.

You can call this function by passing it an image you have previously opened. Refer to the following code:

```
// open the image
cv::Mat image= cv::imread("boldt.jpg",1);
// call function to add noise
salt(image,3000);

// display result
cv::namedWindow("Image");
cv::imshow("Image",image);
```

The resulting image will look as follows:

How it works...

The cv::Mat class includes several methods to access the different attributes of an image. The public member variables, cols and rows, give you the number of columns and rows in the image. For element access, cv::Mat has the at (int y, int x) method, in which x is the column number and y is the row number. However, the type returned by a method must be known at compile time, and since cv::Mat can hold elements of any type, the programmer needs to specify the return type that is expected. This is why the at method has been implemented as a template method. So, when you call it, you must specify the image element type as follows:

```
image.at<uchar>(j,i)= 255;
```

It is important to note that it is the programmer's responsibility to make sure that the type specified matches the type contained in the matrix. The at method does not perform any type conversion.

In color images, each pixel is associated with three components: the red, green, and blue channels. Therefore, a cv::Mat class that contains a color image will return a vector of three 8-bit values. OpenCV has defined a type for such short vectors, and it is called cv::Vec3b. This is a vector of three unsigned characters. This explains why the element access to the pixels of a color pixel is written as follows:

```
image.at<cv::Vec3b>(j,i)[channel]= value;
```

The channel index designates one of the three color channels. OpenCV stores the channel values in the order blue, green, and red (blue is, therefore, channel 0). You can also use the short vector data structure directly and write:

```
image.at<cv::Vec3b>(j, i) = cv::Vec3b(255, 255, 255);
```

Similar vector types also exist for 2-element and 4-element vectors (cv::Vec2b and cv::Vec4b) as well as for other element types. For example, for a 2-element float vector, the last letter of the type name would be replaced by an f, that is, cv::Vec2f. In the case of a short integer, the last letter is replaced with s. This letter is an i for an integer, and a d for a double precision floating point vector. All of these types are defined using the cv::Vec<T,N> template class, where T is the type and N is the number of vector elements.

As a last note, you might have been surprised by the fact that our image-modifying function uses a pass-by-value image parameter. This works because when images are copied, they still share the same image data. So, you do not necessarily have to transmit images by references when you want to modify their content. Incidentally, pass-by-value parameters often make code optimization easier for the compiler.

There's more...

The cv::Mat class has been made generic by defining it using C++ templates.

The cv::Mat_ template class

Using the at method of the cv::Mat class can sometimes be cumbersome because the returned type must be specified as a template argument in each call. In cases where the matrix type is known, it is possible to use the cv::Mat_ class, which is a template subclass of cv::Mat. This class defines a few extra methods but no new data attributes so that pointers or references to one class can be directly converted to another class. Among the extra methods, there is operator(), which allows direct access to matrix elements. Therefore, if image is a cv::Mat variable that corresponds to a uchar matrix, then you can write the following code:

```
// use image with a Mat_ template
cv::Mat_<uchar> img(image);
img(50,100)= 0; // access to row 50 and column 100
```

Since the type of the cv::Mat_ elements is declared when the variable is created, the operator() method knows at compile time which type is to be returned. Other than the fact that it is shorter to write, using the operator() method provides exactly the same result as the at method.

See also

- The *There's more...* section of the *Scanning an image with pointers* recipe explains how to create a function with input and output parameters
- The *Writing efficient image-scanning loops* recipe proposes a discussion on the efficiency of the at method

Scanning an image with pointers

In most image-processing tasks, you need to scan all pixels of the image in order to perform a computation. Considering the large number of pixels that will need to be visited, it is essential that you perform this task in an efficient way. This recipe, and the next one, will show you different ways of implementing efficient scanning loops. This recipe uses the pointer arithmetic.

Getting ready

We will illustrate the image-scanning process by accomplishing a simple task: reducing the number of colors in an image.

Color images are composed of 3-channel pixels. Each of these channels corresponds to the intensity value of one of the three primary colors, red, green, and blue. Since each of these values is an 8-bit unsigned character, the total number of colors is 256x256x256, which is more than 16 million colors. Consequently, to reduce the complexity of an analysis, it is sometimes useful to reduce the number of colors in an image. One way to achieve this goal is to simply subdivide the RGB space into cubes of equal sizes. For example, if you reduce the number of colors in each dimension by 8, then you would obtain a total of 32x32x32 colors. Each color in the original image is then assigned a new color value in the color-reduced image that corresponds to the value in the center of the cube to which it belongs.

Therefore, the basic color reduction algorithm is simple. If N is the reduction factor, divide by N the value of each pixel (integer division is assumed here, therefore, the reminder is lost) then multiply the result by N. This will give you the multiple of N just below the input pixel value. Add N/2 and you obtain the central position of the interval between two adjacent multiples of N. If you repeat this process for each 8-bit channel value, then you will obtain a total of 256/N x 256/N x 256/N possible color values.

How to do it...

The signature of our color reduction function will be as follows:

```
void colorReduce(cv::Mat image, int div=64);
```

The user provides an image and the per-channel reduction factor. Here, the processing is done in-place, that is, the pixel values of the input image are modified by the function. See the *There's more...* section of this recipe for a more general function signature with input and output arguments.

The processing is simply done by creating a double loop that goes over all pixel values as follows:

```
void colorReduce(cv::Mat image, int div=64) {

    int nl= image.rows; // number of lines
    // total number of elements per line
    int nc= image.cols * image.channels();
    for (int j=0; j<nl; j++) {
```

```
    // get the address of row j
    uchar* data= image.ptr<uchar>(j);

    for (int i=0; i<nc; i++) {

      // process each pixel --------------------

      data[i]= data[i]/div*div + div/2;

      // end of pixel processing ----------------
    } // end of line
  }
}
```

This function can be tested using the following code snippet:

```
// read the image
image= cv::imread("boldt.jpg");
// process the image
colorReduce(image,64);
// display the image
cv::namedWindow("Image");
cv::imshow("Image",image);
```

This will give you, for example, the following image:

How it works...

In a color image, the first three bytes of the image data buffer are the 3 channel values of the upper-left pixel, the next three bytes are the values of the second pixel of the first row, and so on (remember that OpenCV uses, by default, the BGR channel order). An image of width W and height H would then require a memory block of WxHx3 uchars. However, for efficiency reasons, the length of a row can be padded with a few extra pixels. This is because image processing can sometimes be made more efficient when rows are multiples of 8 for example; this way they better align with the local memory configuration. Obviously, these extra pixels are not displayed or saved; their exact values are ignored. OpenCV designates the length of a padded row as the effective width. Obviously, if the image has not been padded with extra pixels, the effective width will be equal to the real image width. We have already learned that the cols and rows attributes give you the image's width and height; similarly, the step data attribute gives you the effective width in number of bytes. Even if your image is of a type other than uchar, the step data will still give you the number of bytes in a row. The size of a pixel element is given by the elemSize method (for example, for a 3-channel short integer matrix (CV_16SC3), elemSize will return 6). Recall that the number of channels in the image is given by the nchannels method (which will be 1 for a gray-level image and 3 for a color image). Finally, the total method returns the total number of pixels (that is, the matrix entries) in the matrix.

The number of pixel values per row is then given by the following code:

```
int nc= image.cols * image.channels();
```

To simplify the computation of the pointer arithmetic, the cv::Mat class offers a method that directly gives you the starting address of an image row. This is the ptr method. It is a template method that returns the address of row number j:

```
uchar* data= image.ptr<uchar>(j);
```

Note that in the processing statement, we could have equivalently used the pointer arithmetic to move from column to column. So, we could have written the following code:

```
*data++= *data/div*div + div2;
```

There's more…

The color reduction function presented in this recipe provides just one way of accomplishing this task. You could also use other color reduction formulas. A more general version of the function would also allow the specification of distinct input and output images. The image scanning can also be made more efficient by taking into account the continuity of the image data. Finally, it is also possible to use regular low-level pointer arithmetic to scan the image buffer. All of these elements are discussed in the following subsections.

Other color reduction formulas

In our example, color reduction is achieved by taking advantage of integer division that floors the division result to the nearest lower integer as follows:

```
data[i]= (data[i]/div)*div + div/2;
```

The reduced color could have also been computed from the modulo operator using which we can obtain the multiple of `div` immediately below as follows:

```
data[i]= data[i] - data[i]%div + div/2;
```

Another option would be to use bitwise operators. Indeed, if we restrict the reduction factor to a power of 2, that is, `div=pow(2,n)`, then masking the first n bits of the pixel value would give us the nearest lower multiple of `div`. This mask would be computed by a simple bit shift as follows:

```
// mask used to round the pixel value
uchar mask= 0xFF<<n; // e.g. for div=16, mask= 0xF0
```

The color reduction would be given by the following code:

```
*data &= mask;       // masking
*data++ += div>>1;   // add div/2;
// bitwise OR could also be used above instead of +
```

In general, bitwise operations might lead to very efficient code, so they could constitute a powerful alternative when efficiency is a requirement.

Having input and output arguments

In our color reduction example, the transformation is directly applied to the input image, which is called an in-place transformation. This way, no extra image is required to hold the output result, which could save on the memory usage when this is a concern. However, in some applications, the user might want to keep the original image intact. The user would then be forced to create a copy of the image before calling the function. Note that the easiest way to create an identical deep copy of an image is to call the clone() method; for example, take a look at the following code:

```
// read the image
image= cv::imread("boldt.jpg");
// clone the image
cv::Mat imageClone= image.clone();
// process the clone
// orginal image remains untouched
colorReduce(imageClone);
// display the image result
cv::namedWindow("Image Result");
cv::imshow("Image Result",imageClone);
```

This extra overhead can be avoided by defining a function that gives the user the option to either use or not use in-place processing. The signature of the method would then be as follows:

```
void colorReduce(const cv::Mat &image, // input image
                 cv::Mat &result,      // output image
                 int div=64);
```

Note that the input image is now passed as a const reference, which means that this image will not be modified by the function. The output image is passed as a reference such that the calling function will see the output argument modified by this call. When in-place processing is preferred, the same image is specified as the input and output:

```
colorReduce(image,image);
```

If not, another cv::Mat instance can be provided:

```
cv::Mat result;
colorReduce(image,result);
```

The key here is to first verify whether the output image has an allocated data buffer with a size and pixel type that matches the one of the input image. Very conveniently, this check is encapsulated inside the `create` method of `cv::Mat`. This is the method that is to be used when a matrix must be reallocated with a new size and type. If, by chance, the matrix already has the size and type specified, then no operation is performed and the method simply returns without touching the instance.

Therefore, our function should simply start with a call to `create` that builds a matrix (if necessary) of the same size and type as the input image:

```
result.create(image.rows,image.cols,image.type());
```

The allocated memory block has a size of `total()*elemSize()`. The scanning is then done with two pointers:

```
for (int j=0; j<nl; j++) {

    // get the addresses of input and output row j
    const uchar* data_in= image.ptr<uchar>(j);
    uchar* data_out= result.ptr<uchar>(j);

    for (int i=0; i<nc*nchannels; i++) {

        // process each pixel ---------------------

        data_out[i]= data_in[i]/div*div + div/2;

        // end of pixel processing ----------------

    } // end of line
}
```

In cases where the same image is provided as the input and output, this function becomes completely equivalent to the first version presented in this recipe. If another image is provided as the output, the function will work correctly, irrespective of whether the image has or has not been allocated prior to the function call.

Finally, note that the two parameters of this new function could have been declared as `cv::InputArray` and `cv::OutputArray`. As discussed in Chapter 1, *Playing with Images*, these would provide the same behavior but bring extra flexibility in terms of the argument type they can accept.

Efficient scanning of continuous images

We previously explained that, for efficiency reasons, an image can be padded with extra pixels at the end of each row. However, it is interesting to note that when the image is unpadded, it can also be seen as a long one-dimensional array of WxH pixels. A convenient cv::Mat method can tell us whether the image has been padded or not. This is the isContinuous method that returns true if the image does not include padded pixels. Note that we could also check the continuity of the matrix by writing the following test:

```
// check if size of a line (in bytes)
// equals the number of columns times pixel size in bytes
image.step == image.cols*image.elemSize();
```

To be complete, this test should also check whether the matrix has only one line; in which case, it is continuous by definition. Nevertheless, always use the isContinuous method to test the continuity condition. In some specific processing algorithms, you can take advantage of the continuity of the image by processing it in one single (longer) loop. Our processing function would then be written as follows:

```
void colorReduce(cv::Mat image, int div=64) {

    int nl= image.rows; // number of lines
    // total number of elements per line
    int nc= image.cols * image.channels();

    if (image.isContinuous())   {
      // then no padded pixels
      nc= nc*nl;
      nl= 1;  // it is now a 1D array
    }
      int n= staic_cast<int>(
        log(static_cast<double>(div))/log(2.0) + 0.5);
      // mask used to round the pixel value
      uchar mask= 0xFF<<n; // e.g. for div=16, mask= 0xF0
      uchar div2 = div >> 1; // div2 = div/2

      // this loop is executed only once
      // in case of continuous images
      for (int j=0; j<nl; j++) {

        uchar* data= image.ptr<uchar>(j);

        for (int i=0; i<nc; i++) {

          *data &= mask;
          *data++ += div2;
```

```
            } // end of line
        }
    }
```

Now, when the continuity test tells us that the image does not contain padded pixels, we eliminate the outer loop by setting the width to 1 and the height to WxH. Note that there is also a `reshape` method that could have been used here. You would write the following in this case:

```
if (image.isContinuous())
{
    // no padded pixels
    image.reshape(1,    // new number of channels
                  1);   // new number of rows
}

int nl= image.rows; // number of lines
int nc= image.cols * image.channels();
```

The `reshape()` method changes the matrix dimensions without requiring any memory copying or reallocation. The first parameter is the new number of channels and the second one is the new number of rows. The number of columns is readjusted accordingly.

In these implementations, the inner loop processes all image pixels in a sequence.

Low-level pointer arithmetic

In the `cv::Mat` class, the image data is contained in a memory block of unsigned chars. The address of the first element of this memory block is given by the data attribute that returns an unsigned char pointer. So, to start your loop at the beginning of the image, you could have written the following code:

```
uchar *data= image.data;
```

And moving from one row to the next could have been done by moving your row pointer using the effective width as follows:

```
data+= image.step;   // next line
```

The `step` attribute gives you the total number of bytes (including the padded pixels) in a line. In general, you can obtain the address of the pixel at row j and column i as follows:

```
// address of pixel at (j,i) that is &image.at(j,i)
data= image.data+j*image.step+i*image.elemSize();
```

However, even if this would work in our example, it is not recommended that you proceed this way.

See also

- The *Writing efficient image-scanning loops* recipe in this chapter proposes a discussion on the efficiency of the scanning methods presented here
- The *Exploring the cv::Mat data structure* recipe in Chapter 1, *Playing with Images* contains more information on the attributes and methods of the cv::Mat class. It also discusses the related classes such as the cv::InputArray and cv::OutputArray classes.

Scanning an image with iterators

In object-oriented programming, looping over a data collection is usually done using iterators. Iterators are specialized classes that are built to go over each element of a collection, hiding how the iteration over each element is specifically done for a given collection. This application of the information-hiding principle makes scanning a collection easier and safer. In addition, it makes it similar in form no matter what type of collection is used. The **Standard Template Library** (**STL**) has an iterator class associated with each of its collection classes. OpenCV then offers a cv::Mat iterator class that is compatible with the standard iterators found in the C++ STL.

Getting ready

In this recipe, we again use the color reduction example described in the previous recipe.

How to do it...

An iterator object for a cv::Mat instance can be obtained by first creating a cv::MatIterator_ object. As is the case with cv::Mat_, the underscore indicates that this is a template subclass. Indeed, since image iterators are used to access the image elements, the return type must be known at the time of compilation. The iterator for a color image is then declared as follows:

```
cv::MatIterator_<cv::Vec3b> it;
```

Alternatively, you can also use the `iterator` type defined inside the `Mat_` template class as follows:

```
cv::Mat_<cv::Vec3b>::iterator it;
```

You then loop over the pixels using the usual `begin` and `end` iterator methods, except that these ones are, again, template methods. Consequently, our color reduction function is now written as follows:

```
void colorReduce(cv::Mat image, int div=64) {
  // div must be a power of 2
  int n= staic_cast<int>(
log(static_cast<double>(div))/log(2.0) + 0.5);
  // mask used to round the pixel value
  uchar mask= 0xFF<<n; // e.g. for div=16, mask= 0xF0
  uchar div2 = div >> 1; // div2 = div/2
  // get iterators
  cv::Mat_<cv::Vec3b>::iterator it= image.begin<cv::Vec3b>();
  cv::Mat_<cv::Vec3b>::iterator itend= image.end<cv::Vec3b>();

  // scan all pixels
  for ( ; it!= itend; ++it) {

    (*it)[0]&= mask;
    (*it)[0]+= div2;
    (*it)[1]&= mask;
    (*it)[1]+= div2;
    (*it)[2]&= mask;
    (*it)[2]+= div2;

  }
}
```

Remember that the iterator here returns a `cv::Vec3b` instance because we are processing a color image. Each color channel element is accessed using the dereferencing operator `[]`. Note that you could also rely on the `cv::Vec3b` overloaded operators and simply write:

```
*it= *it/div*div+offset;
```

This will apply the operations on each element of the short vector.

How it works...

Working with iterators always follows the same pattern no matter what kind of collection is scanned.

First, you create your iterator object using the appropriate specialized class, which in our example is `cv::Mat_<cv::Vec3b>::iterator` (or `cv::MatIterator_<cv::Vec3b>`).

You then obtain an iterator initialized at the starting position (in our example, the upper-left corner of the image). This is done using a `begin` method. With a `cv::Mat` instance of a color image, you obtain it as `image.begin<cv::Vec3b>()`. You can also use arithmetic on the iterator. For example, if you wish to start at the second row of an image, you can initialize your `cv::Mat` iterator at `image.begin<cv::Vec3b>()+image.cols`. The end position of your collection is obtained similarly but using the `end` method. However, the iterator thus obtained is just outside your collection. This is why your iterative process must stop when it reaches the end position. You can also use arithmetic on this iterator; for example, if you wish to stop before the last row, your final iteration would stop when the iterator reaches `image.end<cv::Vec3b>()-image.cols`.

Once your iterator is initialized, you create a loop that goes over all elements until the end is reached. A typical `while` loop will look like the following code:

```
while (it!= itend) {

    // process each pixel ---------------------

    ...

    // end of pixel processing ----------------

    ++it;
}
```

The `++` operator is the one that is to be used to move to the next element. You can also specify a larger step size. For example, `it+=10` would process the image every `10` pixels.

Finally, inside the processing loop, you use the dereferencing `operator*` in order to access the current element, using which, you can read (for example, `element= *it;`) or write (for example, `*it= element;`). Note that it is also possible to create constant iterators that you use if you receive a reference to `const cv::Mat` or if you wish to signify that the current loop does not modify the `cv::Mat` instance. These are declared as follows:

```
cv::MatConstIterator_<cv::Vec3b> it;
```

Or, they can be declared as follows:

```
cv::Mat_<cv::Vec3b>::const_iterator it;
```

There's more...

In this recipe, the start and end positions of the iterator were obtained using the `begin` and `end` template methods. As we did in the first recipe of this chapter, we could have also obtained them using a reference to a `cv::Mat_` instance. This would avoid the need to specify the iterator type in the `begin` and `end` methods since this one is specified when the `cv::Mat_` reference is created.

```
cv::Mat_<cv::Vec3b> cimage(image);
cv::Mat_<cv::Vec3b>::iterator it= cimage.begin();
cv::Mat_<cv::Vec3b>::iterator itend= cimage.end();
```

See also

- The *Writing efficient image-scanning loops* recipe proposes a discussion on the efficiency of iterators when scanning an image.
- Also, if you are not familiar with the concept of iterators in object-oriented programming and how they are implemented in ANSI C++, you should read a tutorial on STL iterators. Simply search the Web with the keywords **STL Iterator** and you will find numerous references on the subject.

Writing efficient image-scanning loops

In the previous recipes of this chapter, we presented different ways of scanning an image in order to process its pixels. In this recipe, we will compare the efficiency of these different approaches.

When you write an image-processing function, efficiency is often a concern. When you design your function, you will frequently need to check the computational efficiency of your code in order to detect any bottleneck in your processing that might slow down your program.

However, it is important to note that unless necessary, optimization should not be done at the price of reducing code clarity. Simple code is indeed, always easier to debug and maintain. Only code portions that are critical to a program's efficiency should be heavily optimized.

How to do it...

In order to measure the execution time of a function or a portion of code, there exists a very convenient OpenCV function called `cv::getTickCount()`. This function gives you the number of clock cycles that have occurred since the last time you started your computer. Since we want to evaluate the execution time, the idea is to get this number of clock cycles before and after the execution of some code. To get the execution time in seconds, we use another method, `cv::getTickFrequency()`. This gives us the number of cycles per second, assuming your CPU has a fixed frequency (which is not necessarily the case for more recent processors). The usual pattern to be used in order to obtain the computational time of a given function (or portion of code) would then be as follows:

```
const int64 start = cv::getTickCount();
colorReduce(image); // a function call
// elapsed time in seconds
double duration = (cv::getTickCount()-start)/
                        cv::getTickFrequency();
```

How it works...

The execution times of the different implementations of the `colorReduce` function from this chapter are reported here. The absolute runtime numbers would differ from one machine to another (here, we used a 2.40 GHz machine equipped with a 64-bit Intel Core i7). It is rather interesting to look at their relative difference. These results are also dependent on the specific compiler that is used to produce the executable file. Our tests report the average time to reduce the colors of our test image that has a resolution of `320x240` pixels. We performed these tests on three different configurations:

1. A 2.5 GHz machine equipped with a 64-bit Intel i5 and the Visual Studio 14 2015 compiler under Windows 10
2. A 3.6 GHz machine 64-bit Intel i7 and gcc 4.9.2 under Ubuntu Linux
3. A 2011 MacBook Pro 2.3 GHz Intel i5 and clang++ 7.0.2

First, we compare the three ways of computing the color reduction as presented in the *There's more...* section of the *Scanning an image with pointers* recipe.

	Configuration 1	Configuration 2	Configuration 3
Integer division	0.867 ms	0.586 ms	1.119 ms
Modulo operator	0.774 ms	0.527 ms	1.106 ms
Bitwise operator	0.015 ms	0.013 ms	0.066 ms

It is interesting to observe that the formula that uses the bitwise operator is much faster than the others. The other two methods have similar running times. It is therefore important to take the time to identify the most efficient way of computing a result in an image loop, as the net impact can be very significant.

In a loop, you should avoid repetitive computations of values that could be precomputed instead. This consumes time, obviously. For example, it would be a bad idea to write the inner of our color reduction function as follows:

```
for (int i=0; i<image.cols * image.channels(); i++) {
    *data &= mask;
    *data++ += div/2;
```

Indeed, in this preceding code, the loop needs to compute the total number of elements in a line and the `div/2` result again and again. A better code is then the following:

```
int nc= image.cols * image.channels();
uchar div2= div>>1;

for (int i=0; i<nc; i++) {
    *(data+i) &= mask;
    *(data+i) += div2;
```

On average, the code with re-computations is 10 times slower than the more optimal solution. Note, however, that some compilers might be able to optimize these kinds of loops and still obtain efficient code.

The version of the color reduction function that uses iterators (and bitwise operators), as shown in the *Scanning an image with iterators* recipe, gives slower results at 0.480 ms, 0.320 ms, and 0.655 ms for our three configurations. The main objective of iterators is to simplify the image-scanning process and make it less prone to errors.

For completeness, we also implemented a version of the function that uses the `at` method for pixel access. The main loop of this implementation would then simply read as follows:

```
for (int j=0; j<nl; j++) {
   for (int i=0; i<nc; i++) {
      image.at<cv::Vec3b>(j,i)[0]=
            image.at<cv::Vec3b>(j,i)[0]/div*div + div/2;
      image.at<cv::Vec3b>(j,i)[1]=
            image.at<cv::Vec3b>(j,i)[1]/div*div + div/2;
      image.at<cv::Vec3b>(j,i)[2]=
            image.at<cv::Vec3b>(j,i)[2]/div*div + div/2;

   } // end of line
}
```

This implementation has a slower runtime of 0.925 ms, 0.580 ms, and 1.128 ms. This method should then be used only for the random access of image pixels but never when scanning an image.

Also, a shorter loop with few statements is generally more efficiently executed than a longer loop over a single statement, even if the total number of elements processed is the same. Similarly, if you have N different computations to apply to a pixel, apply all of them in one loop rather than writing N successive loops, one for each computation.

We also performed the continuity test that produces one loop in the case of continuous images instead of the regular double loop over lines and columns. We obtained a slight reduction in the runtime by an average factor of 10%. In general, it is a good practice to use this strategy, since it can lead to a significant gain in speed.

There's more...

Multithreading is another way to increase the efficiency of your algorithms, especially since the advent of multicore processors. **OpenMP**, the **Intel Threading Building Blocks (TBB)** and **Posix** are popular APIs that are used in concurrent programming to create and manage your threads. In addition, C++11 now offers built-in support for threads.

See also

- The *Performing simple image arithmetic* recipe presents an implementation of the color-reduction function (described in the *There's more...* section) that uses the OpenCV arithmetic image operators and has a runtime of 0.091 ms, 0.047 ms, and 0.087 for the three test configurations.
- The *Applying look-up tables to modify the image's appearance* recipe of Chapter 4, *Counting the Pixels with Histograms* describes an implementation of the color-reduction function based on a look-up table. The idea is to precompute all intensity reduction values that lead to a runtime of 0.129 ms, 0.098 ms, and 0.206 ms.

Scanning an image with neighbor access

In image processing, it is common to have a processing function that computes a value at each pixel location based on the value of the neighboring pixels. When this neighborhood includes pixels of the previous and next lines, you then need to simultaneously scan several lines of the image. This recipe shows you how to do it.

Getting ready

To illustrate this recipe, we will apply a processing function that sharpens an image. It is based on the Laplacian operator (which will be discussed in Chapter 6, *Filtering the Images*). It is indeed, a well-known result in image processing that if you subtract the Laplacian from an image, the image edges are amplified, thereby giving a sharper image.

This sharpened value is computed as follows:

```
sharpened_pixel= 5*current-left-right-up-down;
```

Here, `left` is the pixel that is immediately on the left-hand side of the current one, `up` is the corresponding one on the previous line, and so on.

How to do it...

This time, the processing cannot be accomplished in-place. Users need to provide an output image. The image scanning is done using three pointers, one for the current line, one for the line above, and another one for the line below. Also, since each pixel computation requires access to the neighbors, it is not possible to compute a value for the pixels of the first and last row of the image as well as the pixels of the first and last column. The loop can then be written as follows:

```cpp
void sharpen(const cv::Mat &image, cv::Mat &result) {

  // allocate if necessary
  result.create(image.size(), image.type());
  int nchannels= image.channels(); // get number of channels
  // for all rows (except first and last)
  for (int j= 1; j<image.rows-1; j++) {

    const uchar* previous= image.ptr<const uchar>(j-1);// previous row
    const uchar* current= image.ptr<const uchar>(j);   // current row
    const uchar* next= image.ptr<const uchar>(j+1);    // next row

    uchar* output= result.ptr<uchar>(j); // output row

    for (int i=nchannels; i<(image.cols-1)*nchannels; i++) {

      // apply sharpening operator
      *output++= cv::saturate_cast<uchar>(
              5*current[i]-current[i-nchannels]-
              current[i+nchannels]-previous[i]-next[i]);
    }
  }

  // Set the unprocessed pixels to 0
  result.row(0).setTo(cv::Scalar(0));
  result.row(result.rows-1).setTo(cv::Scalar(0));
  result.col(0).setTo(cv::Scalar(0));
  result.col(result.cols-1).setTo(cv::Scalar(0));
}
```

Note how we wrote the function such that it would work on both gray-level and color images. If we apply this function on a gray-level version of our test image, the following result is obtained:

How it works...

In order to access the neighboring pixels of the previous and next row, you must simply define additional pointers that are jointly incremented. You then access the pixels of these lines inside the scanning loop.

In the computation of the output pixel value, the `cv::saturate_cast` template function is called on the result of the operation. This is because, often, a mathematical expression applied on pixels leads to a result that goes outside the range of the permitted pixel values (that is, below 0 or over 255). The solution is then to bring the values back inside this 8-bit range. This is done by changing negative values to 0 and values over 255 to 255. This is exactly what the `cv::saturate_cast<uchar>` function is doing. In addition, if the input argument is a floating point number, then the result is rounded to the nearest integer. You can obviously use this function with other types in order to guarantee that the result will remain within the limits defined by this type.

Border pixels that cannot be processed because their neighborhood is not completely defined need to be handled separately. Here, we simply set them to 0. In other cases, it could be possible to perform a special computation for these pixels, but most of the time, there is no point in spending time to process these very few pixels. In our function, these border pixels are set to 0 using two special methods, `row` and `col`. They return a special `cv::Mat` instance composed of a single-line ROI (or a single-column ROI) as specified in a parameter (remember, we discussed region of interest in the previous chapter). No copy is made here; therefore if the elements of this 1D matrix are modified, they will also be modified in the original image. This is what we do when the `setTo` method is called. This method assigns a value to all elements of a matrix, as follows:

```
result.row(0).setTo(cv::Scalar(0));
```

The preceding statement assigns the value of 0 to all pixels of the first line of the result image. In the case of a 3-channel color image, you would use `cv::Scalar(a,b,c)` to specify the three values to be assigned to each channel of the pixel.

There's more...

When a computation is done over a pixel neighborhood, it is common to represent this with a kernel matrix. This kernel describes how the pixels involved in the computation are combined in order to obtain the desired result. For the sharpening filter used in this recipe, the kernel would be as follows:

0	-1	0
-1	5	-1
0	-1	0

Unless stated otherwise, the current pixel corresponds to the center of the kernel. The value in each cell of the kernel represents a factor that multiplies the corresponding pixel. The result of the application of the kernel on a pixel is then given by the sum of all these multiplications. The size of the kernel corresponds to the size of the neighborhood (here, 3x3).

Using this representation, it can be seen that, as required by the sharpening filter, the four horizontal and vertical neighbors of the current pixel are multiplied by −1, while the current pixel is multiplied by 5. Applying a kernel to an image is more than a convenient representation; it is the basis for the concept of convolution in signal processing. The kernel defines a filter that is applied to the image.

Since filtering is a common operation in image processing, OpenCV has defined a special function that performs this task: the `cv::filter2D` function. To use this, you just need to define a kernel (in the form of a matrix). The function is then called with the image and the kernel, and it returns the filtered image. Using this function, it is therefore easy to redefine our sharpening function as follows:

```
void sharpen2D(const cv::Mat &image, cv::Mat &result) {

    // Construct kernel (all entries initialized to 0)
    cv::Mat kernel(3,3,CV_32F,cv::Scalar(0));
    // assigns kernel values
    kernel.at<float>(1,1)= 5.0;
    kernel.at<float>(0,1)= -1.0;
    kernel.at<float>(2,1)= -1.0;
    kernel.at<float>(1,0)= -1.0;
    kernel.at<float>(1,2)= -1.0;

    //filter the image
    cv::filter2D(image,result,image.depth(),kernel);
}
```

This implementation produces exactly the same result as the previous one (and with the same efficiency). If you input a color image, then the same kernel will be applied to all three channels. Note that it is particularly advantageous to use the `filter2D` function with a large kernel, as it uses, in this case, a more efficient algorithm.

See also

- Chapter 6, *Filtering the Images*, provides more explanations on the concept of image filtering

Performing simple image arithmetic

Images can be combined in different ways. Since they are regular matrices, they can be added, subtracted, multiplied, or divided. OpenCV offers various image arithmetic operators, and their use is discussed in this recipe.

Getting ready

Let's work with a second image that we will combine with our input image using an arithmetic operator. The following represents this second image:

How to do it...

Here, we add two images. This is useful when we want to create some special effects or to overlay information over an image. We do this by calling the `cv::add` function, or more precisely here, the `cv::addWeighted` function, since we want a weighted sum as follows:

```
cv::addWeighted(image1,0.7,image2,0.9,0.,result);
```

The operation results in a new image:

How it works...

All binary arithmetic functions work the same way. Two inputs are provided and a third parameter specifies the output. In some cases, weights that are used as scalar multipliers in the operation can be specified. Each of these functions comes in several flavors; `cv::add` is a good example of a function that is available in many forms:

```cpp
// c[i]= a[i]+b[i];
cv::add(imageA,imageB,resultC);
// c[i]= a[i]+k;
cv::add(imageA,cv::Scalar(k),resultC);
// c[i]= k1*a[i]+k2*b[i]+k3;
cv::addWeighted(imageA,k1,imageB,k2,k3,resultC);
// c[i]= k*a[i]+b[i];
cv::scaleAdd(imageA,k,imageB,resultC);
```

For some functions, you can also specify a mask:

```cpp
// if (mask[i]) c[i]= a[i]+b[i];
cv::add(imageA,imageB,resultC,mask);
```

If you apply a mask, the operation is performed only on pixels for which the mask value is not null (the mask must be 1-channel). Have a look at the different forms of `cv::subtract`, `cv::absdiff`, `cv::multiply`, and `cv::divide` functions. Bitwise operators (operators applied to each individual bit of the pixels' binary representation) are also available: `cv::bitwise_and`, `cv::bitwise_or`, `cv::bitwise_xor`, and `cv::bitwise_not`. The `cv::min` and `cv::max` operators, which find the per-element maximum or minimum pixel value, are also very useful.

In all cases, the `cv::saturate_cast` function (see the preceding recipe) is always used to make sure that the results stay within the defined pixel value domain (that is, to avoid overflow or underflow).

The images must have the same size and type (the output image will be reallocated if it does not match the input size). Also, since the operation is performed per-element, one of the input images can be used as the output.

Several operators that take a single image as the input are also available: `cv::sqrt`, `cv::pow`, `cv::abs`, `cv::cuberoot`, `cv::exp`, and `cv::log`. In fact, there exists an OpenCV function for almost any operation you have to apply on image pixels.

There's more...

It is also possible to use the usual C++ arithmetic operator on the `cv::Mat` instances or on the individual channels of `cv::Mat` instances. The two following subsections explain how to do this.

Overloaded image operators

Very conveniently, most arithmetic functions have their corresponding operator overloaded in OpenCV. Consequently, the call to `cv::addWeighted` can instead be written as follows:

```
result= 0.7*image1+0.9*image2;
```

The preceding code is a more compact form that is also easier to read. These two ways of writing the weighted sum are equivalent. In particular, the `cv::saturate_cast` function will still be called in both cases.

Most C++ operators have been overloaded. Among them are the bitwise operators &, |, ^, and ~; the min, max, and abs functions. The comparison operators <, <=, ==, !=, >, and >= have also been overloaded, and they return an 8-bit binary image. You will also find the m1*m2 matrix multiplication (where m1 and m2 are both cv::Mat instances), the m1.inv() matrix inversion, the m1.t() transpose, the m1.determinant() determinant, the v1.norm() vector norm, the v1.cross(v2) cross-product, the v1.dot(v2) dot product, and so on. When this makes sense, you also have the corresponding compound assignment operator defined (the += operator, as an example).

In the *Writing efficient image-scanning loops* recipe, we presented a color-reduction function that was written using loops that scan the image pixels to perform some arithmetic operations on them. From what we learned here, this function could be rewritten simply using arithmetic operators on the input image as follows:

```
image=(image&cv::Scalar(mask,mask,mask))
             +cv::Scalar(div/2,div/2,div/2);
```

The use of cv::Scalar is due to the fact that we are manipulating a color image. Using the image operators makes the code so simple, and the programmer so productive, that you should consider their use in most situations.

Splitting the image channels

Sometimes you want to process the different channels of an image independently. For example, you might want to perform an operation only on one channel of the image. You can, of course, achieve this in an image-scanning loop. However, you can also use the cv::split function that will copy the three channels of a color image into three distinct cv::Mat instances. Suppose we want to add our rain image to the blue channel only. The following is how we would proceed:

```
// create vector of 3 images
std::vector<cv::Mat> planes;
// split 1 3-channel image into 3 1-channel images
cv::split(image1,planes);
// add to blue channel
planes[0]+= image2;
// merge the 3 1-channel images into 1 3-channel image
cv::merge(planes,result);
```

The cv::merge function performs the inverse operation, that is, it creates a color image from three 1-channel images.

Remapping an image

In the recipes of this chapter, you learned how to read and modify the pixel values of an image. The last recipe will teach you how to modify the appearance of an image by moving its pixels. The pixel values are not changed by this process; it is rather the position of each pixel that is remapped to a new location. This is useful in order to create special effects on an image or to correct image distortions caused, for example, by a lens.

How to do it...

In order to use the OpenCV `remap` function, you simply have to first define the map to be used in the remapping process. Second, you have to apply this map on an input image. Obviously, it is the way you define your map that will determine the effect that will be produced. In our example, we define a transformation function that will create a wavy effect on the image:

```
// remapping an image by creating wave effects
void wave(const cv::Mat &image, cv::Mat &result) {

  // the map functions
  cv::Mat srcX(image.rows,image.cols,CV_32F);
  cv::Mat srcY(image.rows,image.cols,CV_32F);

  // creating the mapping
  for (int i=0; i<image.rows; i++) {
    for (int j=0; j<image.cols; j++) {

      // new location of pixel at (i,j)
      srcX.at<float>(i,j)= j; // remain on same column
                              // pixels originally on row i are now
                              // moved following a sinusoid
      srcY.at<float>(i,j)= i+5*sin(j/10.0);
    }
  }

  // applying the mapping
  cv::remap(image,            // source image
            result,           // destination image
            srcX,             // x map
            srcY,             // y map
            cv::INTER_LINEAR); // interpolation method
}
```

The result is as follows:

How it works...

The objective of remapping is to produce a new version of an image in which pixels have changed in position. To construct this new image, we need to know what the original position is for each pixel in the destination image. The mapping function that is needed is therefore the one that will give us the original pixel positions as a function of the new pixel positions. This is called **backward mapping** because the transformation describes how the pixels of the new images are mapped back to the original image. In OpenCV, backward mapping is described using two maps: one for the x-coordinates and one for the y-coordinates. They are both represented by floating point cv::Mat instances:

```
// the map functions
cv::Mat srcX(image.rows,image.cols,CV_32F); // x-map
cv::Mat srcY(image.rows,image.cols,CV_32F); // y-map
```

The size of these matrices will define the size of the destination image. The value of the `(i,j)` pixel of the destination image can then be read in the source image using the following line of code:

```
( srcX.at<float>(i,j) , srcY.at<float>(i,j) )
```

For example, a simple image flip effect like the one we demonstrated in `Chapter 1`, *Playing with Images*, can be created by the following maps:

```
// creating the mapping
for (int i=0; i<image.rows; i++) {
  for (int j=0; j<image.cols; j++) {

    // horizontal flipping
    srcX.at<float>(i,j)= image.cols-j-1;
    srcY.at<float>(i,j)= i;
  }
}
```

To generate the resulting image, you simply call the OpenCV `remap` function:

```
// applying the mapping
cv::remap(image,              // source image
          result,             // destination image
          srcX,               // x map
          srcY,               // y map
          cv::INTER_LINEAR);  // interpolation method
```

It is interesting to note that the two maps contain floating-point values. Consequently, a pixel in the destination can map back to a non-integral value (that is, a location between pixels). This is very convenient because this allows us to define the mapping function of our choice. For instance, in our remapping example, we used a `sinusoidal` function to define our transformation. However, this also means that we have to interpolate the value of virtual pixels in between real pixels. There exist different ways of performing pixel interpolation, and the last parameter of the `remap` function allows us to select the method that will be used. Pixel interpolation is an important concept in image processing; this subject will be discussed in `Chapter 6`, *Filtering the Images*.

See also

- The *There's more...* section of the *Filtering images using low-pass filters* recipe of Chapter 6, *Filtering the Images*, explains the concept of pixel interpolation
- The *Calibrating a camera* recipe of Chapter 11, *Reconstructing 3D Scenes*, uses remapping to correct lens distortions in an image
- The *Computing a homography between two images* recipe of Chapter 10, *Estimating Projective Relations in Images*, uses perspective image warping to build an image panorama

3
Processing the Colors of an Image

In this chapter, we will cover the following recipes:

- Comparing colors using the Strategy design pattern
- Segmenting an image with the GrabCut algorithm
- Converting color representations
- Representing colors with hue, saturation, and brightness

Introduction

The ability to see the world in colors is one of the important characteristics of the human visual system. The retina of the human eye includes specialized photoreceptors, called cones, which are responsible for the perception of colors. There are three types of cones that differ in the wavelength range of light they absorb; using the stimuli from these different cells, the human brain is able to create color perception. Most other animals only have rod cells, which are photoreceptors with better light sensitivity but that cover the full spectrum of visible light without color discrimination. In the human eye, rods are mainly located at the periphery of the retina, while the cones are concentrated in the central part.

In digital imaging, colors are generally reproduced by using the red, green, and blue additive primary colors. These have been selected because when they are combined together, they can produce a wide gamut of different colors. In fact, this choice of primaries mimics well the trichromatic color perception of the human visual system as the different cone cells have sensitivity located around the red, green, and blue spectrum. In this chapter, you will play with the pixel color and see how an image can be segmented based on the color information. In addition, you will learn that it can sometimes be useful to use a different color representation when performing color image processing.

Comparing colors using the Strategy design pattern

Let's say we want to build a simple algorithm that will identify all of the pixels in an image that have a given color. For this, the algorithm has to accept an image and a color as input and will return a binary image showing the pixels that have the specified color. The tolerance with which we want to accept a color will be another parameter to be specified before running the algorithm.

In order to accomplish this objective, this recipe will use the **Strategy design pattern**. This object-oriented design pattern constitutes an excellent way of encapsulating an algorithm in a class. It becomes then easier to replace a given algorithm with another one, or to chain several algorithms together in order to build a more complex process. In addition, this pattern facilitates the deployment of an algorithm by hiding as much of its complexity as possible behind an intuitive programming interface.

How to do it...

Once an algorithm has been encapsulated in a class using the Strategy design pattern, it can be deployed by creating an instance of this class. Typically, the instance will be created when the program is initialized. At the time of construction, the class instance will initialize the different parameters of the algorithm with their default values so that it will immediately be ready to be used. The algorithm's parameter values can also be read and set using appropriate methods. In the case of an application with a GUI, these parameters can be displayed and modified using different widgets (text fields, sliders, and so on) so that a user can easily play with them.

We will show you the structure of a `Strategy` class in the next section; let's start with an example of how it can be deployed and used. Let's write a simple `main` function that will run our proposed color detection algorithm:

```
int main()
{
  //1. Create image processor object
  ColorDetector cdetect;

  //2. Read input image
  cv::Mat image= cv::imread("boldt.jpg");
  if (image.empty()) return 0;

  //3. Set input parameters
  cdetect.setTargetColor(230,190,130);   // here blue sky

  //4. Process the image and display the result
  cv::namedWindow("result");
  cv::Mat result = cdetect.process(image);
  cv::imshow("result",result);

  cv::waitKey();
  return 0;
}
```

Running this program to detect a blue sky in the colored version of the *Castle* image presented in the previous chapter produces the following output:

Here, a white pixel indicates a positive detection of the sought color, and black indicates negative.

Obviously, the algorithm we encapsulated in this class is relatively simple (as we will see next, it is composed of just one scanning loop and one tolerance parameter). The Strategy design pattern becomes really powerful when the algorithm to be implemented is more complex, has many steps, and includes several parameters.

How it works...

The core process of this algorithm is easy to build. It is a simple scanning loop that goes over each pixel, comparing its color with the target color. Using what we learned in the *Scanning an image with iterators* recipe of the previous chapter, this loop can be written as follows:

```
// get the iterators
cv::Mat_<cv::Vec3b>::const_iterator it= image.begin<cv::Vec3b>();
cv::Mat_<cv::Vec3b>::const_iterator itend= image.end<cv::Vec3b>();
cv::Mat_<uchar>::iterator itout= result.begin<uchar>();

//for each pixel
for ( ; it!= itend; ++it, ++itout) {

  // compute distance from target color
  if (getDistanceToTargetColor(*it)<=maxDist) {
    *itout= 255;
  } else {
   *itout= 0;
  }
}
```

The cv::Mat variable image refers to the input image, while result refers to the binary output image. Therefore, the first step consists of setting up the required iterators. The scanning loop then becomes easy to implement. Note that the input image iterators are declared const as the values of their elements are not modified. The distance between the current pixel color and the target color is evaluated for each pixel in order to check whether it is within the tolerance parameter defined by maxDist. If that is the case, the value 255 (white) is then assigned to the output image; if not, 0 (black) is assigned. To compute the distance to the target color, the getDistanceToTargetColor method is used. There are different ways to compute this distance.

One could, for example, calculate the Euclidean distance between the three vectors that contain the RGB color values. To keep this computation simple, we sum the absolute differences of the RGB values (this is also known as the **city-block distance**). Note that in modern architecture, a floating-point Euclidean distance can be faster to compute than a simple city-block distance (in addition, you can also use squared Euclidean distances to avoid the costly square-root); this is also something to take into consideration in your design. Also, for more flexibility, we write the `getDistanceToTargetColor` method in terms of a `getColorDistance` method, as follows:

```
// Computes the distance from target color.
int getDistanceToTargetColor(const cv::Vec3b& color) const {
  return getColorDistance(color, target);
}
// Computes the city-block distance between two colors.
int getColorDistance(const cv::Vec3b& color1,
const cv::Vec3b& color2) const {
  return abs(color1[0]-color2[0])+
         abs(color1[1]-color2[1])+
         abs(color1[2]-color2[2]);
}
```

Note how we used `cv::Vec3d` to hold the three unsigned chars that represent the RGB values of a color. The `target` variable obviously refers to the specified target color, and as we will see, it is defined as a member variable in the class algorithm that we will define. Now, let's complete the definition of the processing method. Users will provide an input image, and the result will be returned once the image scanning is completed:

```
cv::Mat ColorDetector::process(const cv::Mat &image) {

  // re-allocate binary map if necessary
  // same size as input image, but 1-channel
  result.create(image.size(),CV_8U);

  // processing loop above goes here
  return result;
}
```

Each time this method is called, it is important to check if the output image that contains the resulting binary map needs to be reallocated to fit the size of the input image. This is why we use the `create` method of `cv::Mat`. Remember that this method will only proceed to reallocation if the specified size and/or depth do not correspond to the current image structure.

Now that we have the core processing method defined, let's see what additional methods should be added in order to deploy this algorithm. We have previously determined what input and output data our algorithm requires. Therefore, we define the class attributes that will hold this data:

```
class ColorDetector {
  private:

    // minimum acceptable distance
    int maxDist;
    // target color
    cv::Vec3b target;

    // image containing resulting binary map
    cv::Mat result;
```

In order to create an instance of the class that encapsulates our algorithm (which we have named `ColorDetector`), we need to define a constructor. Remember that one of the objectives of the Strategy design pattern is to make algorithm deployment as easy as possible. The simplest constructor that can be defined is an empty one. It will create an instance of the class algorithm in a valid state. We then want the constructor to initialize all the input parameters to their default values (or the values that are known to generally give a good result). In our case, we decided that a distance of `100` is generally an acceptable tolerance parameter. We also set the default target color. We chose black for no particular reason. The idea is to make sure we always start with predictable and valid input values:

```
// empty constructor
// default parameter initialization here
ColorDetector() : maxDist(100), target(0,0,0) {}
```

Another option would have been not create an empty constructor and rather force the user to input a target color and a color distance in a more elaborated constructor:

```
// another constructor with target and distance
ColorDetector(uchar blue, uchar green, uchar red, int mxDist);
```

At this point, a user who creates an instance of our class algorithm can immediately call the process method with a valid image and obtain a valid output. This is another objective of the Strategy pattern, that is, to make sure that the algorithm always runs with valid parameters. Obviously, the users of this class will want to use their own settings. This is done by providing the user with the appropriate getters and setters. Let's start with the `color` tolerance parameter:

```
// Sets the color distance threshold
// Threshold must be positive,
// otherwise distance threshold is set to 0.
```

```
void setColorDistanceThreshold(int distance) {

  if (distance<0)
    distance=0;
    maxDist= distance;
  }

  // Gets the color distance threshold
  int getColorDistanceThreshold() const {
    return maxDist;
  }
```

Note how we first check the validity of the input. Again, this is to make sure that our algorithm will never be run in an invalid state. The target color can be set in a similar manner, as follows:

```
  // Sets the color to be detected
  void setTargetColor(uchar blue,
                      uchar green,
                      uchar red) {
    // BGR order
    target = cv::Vec3b(blue, green, red);
  }
  // Sets the color to be detected
  void setTargetColor(cv::Vec3b color) {
    target= color;
  }

  // Gets the color to be detected
  cv::Vec3b getTargetColor() const {
    return target;
  }
```

This time, it is interesting to note that we have provided the user with two definitions of the setTargetColor method. In the first version of the definition, the three color components are specified as three arguments, while in the second version, cv::Vec3b is used to hold the color values. Again, the objective is to facilitate the use of our class algorithm. The users can simply select the setter that best fits their needs.

There's more...

The example algorithm used in this recipe consisted of identifying the pixels of an image that has a color sufficiently close to a specified target color. This computation could have been done otherwise. Interestingly, an OpenCV function performs a similar task in order to extract a connected component of a given color. Also, the implementation of a Strategy design pattern could be complemented using function objects. Finally, OpenCV has defined a base class, cv::Algorithm, that implements the Strategy design pattern concepts.

Computing the distance between two color vectors

To compute the distance between two color vectors, we used the following simple formula:

```
return abs(color[0]-target[0])+
       abs(color[1]-target[1])+
       abs(color[2]-target[2]);
```

However, OpenCV includes a function to compute the Euclidean norm of a vector. Consequently, we could have computed our distance as follows:

```
return static_cast<int>(
       cv::norm<int,3>(cv::Vec3i(color[0]-target[0],
                                 color[1]-target[1],
                                 color[2]-target[2])));
```

A very similar result would then be obtained using this definition of the getDistance method. Here, we use cv::Vec3i (a 3-vector array of integers) because the result of the subtraction is an integer value.

It is also interesting to recall from Chapter 2, *Manipulating Pixels*, that the OpenCV matrix and vector data structures include a definition of the basic arithmetic operators. Consequently, one could have proposed the following definition for the distance computation:

```
return static_cast<int>( cv::norm<uchar,3>(color-target));// wrong!
```

This definition may look right at the first glance; however, it is wrong. This is because all these operators always include a call to `saturate_cast` (see the *Scanning an image with neighbor access* recipe in the previous chapter) in order to ensure that the results stay within the domain of the input type (here, it is `uchar`). Therefore, in the cases where the target value is greater than the corresponding color value, the value `0` will be assigned instead of the negative value that one would have expected. A correct formulation would then be as follows:

```
cv::Vec3b dist;
cv::absdiff(color,target,dist);
return cv::sum(dist)[0];
```

However, using two function calls to compute the distance between two 3-vector arrays is inefficient.

Using OpenCV functions

In this recipe, we used a loop with iterators in order to perform our computation. Alternatively, we could have achieved the same result by calling a sequence of OpenCV functions. The color detection method will then be written as follows:

```
cv::Mat ColorDetector::process(const cv::Mat &image) {
   cv::Mat output;
   // compute absolute difference with target color
   cv::absdiff(image,cv::Scalar(target),output);

   // split the channels into 3 images
   std::vector<cv::Mat> images;
   cv::split(output,images);

   // add the 3 channels (saturation might occurs here)
   output= images[0]+images[1]+images[2];
   // apply threshold
   cv::threshold(output,                      // same input/output image
             output,
             maxDist,                         // threshold (must be < 256)
             255,                             // max value
             cv::THRESH_BINARY_INV);  // thresholding mode

   return output;
}
```

This method uses the `absdiff` function, which computes the absolute difference between the pixels of an image and, in this case, a scalar value. Instead of a scalar value, another image can be provided as the second argument to this function. In the latter case, a pixel-by-pixel difference will be applied; consequently, the two images must be of the same size. The individual channels of the difference image are then extracted using the `split` function (discussed in the *There's more...* section of the *Performing simple image arithmetic* recipe of `Chapter 2`, *Manipulating Pixels*) in order to be able to add them together. It is important to note that the result of this sum may sometimes be greater than 255, but because saturation is always applied, the result will be stopped at 255. The consequence is that with this version, the `maxDist` parameter must also be less than 256; this should be corrected if you consider this behavior unacceptable.

The last step is to create a binary image by using the `cv::threshold` function. This function is commonly used to compare all the pixels with a threshold value (the third parameter), and in the regular thresholding mode (`cv::THRESH_BINARY`), it assigns the defined maximum value (the fourth parameter) to all the pixels greater than the specified threshold and 0 to the other pixels. Here, we used the inverse mode (`cv::THRESH_BINARY_INV`) in which the defined maximum value is assigned to the pixels that have a value lower than or equal to the threshold. Of interest are also the `cv::THRESH_TOZERO` and `cv::THRESH_TOZERO_INV` modes, which leave the pixels greater than or lower than the threshold unchanged.

Using the OpenCV functions is generally a good idea. You can then quickly build complex applications and potentially reduce the number of bugs. The result is often more efficient (thanks to the optimization efforts invested by the OpenCV contributors). However, when many intermediate steps are performed, you may find that the resulting method consumes more memory.

The floodFill function

Our `ColorDetector` class identifies the pixels in an image that have a color similar to a given target color. The decision to accept or not a pixel is simply made on a per-pixel basis. The `cv::floodFill` function proceeds in a very similar way with one important difference: in this case, the decision to accept a pixel also depends on the state of its neighbors. The idea is to identify a connected area of a certain color. The user specifies a starting pixel location and tolerance parameters that determine color similarity.

The seed pixel defines the color that is seek and from this seed location, the neighbors are considered in order to identify pixels of similar color; then the neighbors of the accepted neighbors are also considered and so on. This way, one area of constant color will be extracted from the image. For example, to detect the blue sky area in our example image, you could proceed as follows:

```
cv::floodFill(image,                        // input/ouput image
         cv::Point(100, 50),                // seed point
         cv::Scalar(255, 255, 255),         // repainted color
         (cv::Rect*)0,                      // bounding rect of the repainted set
         cv::Scalar(35, 35, 35),            // low/high difference threshold
         cv::Scalar(35, 35, 35),            // identical most of the time
         cv::FLOODFILL_FIXED_RANGE);        // pixels compared to seed
```

The seed pixel (100, 50) is located in the sky. All connected pixels will be tested and the ones having a similar color will be repainted in a new color specified by the third parameter. To determine if a color is similar or not, different thresholds are defined independently for values that are higher or lower than the reference color. Here, we used fixed range mode, which implies that the tested pixels will all be compared to the seed pixel's color. The default mode is the one where each tested pixel is compared to the color of its neighbors. The result obtained is as follows:

A single connected area is repainted by the algorithm (here, we painted the sky in white). Therefore, even if there are some pixels somewhere else with a similar color (in the water, for instance), these ones would not be identified unless they were connected to the sky area.

Functor or function object

Using the C++ operator overloading, it is possible to create a class for which its instances behave as functions. The idea is to overload the `operator()` method so that a call to the processing method of a class looks exactly like a simple function call. The resulting class instance is called a function object, or a **functor**. Often, a functor includes a full constructor such that it can be used immediately after being created. For example, you can define the full constructor of your `ColorDetector` class as follows:

```
// full constructor
ColorDetector(uchar blue, uchar green, uchar red, int  maxDist=100):
               maxDist(maxDist) {

  // target color
  setTargetColor(blue, green, red);
}
```

Obviously, you can still use the setters and getters that have been defined previously. The functor method can be defined as follows:

```
cv::Mat operator()(const cv::Mat &image) {
  // color detection code here
}
```

To detect a given color with this functor method, simply write the following code snippet:

```
ColorDetector colordetector(230,190,130,  // color
                            100);          // threshold
cv::Mat result= colordetector(image);      // functor call
```

As you can see, the call to the color detection method now looks like a function call.

The OpenCV base class for algorithms

OpenCV offers many algorithms that perform various computer vision tasks. To facilitate their use, most of these algorithms have been made subclass of a generic base class called `cv::Algorithm`. This one implements some of the concepts dictated by the Strategy design pattern. First, all these algorithms are created dynamically using a specialized static method that makes sure that the algorithm is always created in a valid state (that is, with valid default values for the unspecified parameters). Let's consider, for example, one of these subclasses, `cv::ORB`; this one is an interest point operator that will be discussed in the *Detecting FAST features at Multiple Scales* recipe in `Chapter 8`, *Detecting Interest Points*. Here, we simply use it as an illustrative example of an algorithm.

An instance of this algorithm is therefore created as follows:

```
cv::Ptr<cv::ORB> ptrORB = cv::ORB::create(); // default state
```

Once created, the algorithm can then be used. For example, the generic methods `read` and `write` can be used to load or store the state of the algorithm. The algorithms also have specialized methods (in the case of ORB, for example, the methods `detect` and `compute` can be used to trigger its main computational units). Algorithms also have specialized setter methods that allows specifying their internal parameters. Note that we could have declared the pointer as `cv::Ptr<cv::Algorithm>` but, in this case, we would not be able to use its specialized methods.

See also

- The policy-based class design, introduced by A. Alexandrescu, is an interesting variant of the Strategy design pattern in which algorithms are selected at compile time
- The *Converting color representation* recipe introduces the concept of perceptually uniform color spaces to achieve more intuitive color comparison

Segmenting an image with the GrabCut algorithm

The previous recipe showed how color information can be useful to segment an image into area corresponding to specific elements of a scene. Objects often have distinctive colors, and these ones can often be extracted by identifying areas of similar colors. OpenCV proposes an implementation of a popular algorithm for image segmentation: the **GrabCut** algorithm. GrabCut is a complex and computationally expensive algorithm, but it generally produces very accurate results. It is the best algorithm to use when you want to extract a foreground object in a still image (for example, to cut and paste an object from one picture to another).

How to do it...

The `cv::grabCut` function is easy to use. You just need to input an image and label some of its pixels as belonging to the background or to the foreground. Based on this partial labeling, the algorithm will then determine a foreground/ background segmentation for the complete image.

One way to specify a partial foreground/background labeling for an input image is by defining a rectangle inside which the foreground object is included:

```
// define bounding rectangle
// the pixels outside this rectangle
// will be labeled as background
cv::Rect rectangle(5,70,260,120);
```

This defines the following area in the image:

All the pixels outside this rectangle will then be marked as background. In addition to the input image and its segmentation image, calling the `cv::grabCut` function requires the definition of two matrices, which will contain the models built by the algorithm as follows:

```
cv::Mat result;                    // segmentation (4 possible values)
cv::Mat bgModel,fgModel;           // the models (internally used)
// GrabCut segmentation
cv::grabCut(image,                 // input image
            result,                // segmentation result
```

```
rectangle,                // rectangle containing foreground
bgModel,fgModel,          // models
5,                        // number of iterations
cv::GC_INIT_WITH_RECT);   // use rectangle
```

Note how we specified that we are using the bounding rectangle mode with the cv::GC_INIT_WITH_RECT flag as the last argument of the function (the next section, *How it works...*, will discuss the other available mode). The input/output segmentation image can have one of the following four values:

- cv::GC_BGD: This is the value of the pixels that certainly belong to the background (for example, pixels outside the rectangle in our example)
- cv::GC_FGD: This is the value of the pixels that certainly belong to the foreground (there are none in our example)
- cv::GC_PR_BGD: This is the value of the pixels that probably belong to the background
- cv::GC_PR_FGD: This is the value of the pixels that probably belong to the foreground (that is, the initial value of the pixels inside the rectangle in our example)

We get a binary image of the segmentation by extracting the pixels that have a value equal to cv::GC_PR_FGD. This is accomplished with the following code:

```
// Get the pixels marked as likely foreground
cv::compare(result,cv::GC_PR_FGD,result,cv::CMP_EQ);
// Generate output image
cv::Mat foreground(image.size(),CV_8UC3,cv::Scalar(255,255,255));
image.copyTo(foreground,// bg pixels are not copied result);
```

To extract all the foreground pixels, that is, with values equal to cv::GC_PR_FGD or cv::GC_FGD, it is possible to check the value of the first bit, as follows:

```
// checking first bit with bitwise-and
result= result&1; // will be 1 if FG
```

This is possible because these constants are defined as values 1 and 3, while the other two (cv::GC_BGD and cv::GC_PR_BGD) are defined as 0 and 2. In our example, the same result is obtained because the segmentation image does not contain the cv::GC_FGD pixels (only the cv::GC_BGD pixels have been inputted).

The following image is then obtained:

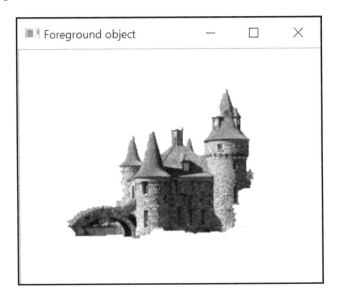

How it works...

In the preceding example, the GrabCut algorithm was able to extract the foreground object by simply specifying a rectangle inside which this objects (the castle) was contained. Alternatively, one could also assign the values cv::GC_BGD and cv::GC_FGD to some specific pixels of the input image, which are provided by using a mask image as the second argument of the cv::grabCut function. You would then specify GC_INIT_WITH_MASK as the input mode flag. These input labels could be obtained, for example, by asking a user to interactively mark a few elements of the image. It is also possible to combine these two input modes.

Using this input information, the GrabCut algorithm creates the background/foreground segmentation by proceeding as follows. Initially, a foreground label (cv::GC_PR_FGD) is tentatively assigned to all the unmarked pixels. Based on the current classification, the algorithm groups the pixels into clusters of similar colors (that is, K clusters for the background and K clusters for the foreground). The next step is to determine a background/ foreground segmentation by introducing boundaries between the foreground and background pixels.

This is done through an optimization process that tries to connect pixels with similar labels, and that imposes a penalty for placing a boundary in the regions of relatively uniform intensity. This optimization problem can be efficiently solved using the Graph Cuts algorithm, a method that can find the optimal solution of a problem by representing it as a connected graph on which cuts are applied in order to compose an optimal configuration. The obtained segmentation produces new labels for the pixels.

The clustering process can then be repeated, and a new optimal segmentation is found again, and so on. Therefore, the GrabCut algorithm is an iterative procedure that gradually improves the segmentation result. Depending on the complexity of the scene, a good solution can be found in more or less number of iterations (in easy cases, one iteration would be enough).

This explains the argument of the function where the user can specify the number of iterations to be applied. The two internal models maintained by the algorithm are passed as an argument of the function (and returned). Therefore, it is possible to call the function with the models of the last run again if one wishes to improve the segmentation result by performing additional iterations.

See also

- The article *GrabCut: Interactive Foreground Extraction using Iterated Graph Cuts* in *ACM Transactions on Graphics (SIGGRAPH) volume 23, issue 3, August 2004, C. Rother, V. Kolmogorov, and A. Blake* describes the GrabCut algorithm in detail
- The *Segmenting images using watersheds* recipe in `Chapter 5`, *Transforming Images with Morphological Operations*, presents another image segmentation algorithm

Converting color representations

The RGB color space is based on the use of the red, green, and blue additive primary colors. We saw in the first recipe of this chapter that these primaries have been chosen because they can produce a good range of colors well aligned with the human visual system. It is often the default color space in digital imagery because this is the way color images are acquired, that is, through the use of red, green, and blue filters. Additionally, the red, green, and blue channels are normalized such that when combined in equal amounts, a gray-level intensity is obtained, that is, from black (`0,0,0`) to white (`255,255,255`).

Unfortunately, computing the distance between the colors using the RGB color space is not the best way to measure the similarity between two given colors. Indeed, RGB is not a **perceptually uniform color space**. This means that two colors at a given distance might look very similar, while two other colors separated by the same distance might look very different.

To solve this problem, other color representations that have the property of being perceptually uniform have been introduced. In particular, the **CIE L*a*b*** is one such color model. By converting our images to this representation, the Euclidean distance between an image pixel and the target color will then be a meaningful measure of the visual similarity between the two colors. In this recipe, we will show you how to convert colors from one representation to another in order to work with other color spaces.

How to do it...

Conversion of images between different color spaces is easily done through the use of the `cv::cvtColor` OpenCV function. Let's revisit the `ColorDetector` class of the first recipe of this chapter, *Comparing colors using the Strategy design pattern*. We now convert the input image to the CIE L*a*b* color space at the beginning of the process method:

```
cv::Mat ColorDetector::process(const cv::Mat &image) {

    // re-allocate binary map if necessary
    // same size as input image, but 1-channel
    result.create(image.rows,image.cols,CV_8U);

    // Converting to Lab color space
    cv::cvtColor(image, converted, CV_BGR2Lab);

    // get the iterators of the converted image
    cv::Mat_<cv::Vec3b>::iterator it=  converted.begin<cv::Vec3b>();
    cv::Mat_<cv::Vec3b>::iterator itend= converted.end<cv::Vec3b>();
    // get the iterator of the output image
    cv::Mat_<uchar>::iterator itout= result.begin<uchar>();

    // for each pixel
    for ( ; it!= itend; ++it, ++itout) {
```

The `converted` variable contains the image after color conversion. In the `ColorDetector` class, it is defined as a class attribute:

```
class ColorDetector {
  private:
  // image containing color converted image
  cv::Mat converted;
```

You also need to convert the input target color. You can do this by creating a temporary image that contains only one pixel. Note that you need to keep the same signature as in the earlier recipes, that is, the user continues to supply the target color in RGB:

```
// Sets the color to be detected
void setTargetColor(unsigned char red, unsigned char green,
                    unsigned char blue) {

  // Temporary 1-pixel image
  cv::Mat tmp(1,1,CV_8UC3);
  tmp.at<cv::Vec3b>(0,0)= cv::Vec3b(blue, green, red);

  // Converting the target to Lab color space
  cv::cvtColor(tmp, tmp, CV_BGR2Lab);

  target= tmp.at<cv::Vec3b>(0,0);
}
```

If the application of the preceding recipe is compiled with this modified class, it will now detect the pixels of the target color using the CIE L*a*b* color model.

How it works...

When an image is converted from one color space to another, a linear or nonlinear transformation is applied on each input pixel to produce the output pixels. The pixel type of the output image will match the one of the input image. Even if you work with 8-bit pixels most of the time, you can also use a color conversion with floating-point images (in which case, the pixel values are generally assumed to vary between 0 and 1.0) or with integer images (with pixels generally varying between 0 and 65535). However, the exact domain of the pixel values depends on the specific color space and destination image type. For example, with the CIE L*a*b* color space, the L channel, which represents the brightness of each pixel, varies between 0 and 100, and it is rescaled between 0 and 255 in the case of the 8-bit images.

The a and b channels correspond to the chromaticity components. These channels contain information about the color of a pixel, independent of its brightness. Their values vary between −127 and 127; for 8-bit images, 128 is added to each value in order to make it fit within the 0 to 255 interval. However, note that the 8-bit color conversion will introduce rounding errors that will make the transformation imperfectly reversible.

Most commonly used color spaces are available. It is just a question of providing the right color space conversion code to the OpenCV function (for CIE L*a*b*, this code is CV_BGR2Lab). Among these is YCrCb, which is the color space used in JPEG compression. To convert a color space from BGR to YCrCb, the code will be CV_BGR2YCrCb. Note that all the conversions that involve the three regular primary colors, red, green, and blue, are available in the RGB and BGR order.

The **CIE L*u*v*** color space is another perceptually uniform color space. You can convert from BGR to CIE L*u*v by using the CV_BGR2Luv code. Both L*a*b* and L*u*v* use the same conversion formula for the brightness channel but use a different representation for the chromaticity channels. Also, note that since these two color spaces distort the RGB color domain in order to make it perceptually uniform, these transformations are nonlinear (therefore, they are costly to compute).

There is also the CIE XYZ color space (with the CV_BGR2XYZ code). It is a standard color space used to represent any perceptible color in a device-independent way. In the computation of the L*u*v and L*a*b color spaces, the XYZ color space is used as an intermediate representation. The transformation between RGB and XYZ is linear. It is also interesting to note that the Y channel corresponds to a gray-level version of the image.

HSV and HLS are interesting color spaces because they decompose the colors into their hue and saturation components plus the value or luminance component, which is a more natural way for humans to describe colors. The next recipe will present this color space.

You can also convert color images to gray-level intensities. The output will be a one-channel image:

```
cv::cvtColor(color, gray, CV_BGR2Gray);
```

It is also possible to do the conversion in the other direction, but the three channels of the resulting color image will then be identically filled with the corresponding values in the gray-level image.

See also

- The *Using the mean shift algorithm to find an object* recipe in `Chapter 4`, *Counting the Pixels with Histograms,* uses the HSV color space in order to find an object in an image.
- Many good references are available on the color space theory. Among them, the following is a complete reference: *The Structure and Properties of Color Spaces and the Representation of Color Images, E. Dubois, Morgan and Claypool Publishers, 2009.*

Representing colors with hue, saturation, and brightness

In this chapter, we played with image colors. We used different color spaces and tried to identify image areas of uniform color. The RGB color space was initially considered, and although it is an effective representation for the capture and display of colors in electronic imaging systems, this representation is not very intuitive. Indeed, this is not the way humans think about colors; they most often describe colors in terms of their tint, brightness, or colorfulness (that is, whether it is a vivid or pastel color). A color space based on the concept of hue, saturation, and brightness has then been introduced to help users to specify the colors using properties that are more intuitive to them. In this recipe, we will explore the concepts of hue, saturation, and brightness as a means to describe colors.

How to do it...

The conversion of a BGR image into another color space is done using the `cv::cvtColor` function that was explored in the previous recipe. Here, we will use the `CV_BGR2HSV` conversion code:

```
// convert into HSV space
cv::Mat hsv;
cv::cvtColor(image, hsv, CV_BGR2HSV);
```

We can go back to the BGR space using the CV_HSV2BGR code. We can visualize each of the HSV components by splitting the converted image channels into three independent images, as follows:

```
// split the 3 channels into 3 images
std::vector<cv::Mat> channels;
cv::split(hsv,channels);
// channels[0] is the Hue
// channels[1] is the Saturation
// channels[2] is the Value
```

Note that the third channel is the value of the color, that is, an approximate measure of the brightness of the color. Since we are working on 8-bit images, OpenCV rescales the channel values to cover the 0 to 255 range (except for the hue, which is rescaled between 0 and 0180 as it will be explained in the next section). This is very convenient as we are able to display these channels as gray-level images.

The value channel of the castle image will then look as follows:

The same image in the saturation channel will look as follows:

Finally, the image with the hue channel is as follows:

These images are interpreted in the next section.

How it works...

The hue/saturation/value color space has been introduced because this representation corresponds to the way humans tend to naturally organize colors. Indeed, humans prefer to describe colors with intuitive attributes such as tint, colorfulness, and brightness. These three attributes are the basis of most phenomenal color spaces. **Hue** designates the dominant color; the names that we give to colors (such as green, yellow, blue, and red) correspond to the different hue values. **Saturation** tells us how vivid the color is; pastel colors have low saturation, while the colors of the rainbow are highly saturated. Finally, brightness is a subjective attribute that refers to the luminosity of a color. Other phenomenal color spaces use the concept of color **value** or color **lightness** as a way to characterize the relative color intensity.

These color components try to mimic the intuitive human perception of colors. In consequence, there is no standard definition for them. In the literature, you will find several different definitions and formulae of the hue, saturation, and brightness. OpenCV proposes two implementations of phenomenal color spaces: the HSV and the HLS color spaces. The conversion formulas are slightly different, but they give very similar results.

The value component is probably the easiest to interpret. In the OpenCV implementation of the HSV space, it is defined as the maximum value of the three BGR components. It is a very simplistic implementation of the brightness concept. For a definition of brightness that matches the human visual system better, you should use the L channel of the perceptually uniform L*a*b* and L*u*v* color spaces. For example, the L channel takes into account the fact that a green color appears to human brighter than, for instance, a blue color of same intensity.

To compute the saturation, OpenCV uses a formula based on the minimum and maximum values of the BGR components:

$$S = (\max(R,G,B) - \min(R,G,B))/\max(R,G,B)$$

The idea is that a grayscale color in which the three R, G, and B components are all equal will correspond to a perfectly desaturated color; therefore, it will have a saturation value of 0. Saturation is a value between 0 and 1.0. For 8-bit images, saturation is rescaled to a value between 0 and 255, and when displayed as a gray-level image, brighter areas correspond to the colors that have a higher saturation color.

For example, from the saturation image in the previous section, it can be seen that the blue of the water is more saturated than the light blue pastel color of the sky, as expected. The different shades of gray have, by definition, a saturation value equal to zero (because, in this case, all three BGR components are equal). This can be observed on the different roofs of the castle, which are made of a dark gray stone. Finally, in the saturation image, you may have noticed some white spots located in areas that correspond to very dark regions of the original image. These are a consequence of the used definition for saturation. Indeed, because saturation measures only the relative difference between the maximum and minimum BGR values, a triplet such as (1,0,0) gives a perfect saturation of 1.0, even if this color would be seen as black. Consequently, the saturation values measured in dark regions are unreliable and should not be considered.

The hue of a color is generally represented by an angle value between 0 and 360, with the red color at 0 degrees. In the case of an 8-bit image, OpenCV divides this angle by two to fit within the 1-byte range. Therefore, each hue value corresponds to a given color tint independent of its brightness and saturation. For example, both the sky and the water have the same hue value, approximately 200 degrees (intensity, 100), which corresponds to the blue shade; the green color of the trees in the background has a hue of around 90 degrees. It is important to note that hue is less reliable when evaluated for colors that have a very low saturation.

The HSB color space is often represented by a cone, where each point inside corresponds to a particular color. The angular position corresponds to the hue of the color, the saturation is the distance from the central axis, and the brightness is given by the height. The tip of the cone corresponds to the black color for which the hue and saturation are undefined:

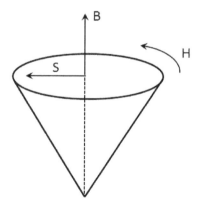

We can also generate an artificial image that will illustrate the different hue/saturation combinations.

```
cv::Mat hs(128, 360, CV_8UC3);
for (int h = 0; h < 360; h++) {
  for (int s = 0; s < 128; s++) {
    hs.at<cv::Vec3b>(s, h)[0] = h/2;     // all hue angles
    // from high saturation to low
    hs.at<cv::Vec3b>(s, h)[1] = 255-s*2;
    hs.at<cv::Vec3b>(s, h)[2] = 255;     // constant value
  }
}
```

The columns of the following screenshot show the different possible hues (from 0 to 180), while the different lines illustrate the effect of saturation; the top part of the image shows fully saturated colors while the bottom part corresponds to unsaturated colors. A brightness value of 255 has been attributed to all the displayed colors:

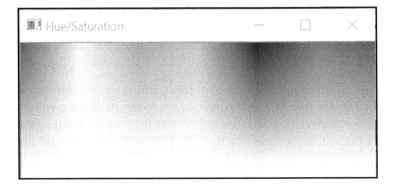

Interesting effects can be created by playing with the HSV values. Several color effects that can be created using photo editing software are accomplished from this color space. For example, you may decide to modify an image by assigning a constant brightness to all the pixels of an image without changing the hue and saturation. This can be done as follows:

```
// convert into HSV space
cv::Mat hsv;
cv::cvtColor(image, hsv, CV_BGR2HSV);
// split the 3 channels into 3 images
std::vector<cv::Mat> channels;
cv::split(hsv,channels);
// Value channel will be 255 for all pixels
channels[2]= 255;
// merge back the channels
cv::merge(channels,hsv);
// reconvert to BGR
```

```
cv::Mat newImage;
cv::cvtColor(hsv,newImage,CV_HSV2BGR);
```

This gives the following image, which now looks like a drawing.

There's more...

The HSV color space can also be very convenient to use when you want to look for objects of specific colors.

Using colors for detection – skin tone detection

Color information can be very useful for the initial detection of specific objects. For example, the detection of road signs in a driver-assistance application could rely on the colors of standard signs in order to quickly identify potential road sign candidates. The detection of skin color is another example in which the detected skin regions could be used as an indicator of the presence of a human in an image; this approach is very often used in gesture recognition where skin tone detection is used to detect hand positions.

In general, to detect an object using color, you first need to collect a large database of image samples that contain the object captured from different viewing conditions. These will be used to define the parameters of your classifier. You also need to select the color representation that you will use for classification. For skin tone detection, many studies have shown that skin color from the diverse ethnical groups clusters well in the hue/saturation space. For this reason, we will simply use the hue and saturation values to identify the skin tones in the following image:

We have defined a function that classifies the pixels of an image as skin or non-skin simply based on an interval of values (the minimum and maximum hue, and the minimum and maximum saturation):

```
void detectHScolor(const cv::Mat& image,    // input image
            double minHue, double maxHue,    // Hue interval
            double minSat, double maxSat,    // saturation interval
            cv::Mat& mask) {                 // output mask

    // convert into HSV space
    cv::Mat hsv;
    cv::cvtColor(image, hsv, CV_BGR2HSV);

    // split the 3 channels into 3 images
    std::vector<cv::Mat> channels;
    cv::split(hsv, channels);
    // channels[0] is the Hue
    // channels[1] is the Saturation
    // channels[2] is the Value

    // Hue masking
```

```
cv::Mat mask1; // below maxHue
cv::threshold(channels[0], mask1, maxHue, 255,
              cv::THRESH_BINARY_INV);
cv::Mat mask2; // over minHue
cv::threshold(channels[0], mask2, minHue, 255, cv::THRESH_BINARY);

cv::Mat hueMask; // hue mask
if (minHue < maxHue)
  hueMask = mask1 & mask2;
else // if interval crosses the zero-degree axis
  hueMask = mask1 | mask2;

// Saturation masking
// between minSat and maxSat
cv::Mat satMask; // saturation mask
cv::inRange(channels[1], minSat, maxSat, satMask);

// combined mask
mask = hueMask & satMask;
}
```

Having a large set of skin (and non-skin) samples at our disposal, we could have used a probabilistic approach in which the likelihood of observing a given color in the skin class versus that of observing the same color in the non-skin class would have been estimated. Here, we empirically define an acceptable hue/saturation interval for our test image (remember that the 8-bit version of the hue goes from 0 to 180 and saturation goes from 0 to 255):

```
// detect skin tone
cv::Mat mask;
detectHScolor(image, 160, 10,  // hue from 320 degrees to 20 degrees
              25, 166,         // saturation from ~0.1 to 0.65
              mask);

// show masked image
cv::Mat detected(image.size(), CV_8UC3, cv::Scalar(0, 0, 0));
image.copyTo(detected, mask);
```

The following detection image is obtained as the result:

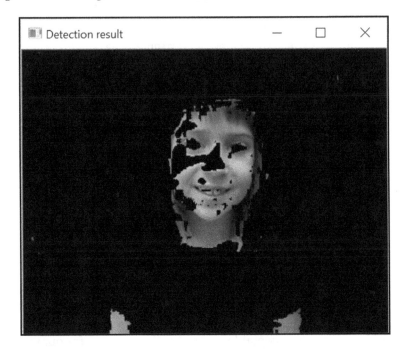

Note that, for simplicity, we have not considered color brightness in the detection. In practice, excluding brighter colors would have reduced the possibility of wrongly detecting a bright reddish colors as skin. Obviously, a reliable and accurate detection of skin color would require a much more elaborate analysis. It is also very difficult to guarantee good detection across different images because many factors influence color rendering in photography, such as white balancing and lighting conditions. Nevertheless, as shown here, using hue/saturation information as an initial detector gives us acceptable results.

See also

- `Chapter 5`, *Transforming Images with Morphological Operations*, shows you how to post-process binary images obtained from detection
- The article, *A survey of skin-color modeling and detection methods, Pattern Recognition, vol. 40, 2007, P. Kakumanu, S. Makrogiannis, N. Bourbakis*, reviews different methods of skin detection

4
Counting the Pixels with Histograms

In this chapter, we will cover the following recipes:

- Computing an image histogram
- Applying look-up tables to modify the image's appearance
- Equalizing the image histogram
- Backprojecting a histogram to detect specific image content
- Using the mean shift algorithm to find an object
- Retrieving similar images using the histogram comparison
- Counting pixels with integral images

Introduction

An image is composed of pixels of different values (colors). The distribution of pixel values across an image constitutes an important characteristic of that image. This chapter introduces the concept of image histograms. You will learn how to compute a histogram and how to use it to modify an image's appearance. Histograms can also be used to characterize an image's content and detect specific objects or textures in an image. Some of these techniques will be presented in this chapter.

Computing an image histogram

An image is made of pixels that have different values. For example, in a 1-channel gray-level image, each pixel has an integer value between 0 (black) and 255 (white). Depending on the picture content, you will find different amounts of each gray shade laid out inside the image.

A **histogram** is a simple table that gives you the number of pixels that have a given value in an image (or sometimes, a set of images). The histogram of a gray-level image will, therefore, have 256 entries (or bins). Bin 0 gives you the number of pixels that have the value 0, bin 1 gives you the number of pixels that have the value 1, and so on. Obviously, if you sum all of the entries of a histogram, you should get the total number of pixels. Histograms can also be normalized so that the sum of the bins equals 1. In this case, each bin gives you the percentage of pixels that have this specific value in the image.

Getting ready

The first three recipes of this chapter will use the following image:

How to do it...

Computing a histogram with OpenCV can be easily done by using the `cv::calcHist` function. This is a general function that can compute the histogram of multiple channel images of any pixel value type and range. Here, we will make this one simpler to use by specializing a class for the case of 1-channel gray-level images. For other types of image, you can always directly use the `cv::calcHist` function, which offers you all the flexibility required. The next section will explain each of its parameters.

For now, the initialization of our specialized class looks as follows:

```
//To create histograms of gray-level images
class Histogram1D {

  private:
    int histSize[1];          // number of bins in histogram
    float hranges[2];         // range of values
    const float* ranges[1];   // pointer to the value ranges
    int channels[1];          // channel number to be examined

  public:
  Histogram1D() {

    // Prepare default arguments for 1D histogram
    histSize[0]= 256;         // 256 bins
    hranges[0]= 0.0;          // from 0 (inclusive)
    hranges[1]= 256.0;        // to 256 (exclusive)
    ranges[0]= hranges;
    channels[0]= 0;           // we look at channel 0
  }
```

With the defined member variables, computing a gray-level histogram can then be accomplished using the following method:

```
// Computes the 1D histogram.
cv::Mat getHistogram(const cv::Mat &image) {

  cv::Mat hist;
  // Compute 1D histogram with calcHist
  cv::calcHist(&image, 1,  // histogram of 1 image only
            channels,  // the channel used
            cv::Mat(), // no mask is used
            hist,      // the resulting histogram
            1,         // it is a 1D histogram
            histSize,  // number of bins
            ranges     // pixel value range
  );
```

```
        return hist;
}
```

Now, your program simply needs to open an image, create a `Histogram1D` instance, and call the `getHistogram` method:

```
// Read input image
cv::Mat image= cv::imread("group.jpg", 0); // open in b&w

// The histogram object
Histogram1D h;

// Compute the histogram
cv::Mat histo= h.getHistogram(image);
```

The `histo` object here is a simple one-dimensional array with 256 entries. Therefore, you can read each bin by simply looping over this array:

```
// Loop over each bin
for (int i=0; i<256; i++)
  cout << "Value " << i << " = "
        <<histo.at<float>(i) << endl;
```

With the image shown at the start of this chapter, some of the displayed values would read as follows:

```
Value 7 = 159
Value 8 = 208
Value 9 = 271
Value 10 = 288
Value 11 = 340
Value 12 = 418
Value 13 = 432
Value 14 = 472
Value 15 = 525
```

It is obviously difficult to extract any intuitive meaning from this sequence of values. For this reason, it is often convenient to display a histogram as a function, for example, using bar graphs. The following methods create such a graph:

```
// Computes the 1D histogram and returns an image of it.
cv::Mat getHistogramImage(const cv::Mat &image, int zoom=1) {

  // Compute histogram first
  cv::Mat hist= getHistogram(image);
  // Creates image
  return getImageOfHistogram(hist, zoom);
}
```

```
// Create an image representing a histogram (static method)
static cv::Mat getImageOfHistogram (const cv::Mat &hist, int zoom) {
  // Get min and max bin values
  double maxVal = 0;
  double minVal = 0;
  cv::minMaxLoc(hist, &minVal, &maxVal, 0, 0);

  // get histogram size
  int histSize = hist.rows;

  // Square image on which to display histogram
  cv::Mat histImg(histSize*zoom, histSize*zoom,
                  CV_8U, cv::Scalar(255));

  // set highest point at 90% of nbins (i.e. image height)
  int hpt = static_cast<int>(0.9*histSize);

  // Draw vertical line for each bin
  for (int h = 0; h < histSize; h++) {

    float binVal = hist.at<float>(h);
    if (binVal>0) {
      int intensity = static_cast<int>(binVal*hpt / maxVal);
      cv::line(histImg, cv::Point(h*zoom, histSize*zoom),
               cv::Point(h*zoom, (histSize - intensity)*zoom),
               cv::Scalar(0), zoom);
    }
  }

  return histImg;
}
```

Using the get ImageOfHistogram method, you can obtain an image of the histogram function in the form of a bar graph that is drawn using lines:

```
//Display a histogram as an image
cv::namedWindow("Histogram");
cv::imshow("Histogram", h.getHistogramImage(image));
```

The result is the following image:

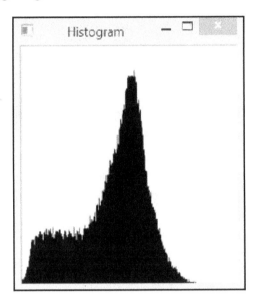

From the preceding histogram, it can be seen that the image exhibits a large peak of mid-gray level values and a good quantity of darker pixels. Coincidentally, these two groups mostly correspond to, respectively, the background and foreground of the image. This can be verified by thresholding the image at the transition between these two groups. A convenient OpenCV function can be used for this, namely the cv::threshold function, which was introduced in the previous chapter. Here, to create our binary image, we threshold the image at the minimum value just before it increases toward the high peak of the histogram (gray value 70):

```cpp
cv::Mat thresholded;              // output binary image
cv::threshold(image,thresholded,70,  // threshold value
              255,                // value assigned to
                                  // pixels over threshold value
              cv::THRESH_BINARY); // thresholding type
```

The resulting binary image clearly shows you the background/foreground segmentation:

How it works...

The `cv::calcHist` function has many parameters to permit its use in many contexts, which are as follows:

```
void calcHist(const Mat*images, // source images
        int nimages,            // number of source images (usually 1)
        const int*channels,     // list the channels to be used
        InputArray mask,        // input mask (pixels to consider)
        OutputArray hist,       // output histogram
        int dims,               // histogram dimension (number of channels)
        const int*histSize,     // number of bins in each dimension
        const float**ranges,    // range of each dimension
        bool uniform=true,      // true if equally spaced bins
        bool accumulate=false)  // to cumulate over several calls
```

Most of the time, your histogram will be one of a single 1-channel or 3-channel image. However, the function allows you to specify a multiple-channel image distributed over several images (that is, several cv::Mat). This is why an array of input images is the first parameter of this function. The sixth parameter, dims, specifies the dimensionality of the histogram, for example, 1 for a 1D histogram. Even if you are analyzing a multichannel image, you do not have to use all its channels in the computation of the histogram. The channels to be considered are listed in the channel array that has the specified dimensionality. In our class implementation, this single channel is channel 0 by default. The histogram itself is described by the number of bins in each dimension (this is the histSize array of integers) and by the minimum (inclusive) and maximum (exclusive) values in each dimension (given by the ranges array of 2-element arrays). It is also possible to define a non-uniform histogram (the second-last parameter would be set to false in that case), in which case, you need to specify the limits of each bin.

As with many OpenCV functions, a mask can be specified, indicating which pixels you want to include in the count (all pixels for which the mask value is 0 are then ignored). Two additional parameters can be specified, both of which are Boolean values. The first one indicates whether the histogram is uniform or not (true is the default). The second allows you to accumulate the result of several histogram computations. If this last parameter is true, then the pixel count of the image will be added to the current values found in the input histogram. This is useful when you want to compute the histogram of a group of images.

The resulting histogram is stored in a cv::Mat instance. Indeed, the cv::Mat class can be used to manipulate general N-dimensional matrices. Recall from Chapter 2, *Manipulating Pixels*, that this class has defined the at method for matrices of dimension 1, 2, and 3. This is why we were able to write the following code when accessing each bin of the 1D histogram in the getHistogramImage method:

```
float binVal = hist.at<float>(h);
```

Note that the values in the histogram are stored as float values.

There's more...

The Histogram1D class presented in this recipe has simplified the cv::calcHist function by restricting it to a 1D histogram. This is useful for gray-level images, but what about color images?

Computing histograms of color images

Using the same cv::calcHist function, we can compute histograms of multichannel images. For example, a class that computes histograms of color BGR images can be defined as follows:

```
class ColorHistogram {

  private:
    int histSize[3];        // size of each dimension
    float hranges[2];       // range of values (same for the 3
  dimensions)
    const float* ranges[3]; // ranges for each dimension
    int channels[3];        // channel to be considered

  public:
  ColorHistogram() {

    // Prepare default arguments for a color histogram
    // each dimension has equal size and range
    histSize[0]= histSize[1]= histSize[2]= 256;
    hranges[0]= 0.0;       // BRG range from 0 to 256
    hranges[1]= 256.0;
    ranges[0]= hranges;    // in this class,
    ranges[1]= hranges;    // all channels have the same range
    ranges[2]= hranges;
    channels[0]= 0;        // the three channels: B
    channels[1]= 1;        // G
    channels[2]= 2;        // R
  }
```

In this case, the histogram will be three-dimensional. Therefore, we need to specify a range for each of the three dimensions. In the case of our BGR image, the three channels have the same [0, 255] range. With the arguments thus prepared, the color histogram is computed by the following method:

```
//Computes the histogram.
cv::Mat getHistogram(const cv::Mat &image) {
  cv::Mat hist;

  //Compute histogram
  cv::calcHist(&image, 1,   // histogram of 1 image only
               channels,    // the channel used
               cv::Mat(),   // no mask is used
               hist,        // the resulting histogram
               3,           // it is a 3D histogram
               histSize,    // number of bins
```

```
                    ranges        // pixel value range
        );

        return hist;
    }
```

A three-dimensional `cv::Mat` instance is returned. When a histogram of 256 bins is selected, this matrix has `(256)^3` elements, which represents more than 16 million entries. In many applications, it would be better to reduce the number of bins in the computation of the histogram. It is also possible to use the `cv::SparseMat` data structure, which is designed to represent large sparse matrices (that is, matrices with very few non-zero elements) without consuming too much memory. The `cv::calcHist` function has a version that returns one such matrix. It is, therefore, simple to modify the previous method in order to use `cv::SparseMatrix`:

```
//Computes the histogram.
cv::SparseMat getSparseHistogram(const cv::Mat &image) {

    cv::SparseMat hist(3,        // number of dimensions
                  histSize,      // size of each dimension
                  CV_32F);

    //Compute histogram
    cv::calcHist(&image, 1,  // histogram of 1 image only
                  channels,  // the channel used
                  cv::Mat(), // no mask is used
                  hist,      // the resulting histogram
                  3,         // it is a 3D histogram
                  histSize,  // number of bins
                  ranges     // pixel value range
    );
    return hist;
}
```

The histogram in this case is three-dimensional, which makes it more difficult to represent. A possible option to illustrate the color distribution in an image could be by showing the individual R, G, and B histograms.

See also

- The *Backprojecting a histogram to detect specific image content* recipe later in this chapter makes use of color histograms in order to detect specific image content

Applying look-up tables to modify the image's appearance

Image histograms capture the way a scene is rendered using the available pixel intensity values. By analyzing the distribution of the pixel values over an image, it is possible to use this information to modify and possibly improve an image. This recipe explains how we can use a simple mapping function, represented by a look-up table, to modify the pixel values of an image. As we will see, look-up tables are often produced from histogram distributions.

How to do it...

A **look-up table** is a simple one-to-one (or many-to-one) function that defines how pixel values are transformed into new values. It is a 1D array with, in the case of regular gray-level images, 256 entries. Entry i of the table gives you the new intensity value of the corresponding gray level, which is expressed as follows:

```
newIntensity= lookup[oldIntensity];
```

The cv::LUT function in OpenCV applies a look-up table to an image in order to produce a new image. Since look-up tables are often built from histograms, we have added this function to our Histogram1D class:

```
static cv::Mat applyLookUp(const cv::Mat& image,    // input image
                           const cv::Mat& lookup) {// 1x256 8U
    // the output image
    cv::Mat result;

    // apply lookup table
    cv::LUT(image,lookup,result);
    return result;
}
```

How it works...

When a look-up table is applied to an image, it results in a new image in which the pixel intensity values have been modified as prescribed by the look-up table. A simple transformation could be defined as follows:

```
//Create an image inversion table
cv::Mat lut(1,256,CV_8U); // 256x1 matrix

for (int i=0; i<256; i++) {
  //0 becomes 255, 1 becomes 254, etc.
  lut.at<uchar>(i)= 255-i;
}
```

This transformation simply inverts the pixel intensities, that is, intensity 0 becomes 255, 1 becomes 254, and so on up to 255 that becomes 0. Applying such a look-up table to an image will produce the negative of the original image.

With the image in the previous recipe, the result is seen here:

There's more...

Look-up tables are useful for any application in which all pixel intensities are given a new intensity value. The transformation, however, has to be global; that is, all pixels of each intensity value must undergo the same transformation.

Stretching a histogram to improve the image contrast

It is possible to improve an image's contrast by defining a look-up table that modifies the original image's histogram. For example, if you observe the histogram of the image shown in the first recipe of this chapter, you will notice that there are practically no pixels in the image with a value higher than 200. We can, therefore, stretch the histogram in order to produce an image with an expanded contrast. To do so, the procedure uses a percentile threshold that defines the percentage of pixels that can be assigned the minimum intensity value (0) and the maximum intensity value (255) in the stretched image.

We must, therefore, find the lowest (imin) and the highest (imax) intensity values so that we have the required number of pixels below or above the specified percentile. This is accomplished by the following loops (where hist is the computed 1D histogram):

```
// number of pixels in percentile
float number= image.total()*percentile;

// find left extremity of the histogram
int imin = 0;
for (float count=0.0; imin < 256; imin++) {
  // number of pixel at imin and below must be > number
  if ((count+=hist.at<float>(imin)) >= number)
    break;
}

// find right extremity of the histogram
int imax = 255;
for (float count=0.0; imax >= 0; imax--) {
  // number of pixel at imax and below must be > number
  if ((count += hist.at<float>(imax)) >= number)
    break;
}
```

The intensity values can then be remapped so that the imin value is repositioned at intensity 0 and the imax value is assigned the value of 255. The in-between i intensities are simply linearly remapped, as follows:

```
255.0*(i-imin)/(imax-imin);
```

The resulting stretched image with a percentile cut-off of 1% is then as follows:

The expanded histogram then looks as follows:

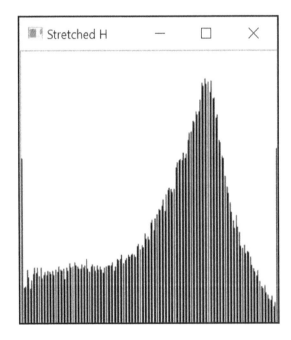

Applying a look-up table to color images

In Chapter 2, *Manipulating Pixels*, we defined a color-reduction function that modifies the BGR values of an image in order to reduce the number of possible colors. We did this by looping through the image's pixels and applying the color-reduction function to each of them. In fact, it would be much more efficient to precompute all color reductions and then modify each pixel by using a look-up table. This is indeed very easy to accomplish from what we learned in this recipe. The new color-reduction function would then be written as follows:

```
void colorReduce(cv::Mat &image, int div=64) {

  // creating the 1D lookup table
  cv::Mat lookup(1,256,CV_8U);

  // defining the color reduction lookup
  for (int i=0; i<256; i++)
    lookup.at<uchar>(i)= i/div*div + div/2;

  // lookup table applied on all channels
  cv::LUT(image,lookup,image);
}
```

The color-reduction scheme is correctly applied here because when a one-dimensional look-up table is applied to a multichannel image, then the same table is individually applied to all channels. When a look-up table has more than one dimension, then it must be applied to an image with the same number of channels.

See also

- The next recipe, *Equalizing the image histogram*, shows you another way to improve the image contrast

Equalizing the image histogram

In the previous recipe, we showed you how the contrast of an image can be improved by stretching a histogram so that it occupies the full range of the available intensity values. This strategy indeed constitutes an easy fix that can effectively improve the quality of an image. However, in many cases, the visual deficiency of an image is not that it uses a too-narrow range of intensities.

Rather, it is that some intensity values are used much more frequently than others. The histogram shown in the first recipe of this chapter is a good example of this phenomenon. The middle-gray intensities are indeed heavily represented, while darker and brighter pixel values are rather rare. One possible way to improve the quality of an image could therefore be to make equal use of all available pixel intensities. This is the idea behind the concept of **histogram equalization**, that is making the image histogram as flat as possible.

How to do it...

OpenCV offers an easy-to-use function that performs histogram equalization. It is called as follows:

```
cv::equalizeHist(image,result);
```

After applying it on our image, the following image is obtained:

This equalized image has the following histogram:

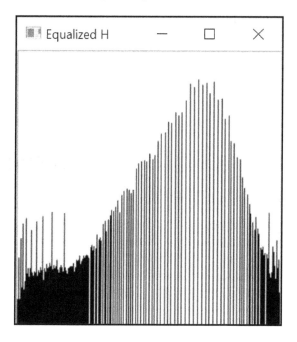

Of course, the histogram cannot be perfectly flat because the look-up table is a global many-to-one transformation. However, it can be seen that the general distribution of the histogram is now more uniform than the original one.

How it works...

In a perfectly uniform histogram, all bins would have an equal number of pixels. This implies that 50 percent of the pixels should have an intensity lower than `128` (the median intensity value), 25 percent should have an intensity lower than `64`, and so on. This observation can be expressed using the rule that in a uniform histogram, `p%` of the pixels must have an intensity value lower than or equal to `255*p%`. The rule used to equalize a histogram is that the mapping of intensity `i` should be at the intensity that corresponds to the percentage of pixels that have an intensity value below `i`. Therefore, the required look-up table can be built from the following equation:

```
lookup.at<uchar>(i)= static_cast<uchar>(255.0*p[i]/image.total());
```

Here, p[i] is the number of pixels that have an intensity lower than or equal to i. The p[i] function is often referred to as a cumulative histogram, that is it is a histogram that contains the count of pixels lower than or equal to a given intensity instead of containing the count of pixels that have a specific intensity value. Recall that image.total() returns the number of pixels in an image, so p[i]/image.total() is a percentage of pixels.

Generally, the histogram equalization greatly improves the image's appearance. However, depending on the visual content, the quality of the result can vary from image to image.

Backprojecting a histogram to detect specific image content

A histogram is an important characteristic of an image's content. If you look at an image area that shows a particular texture or a particular object, then the histogram of this area can be seen as a function that gives the probability that a given pixel belongs to this specific texture or object. In this recipe, you will learn how the concept of **histogram backprojection** can be advantageously used to detect specific image content.

How to do it...

Suppose you have an image and you wish to detect specific content inside it (for example, in the following image, the clouds in the sky). The first thing to do is to select a region of interest that contains a sample of what you are looking for. This region is the one inside the rectangle drawn on the following test image:

In our program, the region of interest is obtained as follows:

```
cv::Mat imageROI;
imageROI= image(cv::Rect(216,33,24,30)); // Cloud region
```

You then extract the histogram of this ROI. This is easily accomplished using the
Histogram1D class defined in the first recipe of this chapter, as follows:

```
Histogram1D h;
cv::Mat hist= h.getHistogram(imageROI);
```

By normalizing this histogram, we obtain a function that gives us the probability that a
pixel of a given intensity value belongs to the defined area, as follows:

```
cv::normalize(histogram,histogram,1.0);
```

Backprojecting a histogram consists of replacing each pixel value in an input image with its
corresponding probability value read in the normalized histogram. An OpenCV function
performs this task as follows:

```
cv::calcBackProject(&image,
        1,              // one image
        channels,       // the channels used,
                        // based on histogram dimension
        histogram,      // the histogram we are backprojecting
        result,         // the resulting back projection image
        ranges,         // the ranges of values
        255.0           // the scaling factor is chosen
                        // such that a probability value of 1 maps to 255
);
```

The `result` is the following probability map. For better readability, we display the negative of the `result` image, with probability of belonging to the reference area ranging from bright (low probability) to dark (high probability):

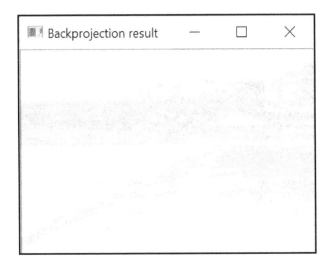

If we apply a threshold on this image, we obtain the most probable cloud pixels:

```
cv::threshold(result, result, threshold, 255, cv::THRESH_BINARY);
```

The result is shown in the following screenshot:

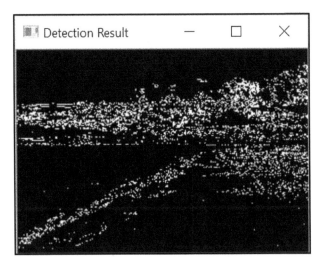

How it works...

The preceding result is disappointing because, in addition to the clouds, other areas have been wrongly detected as well. It is important to understand that the probability function has been extracted from a simple gray-level histogram. Many other pixels in the image share the same intensities as the cloud pixels, and pixels of the same intensity are replaced with the same probability value when backprojecting the histogram. One solution to improve the detection result would be to use the color information. However, in order to do this, we need to modify the call to `cv::calBackProject`. This will be explained in the *There's more...* section.

The `cv::calBackProject` function is similar to the `cv::calcHist` function. The values associated with a pixel refer to one bin of a (potentially multi-dimensional) histogram. But instead of incrementing the bin count, the `cv::calBackProject` function assigns to the corresponding pixel in the output backprojection image the value read in that bin. The first parameter of this function specifies the input images (most of the time, only one). You then need to list the channel numbers you wish to use. The histogram that is passed to the function is, this time, an input parameter; its dimension should match the one of the channel list arrays. As with `cv::calcHist`, the ranges parameter specifies the bin boundaries of the input histogram in the form of an array of float arrays, each specifying the range (minimum and maximum values) of each channel.

The resulting output is an image containing the computed probability map. Since each pixel is replaced by the value found in the histogram at the corresponding bin position, the resulting image has values between `0.0` and `1.0` (assuming a normalized histogram has been provided as input). A last parameter allows you to optionally rescale these values by multiplying them by a given factor.

There's more...

Let's now see how we can use the color information in the histogram backprojection algorithm.

Backprojecting color histograms

Multidimensional histograms can also be backprojected onto an image. Let's define a class that encapsulates the backprojection process. We first define the required attributes and initialize the data as follows:

```
class ContentFinder {
  private:
```

```
        // histogram parameters
        float hranges[2];
        const float* ranges[3];
        int channels[3];
        float threshold;            // decision threshold
        cv::Mat histogram;          // input histogram

    public:
    ContentFinder() : threshold(0.1f) {
        // in this class, all channels have the same range
        ranges[0]= hranges;
        ranges[1]= hranges;
        ranges[2]= hranges;
    }
```

A `threshold` attribute used to create the binary map showing the detection result is introduced. If this parameter is set to a negative value, the raw probability map will be returned. The input histogram is normalized (this is, however, not required) as follows:

```
    // Sets the reference histogram
    void setHistogram(const cv::Mat& h) {
      histogram= h;
      cv::normalize(histogram,histogram,1.0);
    }
```

To backproject the histogram, you simply need to specify the image, the range (we assumed here that all channels have the same range), and the list of channels used. The `find` method performs the backprojection. Two versions of this method are available; the first one that uses the three channels of the image calls the more general version:

```
    // Simplified version in which
    // all channels used, with range [0,256[ by default
    cv::Mat find(const cv::Mat& image) {

      cv::Mat result;
      hranges[0]= 0.0;     // default range [0,256[hranges[1]= 256.0;
      channels[0]= 0;      // the three channels
      channels[1]= 1;
      channels[2]= 2;
      return find(image, hranges[0], hranges[1], channels);
    }

    // Finds the pixels belonging to the histogram
    cv::Mat find(const cv::Mat& image, float minValue, float maxValue,
                 int *channels) {

      cv::Mat result;
```

```
    hranges[0]= minValue;
    hranges[1]= maxValue;
    // histogram dim matches channel list
    for (int i=0; i<histogram.dims; i++)
      this->channels[i]= channels[i];

    cv::calcBackProject(&image, 1, // we only use one image
                channels,     // channels used
                histogram,    // the histogram we are using
                result,       // the back projection image
                ranges,       // the range of values,
                              // for each dimension
                255.0         //the scaling factor is chosen such
                              //that a histogram value of 1 maps to 255
    );
  }

  // Threshold back projection to obtain a binary image
  if (threshold>0.0)
    cv::threshold(result, result, 255.0*threshold,
              255.0, cv::THRESH_BINARY);

  return result;
}
```

Let's now use a BGR histogram on the color version of the image we used previously (see the book's website to see this image in color). This time, we will try to detect the blue sky area. We will first load the color image, define the region of interest, and compute the 3D histogram on a reduced color space, as follows:

```
// Load color image
ColorHistogram hc;
cv::Mat color= cv::imread("waves.jpg");

// extract region of interest
imageROI= color(cv::Rect(0,0,100,45)); // blue sky area

// Get 3D color histogram (8 bins per channel)
hc.setSize(8); // 8x8x8
cv::Mat shist= hc.getHistogram(imageROI);
```

Next, you compute the histogram and use the `find` method to detect the sky portion of the image, as follows:

```
// Create the content finder
ContentFinder finder;
// set histogram to be back-projected
finder.setHistogram(shist);
finder.setThreshold(0.05f);

// Get back-projection of color histogram
Cv::Mat result= finder.find(color);
```

The result of the detection on the color version of the image in the previous section is seen here:

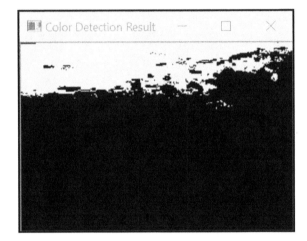

The BGR color space is generally not the best one to identify color objects in an image. Here, to make it more reliable, we reduced the number of colors before computing the histogram (remember that the original BGR space counts more than 16 million colors). The histogram extracted represents the typical color distribution for a sky area. Try to backproject it on another image. It should also detect the sky portion. Note that using a histogram built from multiple sky images should increase the accuracy of this detection.

In this case, computing a sparse histogram would have been better in terms of memory usage. You should be able to redo this exercise using `cv::SparseMat` this time. Also, if you are looking for a bright-colored object, using the hue channel of the HSV color space would probably be more efficient. In other cases, the use of the chromaticity components of a perceptually uniform space (such as L*a*b*) might constitute a better choice.

See also

- The *Using the mean shift algorithm to find an object* recipe uses the HSV color space to detect an object in an image. This is one of the many alternative solutions you can use in the detection of some image content.

- The last two recipes of `Chapter 3`, *Processing the Colors of an Image*, discusses the different color spaces that you could use for histogram backprojection.

Using the mean shift algorithm to find an object

The result of a histogram backprojection is a probability map that expresses the probability that a given piece of image content is found at a specific image location. Suppose we now know the approximate location of an object in an image; the probability map can be used to find the exact location of the object. The most probable location will be the one that maximizes this probability inside a given window. Therefore, if we start from an initial location and iteratively move around in an attempt to increase the local probability measure, it should be possible to find the exact object location. This is what is accomplished by the **mean shift algorithm**.

How to do it...

Suppose we have identified an object of interest here, a baboon's face, as shown in the following image:

This time, we will describe this object by using the hue channel of the HSV color space. This means that we need to convert the image into an HSV one and then extract the hue channel and compute the 1D hue histogram of the defined ROI. Refer to the following code:

```
// Read reference image
cv::Mat image= cv::imread("baboon01.jpg");
// Baboon's face ROI
cv::Rect rect(110, 45, 35, 45);
cv::Mat imageROI= image(rect);
// Get the Hue histogram of baboon's face
int minSat=65;
ColorHistogram hc;
cv::Mat colorhist= hc.getHueHistogram(imageROI,minSat);
```

As can be seen, the hue histogram is obtained using a convenient method that we have added to our `ColorHistogram` class as follows:

```
// Computes the 1D Hue histogram
// BGR source image is converted to HSV
// Pixels with low saturation are ignored
cv::Mat getHueHistogram(const cv::Mat &image, int minSaturation=0) {
```

```
cv::Mat hist;

// Convert to HSV colour space
cv::Mat hsv;
cv::cvtColor(image, hsv, CV_BGR2HSV);

// Mask to be used (or not)
cv::Mat mask;
// creating the mask if required
if (minSaturation>0) {

  // Spliting the 3 channels into 3 images
  std::vector<cv::Mat> v;
  cv::split(hsv,v);

  // Mask out the low saturated pixels
  cv::threshold(v[1],mask,minSaturation,
              255, cv::THRESH_BINARY);
}

//Prepare arguments for a 1D hue histogram
hranges[0]= 0.0;     // range is from 0 to 180
hranges[1]= 180.0;
channels[0]= 0;      // the hue channel

//Compute histogram
cv::calcHist(&hsv, 1,  // histogram of 1 image only
             channels, //the channel used
             mask,     //binary mask
             hist,     //the resulting histogram
             1,        //it is a 1D histogram
             histSize, //number of bins
             ranges    //pixel value range
);

return hist;
}
```

The resulting histogram is then passed to our `ContentFinder` class instance, as follows:

```
ContentFinder finder;
finder.setHistogram(colorhist);
```

Let's now open a second image, where we want to locate the new baboon's face position. This image needs to be converted to the HSV space first, and then we backproject the histogram of the first image. Refer to the following code:

```
image= cv::imread("baboon3.jpg");
```

```
// Convert to HSV space
cv::cvtColor(image, hsv, CV_BGR2HSV);
// Get back-projection of hue histogram
int ch[1]={0};
finder.setThreshold(-1.0f); // no thresholding
cv::Mat result= finder.find(hsv,0.0f,180.0f,ch);
```

Now, from an initial rectangular area (that is, the position of the baboon's face in the initial image), the cv::meanShift algorithm of OpenCV will update the rect object at the new baboon's face location, as follows:

```
// initial window position
cv::Rect rect(110,260,35,40);

// search object with mean shift
cv::TermCriteria criteria(
        cv::TermCriteria::MAX_ITER | cv::TermCriteria::EPS,
        10, // iterate max 10 times
        1); // or until the change in centroid position is less than
1px
cv::meanShift(result,rect,criteria);
```

The initial (red) and new (green) face locations are displayed here:

How it works...

In this example, we used the hue component of the HSV color space in order to characterize the object we were looking for. We made this choice because the baboon's face has a very distinctive pink color; consequently, the pixels' hue should make the face easily identifiable. The first step, therefore, is to convert the image to the HSV color space. The hue component is the first channel of the resulting image when the CV_BGR2HSV flag is used. This is an 8-bit component that varies from 0 to 180 (with cv::cvtColor, the converted image is of the same type as the source image). In order to extract the hue image, the 3-channel HSV image is split into three 1-channel images using the cv::split function. The three images are inserted into a std::vector instance, and the hue image is the first entry of the vector (that is, at index 0).

When using the hue component of a color, it is always important to take its saturation into account (which is the second entry of the vector). Indeed, when the saturation of a color is low, the hue information becomes unstable and unreliable. This is due to the fact that for low-saturated color, the B, G, and R components are almost equal. This makes difficult to determine the exact color that is represented. Consequently, we decided to ignore the hue component of colors with low saturation. That is, they are not counted in the histogram (using the minSat, parameter which masks out pixels with saturation below this threshold in the getHueHistogram method).

The mean shift algorithm is an iterative procedure that locates the local maxima of a probability function. It does this by finding the centroid, or weighted mean, of the data point inside a predefined window. The algorithm then moves the window center to the centroid location and repeats the procedure until the window center converges to a stable point. The OpenCV implementation defines two stopping criteria: a maximum number of iterations (MAX_ITER) and a window center displacement value below which the position is considered to have converged to a stable point (EPS). These two criteria are stored in a cv::TermCriteria instance. The cv::meanShift function returns the number of iterations that have been performed. Obviously, the quality of the result depends on the quality of the probability map provided on the given initial position. Note that here, we used a histogram of colors to represent an image's appearance; it is also possible to use histograms of other features to represent the object (for example, a histogram of edge orientation).

See also

- The mean shift algorithm has been largely used for visual tracking. Chapter 13, *Tracking Visual Motion*, will explore the problem of object tracking in more detail
- The mean shift algorithm has been introduced in the article *Mean Shift: A robust approach toward feature space analysis* by D. Comaniciu and P. Meer in *IEEE transactions on Pattern Analysis and Machine Intelligence*, volume 24, number 5, May 2002
- OpenCV also offers an implementation of the **CamShift** algorithm, which is an improved version of the mean shift algorithm in which the size and the orientation of the window can change

Retrieving similar images using the histogram comparison

Content-based image retrieval is an important problem in computer vision. It consists of finding a set of images that present content that is similar to a given query image. Since we have learned that histograms constitute an effective way to characterize an image's content, it makes sense to think that they can be used to solve the **content-based** image **retrieval** problem.

The key here is to be able to measure the similarity between two images by simply comparing their histograms. A measurement function that will estimate how different, or how similar, two histograms are will need to be defined. Various such measures have been proposed in the past, and OpenCV proposes a few of them in its implementation of the cv::compareHist function.

How to do it...

In order to compare a reference image with a collection of images and find the ones that are the most similar to this query image, we created an ImageComparator class. This class contains a reference to a query image and an input image, together with their histograms. In addition, since we will perform the comparison using color histograms, the ColorHistogram class is used inside our ImageComparator class:

```
class ImageComparator {

  private:
```

```
cv::Mat refH;          // reference histogram
cv::Mat inputH;        // histogram of input image

ColorHistogram hist;   // to generate the histograms
int nBins;             // number of bins used in each color channel

public:
ImageComparator() :nBins(8) {

}
```

To get a reliable similarity measure, the histogram should be computed over a reduced number of bins. Therefore, the class allows you to specify the number of bins to be used in each BGR channel. The query image is specified using an appropriate setter that also computes the reference histogram, as follows:

```
// set and compute histogram of reference image
void setReferenceImage(const cv::Mat& image) {

  hist.setSize(nBins);
  refH= hist.getHistogram(image);
}
```

Finally, a `compare` method compares the reference image with a given input image. The following method returns a score that indicates how similar the two images are:

```
// compare the images using their BGR histograms
double compare(const cv::Mat& image) {

  inputH= hist.getHistogram(image);

  // histogram comparison using intersection
  return cv::compareHist(refH,inputH, cv::HISTCMP_INTERSECT);
}
```

The preceding class can be used to retrieve images that are similar to a given query image. A reference image is provided to the class instance as follows:

```
ImageComparator c;
c.setReferenceImage(image);
```

Here, the query image we used is the color version of the beach image shown in the *Backprojecting a histogram to detect specific image content* recipe earlier in the chapter. This image was compared to the following series of images. The images are shown in order from the most similar to the least similar:

How it works...

Most histogram comparison measures are based on bin-by-bin comparisons. This is why it is important to work with a reduced histogram that will combine neighboring color into the same bin when measuring the similarity of two color histograms. The call to `cv::compareHist` is straightforward. You just input the two histograms and the function returns the measured distance. The specific measurement method you want to use is specified using a flag. In the `ImageComparator` class, the intersection method is used (with the `cv::HISTCMP_INTERSECT` flag). This method simply compares, for each bin, the two values in each histogram and keeps the minimum one. The similarity measure, then, is the sum of these minimum values. Consequently, two images that have histograms with no colors in common would get an intersection value of 0, while two identical histograms would get a value that is equal to the total number of pixels.

The other available methods are the Chi-Square measure (the `cv::HISTCMP_CHISQR` flag), which sums the normalized square difference between the bins; the correlation method (the `cv::HISTCMP_CORREL` flag), which is based on the normalized cross-correlation operator used in signal processing to measure the similarity between two signals; and the Bhattacharyya measure (the `cv::HISTCMP_BHATTACHARYYA` flag) and Kullback-Leibler divergence (the `cv::HISTCMP_KL_DIV` flag), both used in statistics to estimate the similarity between two probabilistic distributions.

See also

- The OpenCV documentation provides a description of the exact formulas used in the different histogram comparison measures.
- Earth Mover Distance is another popular histogram comparison method. It is implemented in OpenCV as the `cv::EMD` function. The main advantage of this method is that it takes into account the values found in adjacent bins to evaluate the similarity of two histograms. It is described in the article *The Earth Mover's Distance as a Metric for Image Retrieval* by *Y. Rubner, C. Tomasi, and L. J. Guibas in Int. Journal of Computer Vision*, Volume 40, No 2, 2000, pp. 99-121.

Counting pixels with integral images

In the previous recipes, we learned that a histogram is computed by going through all the pixels of an image and cumulating a count of how often each intensity value occurs in this image. We have also seen that, sometimes, we are only interested in computing our histogram in a certain area of the image. In fact, having to accumulate a sum of pixels inside an image's subregion is a common task in many computer vision algorithms. Now, suppose you have to compute several such histograms over multiple regions of interest inside your image. All these computations could rapidly become very costly. In such a situation, there is a tool that can drastically improve the efficiency of counting pixels over image subregions: the integral image.

Integral images have been introduced as an efficient way of summing pixels in image regions of interest. They are widely used in applications that involve, for example, computations over sliding windows at multiple scales.

This recipe will explain the principle behind integral images. Our objective here is to show how pixels can be summed over a rectangular region by using only three arithmetic operations. Once we have learned this concept, the *There's more...* section of this recipe will show you two examples where integral images can be advantageously used.

How to do it...

This recipe will play with the following picture, in which a region of interest showing a girl on her bike is identified:

Integral images are useful when you need to sum pixels over several image areas. Normally, if you wish to get the sum of all pixels over a region of interest, you would write the following code:

```
// Open image
cv::Mat image= cv::imread("bike55.bmp",0);
// define image roi (here the girl on bike)
int xo=97, yo=112;
int width=25, height=30;
cv::Mat roi(image,cv::Rect(xo,yo,width,height));
// compute sum
// returns a Scalar to work with multi-channel images
cv::Scalar sum= cv::sum(roi);
```

The `cv::sum` function simply loops over all the pixels of the region and accumulates the sum. Using an integral image, this can be achieved using only three additive operations. However, first you need to compute the integral image, as follows:

```
// compute integral image
cv::Mat integralImage;
cv::integral(image,integralImage,CV_32S);
```

As will be explained in the next section, the same result can be obtained using this simple arithmetic expression on the computed integral image, as follows:

```
// get sum over an area using three additions/subtractions
int sumInt= integralImage.at<int>(yo+height,xo+width)-
            integralImage.at<int>(yo+height,xo)-
            integralImage.at<int>(yo,xo+width)+
            integralImage.at<int>(yo,xo);
```

Both approaches give you the same result. However, computing the integral image is costly, since you have to loop over all the image pixels. The key is that once this initial computation is done, you will only need to add four values to get a sum over a region of interest no matter what the size of this region is. Integral images then become advantageous to use when multiple such pixel sums have to be computed over multiple regions of different sizes.

How it works...

In the previous section, you were introduced to the concept of integral images through a brief demonstration of the magic behind them, that is, how they can be used to cheaply compute the sum of pixels inside rectangular regions. To understand how they work, let's now define what an integral image is. An integral image is obtained by replacing each pixel with the value of the sum of all the pixels located inside the upper-left quadrant delimited by this pixel. The integral image can be computed by scanning the image once. Indeed, the integral value of a current pixel is given by the integral value of the pixel above this current pixel plus the value of the cumulative sum of the current line. The integral image is therefore a new image containing pixel sums. To avoid overflows, this image is usually an image of `int` values (`CV_32S`) or `float` values (`CV_32F`).

For example, in the following figure, pixel A in this integral image would contain the sum of the pixels contained inside the upper-left corner area, which is identified with a double-hatched pattern:

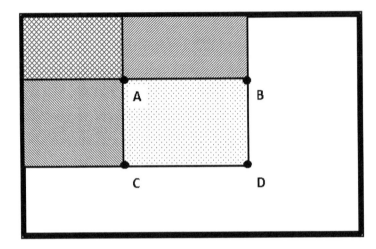

Once the integral image has been computed, any summation over a rectangular region can be easily obtained through four pixel accesses, and here is why. Referring to the preceding figure, we can see that the sum of the pixels inside the region delimited by the pixels **A**, **B**, **C**, and **D** can be obtained by reading the integral value at pixel **D**, from which you subtract the values of the pixels over **B** and to the left-hand side of **C**. However, by doing so, you have subtracted twice the sum of pixels located in the upper-left corner of **A**; this is why you have to re-add the integral sum at **A**. Formally, then, the sum of pixels inside **A**, **B**, **C**, and **D** is given by A−B−C+D. If we use the cv::Mat method to access pixel values, this formula translates to the following:

```
// window at (xo,yo) of size width by height
return (integralImage.at<cv::Vec<T,N>>(yo+height,xo+width)-
         integralImage.at<cv::Vec<T,N>>(yo+height,xo)-
         integralImage.at<cv::Vec<T,N>>(yo,xo+width)+
         integralImage.at<cv::Vec<T,N>>(yo,xo));
```

The complexity of this computation is, therefore, constant, no matter what the size of the region of interest is. Note that, for simplicity, we used the at method of the cv::Mat class, which is not the most efficient way to access pixel values (see Chapter 2, *Manipulating Pixels*). This aspect will be discussed in the *There's more...* section of this recipe, which presents two applications that benefit from the efficiency of the integral image concept.

There's more…

Integral images are used whenever multiple pixel summations must be performed. In this section, we will illustrate the use of integral images by introducing the concept of adaptive thresholding. Integral images are also useful for the efficient computation of histograms over multiple windows. This is also explained in this section.

Adaptive thresholding

Applying a threshold on an image in order to create a binary image could be a good way to extract the meaningful elements of an image. Suppose that you have the following image of a book:

Since you are interested in analyzing the text in this image, you apply a threshold to this image as follows:

```
// using a fixed threshold
cv::Mat binaryFixed;
cv::threshold(image,binaryFixed,70,255,cv::THRESH_BINARY);
```

You obtain the following result:

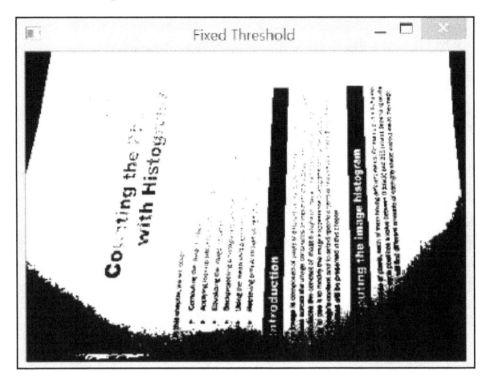

In fact, no matter what value you choose for the threshold, in some parts of the image you get missing text, whereas in other parts, the text disappears under the shadow. To overcome this problem, one possible solution consists of using a local threshold that is computed from each pixel's neighborhood. This strategy is called **adaptive thresholding**, and it consists of comparing each pixel with the mean value of the neighboring pixels. Pixels that clearly differ from their local mean will then be considered as outliers and will be cut off by the thresholding process.

Adaptive thresholding, therefore, requires the computation of a local mean around every pixel. This requires multiple image window summations that can be computed efficiently through the integral image. Consequently, the first step is to compute the following integral image:

```
// compute integral image
cv::Mat iimage;
cv::integral(image,iimage,CV_32S);
```

Now we can go through all the pixels and compute the mean over a square neighborhood. We could use our `IntegralImage` class to do so, but this one uses the inefficient `at` method for pixel access. This time, let's get efficient by looping over the image using the pointers, as we learned in `Chapter 2`, *Manipulating Pixels*. This loop looks as follows:

```
int blockSize= 21;   // size of the neighborhood
int threshold=10;    // pixel will be compared
                     // to (mean-threshold)

// for each row
int halfSize= blockSize/2;
for (int j=halfSize; j<nl-halfSize-1; j++) {

  // get the address of row j
  uchar* data= binary.ptr<uchar>(j);
  int* idata1= iimage.ptr<int>(j-halfSize);
  int* idata2= iimage.ptr<int>(j+halfSize+1);

  // for each pixel of a line
  for (int i=halfSize; i<nc-halfSize-1; i++) {
    // compute sum
    int sum= (idata2[i+halfSize+1]-data2[i-halfSize]-
            idata1[i+halfSize+1]+idata1[i-halfSize])
                                /(blockSize*blockSize);

    // apply adaptive threshold
    if (data[i]<(sum-threshold))
      data[i]= 0;
    else
      data[i]=255;
  }
}
```

In this example, a neighborhood of size `21x21` is used. To compute each mean, we need to access the four integral pixels that delimit the square neighborhood: two located on the line pointed by `idata1` and two on the line pointed by `idata2`. The current pixel is compared to the computed mean, from which we subtract a threshold value (here, set to `10`); this is to make sure that rejected pixels clearly differ from their local mean. The following binary image is then obtained:

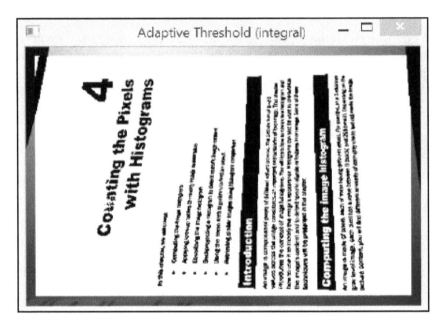

Clearly, this is a much better result than the one we got using a fixed threshold. Adaptive thresholding is a common image-processing technique. As such, it is also implemented in OpenCV as follows:

```
cv::adaptiveThreshold(image,            // input image
        binaryAdaptive,                 // output binary image
        255,                            // max value for output
        cv::ADAPTIVE_THRESH_MEAN_C,     // method
        cv::THRESH_BINARY,              // threshold type
        blockSize,                      // size of the block
        threshold);                     // threshold used
```

This function call produces exactly the same result as the one we obtained using our integral image. In addition, instead of using the local mean for thresholding, this function allows you to use a Gaussian weighted sum (the method flag would be cv::ADAPTIVE_THRESH_GAUSSIAN_C) in this case. It is interesting to note that our implementation is slightly faster than the cv::adaptiveThreshold call.

Finally, it is worth mentioning that we can also write an adaptive thresholding procedure by using the OpenCV image operators. This would be done as follows:

```
cv::Mat filtered;
cv::Mat binaryFiltered;
// box filter compute avg of pixels over a rectangular region
cv::boxFilter(image,filtered,CV_8U,cv::Size(blockSize,blockSize));
// check if pixel greater than (mean + threshold)
binaryFiltered= image>= (filtered-threshold);
```

Image filtering will be covered in Chapter 6, *Filtering the Images*.

Visual tracking using histograms

As we learned in the previous recipes, a histogram constitutes a reliable global representation of an object's appearance. In this section, we will demonstrate the usefulness of integral images by showing you how we can locate an object in an image by searching for an image area that presents a histogram similar to a target object. We accomplished this in the *Using the mean shift algorithm to find an object* recipe by using the concepts of histogram backprojection and local search through mean shift. This time, we will find our object by performing an explicit search for regions of similar histograms over the full image.

In the special case where an integral image is used on a binary image made of 0 and 1 values, the integral sum gives you the number of pixels that have a value of 1 inside the specified region. We will exploit this fact in this recipe to compute the histogram of a gray-level image.

The cv::integral function also works for multichannel images. You can take advantage of this fact to compute histograms of image subregions using integral images. You simply need to convert your image into a multichannel image made of binary planes; each of these planes is associated to a bin of your histogram and shows you which pixels have a value that falls into this bin. The following function creates such multiplane images from a gray-level one:

```
// convert to a multi-channel image made of binary planes
// nPlanes must be a power of 2
void convertToBinaryPlanes(const cv::Mat& input,
```

```
                                cv::Mat& output, int nPlanes) {

   // number of bits to mask out
   int n= 8-static_cast<int>(
                 log(static_cast<double>(nPlanes))/log(2.0));
   // mask used to eliminate least significant bits
   uchar mask= 0xFF<<n;

   // create a vector of binary images
   std::vector<cv::Mat> planes;
   // reduce to nBins by eliminating least significant bits
   cv::Mat reduced= input&mask;
   // compute each binary image plane
   for (int i=0; i<nPlanes; i++) {
     // 1 for each pixel equals to i<<shift
     planes.push_back((reduced==(i<<n))&0x1);
   }

   // create multi-channel image
   cv::merge(planes,output);
}
```

The integral image computations can also be encapsulated into one convenient template class as follows:

```
template <typename T, int N>
class IntegralImage {

  cv::Mat integralImage;

  public:

  IntegralImage(cv::Mat image) {

   // (costly) computation of the integral image
   cv::integral(image,integralImage,
              cv::DataType<T>::type);
  }

  // compute sum over sub-regions of any size
  // from 4 pixel accesses
  cv::Vec<T,N> operator()(int xo, int yo, int width, int height) {

   // window at (xo,yo) of size width by height
   return (integralImage.at<cv::Vec<T,N>>(yo+height,xo+width)-
          integralImage.at<cv::Vec<T,N>>(yo+height,xo)-
          integralImage.at<cv::Vec<T,N>>(yo,xo+width)+
          integralImage.at<cv::Vec<T,N>>(yo,xo));
```

Chapter 4

```
        }

    };
```

We now want to find where the girl on the bicycle, whom we identified in the previous image, is in a subsequent image. Let's first compute the histogram of the girl in the original image. We can accomplish this using the `Histogram1D` class we built in the recipe *Computing an image histogram* of this chapter. Here, we produce a 16-bin histogram as follows:

```
// histogram of 16 bins
Histogram1D h;
h.setNBins(16);
// compute histogram over image roi
cv::Mat refHistogram=  h.getHistogram(roi);
```

The preceding histogram will be used as a referential representation to locate the target object (the girl on her bike) in a subsequent image.

Suppose that the only information we have is that the girl is moving more or less horizontally across the image. Since we will have many histograms to compute at various locations, we compute the integral image as a preliminary step. Refer to the following code:

```
// first create 16-plane binary image
cv::Mat planes;
convertToBinaryPlanes(secondIimage,planes,16);
// then compute integral image
IntegralImage<float,16> intHistogram(planes);
```

To perform the search, we loop over a range of possible locations and compare the current histogram with the referential one. Our goal is to find the location with the most similar histogram. Refer to the following code:

```
double maxSimilarity=0.0;
int xbest, ybest;
// loop over a horizontal strip around girl
// location in initial image
for (int y=110; y<120; y++) {
  for (int x=0; x<secondImage.cols-width; x++) {

    // compute histogram of 16 bins using integral image
    histogram= intHistogram(x,y,width,height);
    // compute distance with reference histogram
    double distance= cv::compareHist(refHistogram,
                                     histogram,
                                     CV_COMP_INTERSECT);
    //find position of most similar histogram
```

```
      if (distance>maxSimilarity) {

        xbest= x;
        ybest= y;
        maxSimilarity= distance;
      }
    }
  }
  //draw rectangle at best location
  cv::rectangle(secondImage, cv::Rect(xbest,ybest,width,height),0));
```

The location with the most similar histogram is then identified as followings:

The white rectangle represents the search area. Histograms of all windows that fit inside this area have been computed. We kept the window size constant, but it could have been a good strategy to also search for slightly smaller or larger windows in order to take into account the eventual changes in scale. Note that in order to limit the complexity of this computation, the number of bins in the histograms to be computed should be kept low. In our example, we reduced this to 16 bins. Consequently, plane 0 of this multiplane image contains a binary image that shows you all pixels that have a value between 0 and 15, while plane 1 shows you pixels with values between 16 and 31, and so on.

The search for an object consisted of computing the histograms of all windows of the given size over a predetermined range of pixels. This represents the computation of `3200` different histograms that have been efficiently computed from our integral image. All the histograms returned by our `IntegralImage` class are contained in a `cv::Vec` object (because of the use of the `at` method). We then use the `cv::compareHist` function to identify the most similar histogram (remember that this function, like most OpenCV functions, can accept either the `cv::Mat` or `cv::Vec` object through the convenient `cv::InputArray` generic parameter type).

See also

- `Chapter 8`, *Detecting Interest Points,* will present the SURF operator that also relies on the use of integral images
- The *Finding objects and faces with a cascade of Haar features* recipe in `Chapter 14`, *Learning from Examples,* presents the Haar features that are computed using integral images
- The *Applying morphological operators on gray-level images* recipe in `Chapter 5`, *Transforming Images with Morphological Operations,* presents an operator that can produce results similar to the presented adaptive thresholding technique
- The article *Robust Fragments-based Tracking using the Integral Histogram* by *A. Adam, E. Rivlin,* and *I. Shimshoni* in the *Proceedings of the International Conference on Computer Vision and Pattern Recognition,* 2006, pp. 798-805, describes an interesting approach that uses integral images to track objects in an image sequence

5
Transforming Images with Morphological Operations

In this chapter, we will cover the following recipes:

- Eroding and dilating images using morphological filters
- Opening and closing images using morphological filters
- Applying morphological operators on gray-level images
- Segmenting images using watersheds
- Extracting distinctive regions using MSER

Introduction

Mathematical morphology is a theory that was developed in the 1960s for the analysis and processing of discrete images. It defines a series of operators that transform an image by probing it with a predefined shape element. The way this shape element intersects the neighborhood of a pixel determines the result of the operation. This chapter presents the most important morphological operators. It also explores the problems of image segmentation and feature detection using algorithms based on morphological operators.

Eroding and dilating images using morphological filters

Erosion and dilation are the most fundamental morphological operators. Therefore, we will present them in this first recipe. The fundamental component in mathematical morphology is the **structuring element**. A structuring element can be simply defined as a configuration of pixels (the square shape in the following figure) on which an origin is defined (also called an **anchor point**). Applying a morphological filter consists of probing each pixel of the image using this structuring element. When the origin of the structuring element is aligned with a given pixel, its intersection with the image defines a set of pixels on which a particular morphological operation is applied (the nine shaded pixels in the following figure). In principle, the structuring element can be of any shape, but most often, a simple shape such as a square, circle, or diamond with the origin at the center is used. Custom structuring elements can be useful to emphasize or eliminate regions of particular shapes.

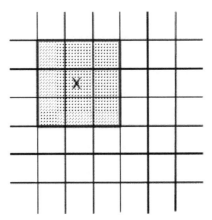

Getting ready

As morphological filters often work on binary images, we will use the binary image that was created through thresholding in the first recipe of the previous chapter. However, since the convention is to have the foreground objects represented by high (white) pixel values and the background objects by low (black) pixel values in morphology, we have negated the image.

In morphological terms, the following image is said to be the **complement** of the image that was created in the previous chapter:

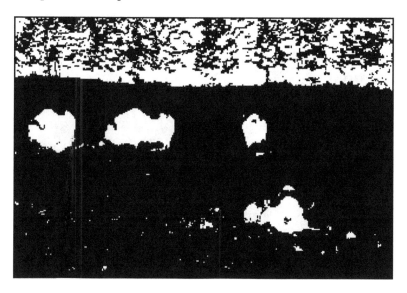

How to do it...

Erosion and dilation are implemented in OpenCV as simple functions, which are cv::erode and cv::dilate. Their usage is straightforward:

```
// Read input image
cv::Mat image= cv::imread("binary.bmp");

// Erode the image
// with the default 3x3 structuring element (SE)
cv::Mat eroded;  // the destination image
cv::erode(image,eroded,cv::Mat());

// Dilate the image
cv::Mat dilated;  // the destination image
cv::dilate(image,dilated,cv::Mat());
```

The two images produced by these function calls are seen in the following images. The first one shows erosion:

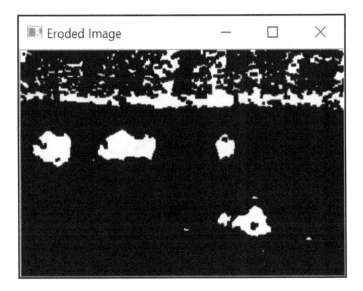

The second image shows the dilation result:

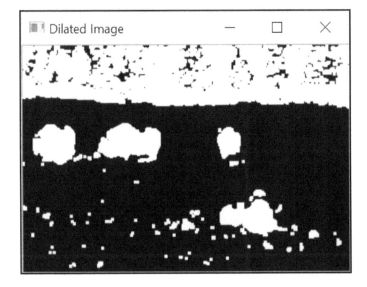

How it works...

As for all morphological filters, the two filters of this recipe operate on sets of pixels defined by a structuring element. Recall that when applied to a given pixel, the anchor point of the structuring element is aligned with this pixel location, and all the pixels that intersect the structuring element are included in the current set. **Erosion** replaces the current pixel with the minimum pixel value found in the defined pixel set. **Dilation** is the complementary operator, and it replaces the current pixel with the maximum pixel value found in the defined pixel set. Since the input binary image contains only black (value 0) and white (value 255) pixels, each pixel is replaced by either a white or black pixel.

A good way to picturize the effect of these two operators is to think in terms of background (black) and foreground (white) objects. With erosion, if the structuring element when placed at a given pixel location touches the background (that is, one of the pixels in the intersecting set is black), then this pixel will be sent to the background. In the case of dilation, if the structuring element on a background pixel touches a foreground object, then this pixel will be assigned a white value. This explains why the size of the objects has been reduced (the shape has been eroded) in the eroded image while it has been expanded in the dilated image. Note how some of the small objects (which can be considered as "noisy" background pixels) have also been completely eliminated in the eroded image. Similarly, the dilated objects are now larger, and some of the "holes" inside them have been filled. By default, OpenCV uses a 3x3 square structuring element. This default structuring element is obtained when an empty matrix (that is, cv::Mat()) is specified as the third argument in the function call, as it was done in the preceding example. You can also specify a structuring element of the size (and shape) you want by providing a matrix in which the nonzero element defines the structuring element. For example, to apply a 7x7 structuring element, you would proceed as follows:

```
// Erode the image with a larger SE
// create a 7x7 mat with containing all 1s
cv::Mat element(7,7,CV_8U,cv::Scalar(1));
// erode the image with that SE
cv::erode(image,eroded,element);
```

The effect is much more destructive in this case, as shown in the following screenshot:

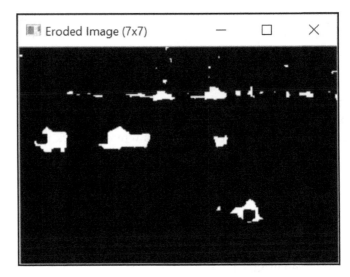

Another way to obtain a similar result is to repetitively apply the same structuring element on an image. The two functions have an optional parameter to specify the number of repetitions:

```
// Erode the image 3 times
cv::erode(image,eroded,cv::Mat(),cv::Point(-1,-1), 3);
```

The `cv::Point(-1,-1)` argument means that the origin is at the center of the matrix (default); it can be defined anywhere on the structuring element. The image that is obtained will be identical to the image we obtained with the 7x7 structuring element. Indeed, eroding an image twice is similar to eroding an image with a structuring element dilated with itself. This also applies to dilation.

Finally, since the notion of background/foreground is arbitrary, we can make the following observation (which is a fundamental property of the erosion/dilation operators). Eroding the foreground objects with a structuring element can be seen as a dilation of the background part of the image. In other words, we can make the following observations:

- The erosion of an image is equivalent to the complement of the dilation of the complement image
- The dilation of an image is equivalent to the complement of the erosion of the complement image

There's more...

Note that even though we applied our morphological filters on binary images here, these filters can be applied on gray-level or even color images with the same definitions. The third recipe of this chapter will present few morphological operators and their effect on gray-level images.

Also, note that the OpenCV morphological functions support in-place processing. This means that you can use the input image as the destination image, as follows:

```
cv::erode(image,image,cv::Mat());
```

OpenCV will create the required temporary image for you for this to work properly.

See also

- The *Opening and closing images using morphological filters* recipe applies the erosion and dilation filters in cascade to produce new operators
- The *Applying morphological operators on gray-level images* recipe introduces other morphological operators that can usefully be applied to gray-level images

Opening and closing images using morphological filters

The previous recipe introduced you to the two fundamental morphological operators: dilation and erosion. From these, other operators can be defined. The next two recipes will present some of them. The opening and closing operators are presented in this recipe.

How to do it...

In order to apply higher-level morphological filters, you need to use the `cv::morphologyEx` function with the appropriate function code. For example, the following call will apply the closing operator:

```
// Close the image
cv::Mat element5(5,5,CV_8U,cv::Scalar(1));
cv::Mat closed;
cv::morphologyEx(image,closed,    // input and output images
```

```
cv::MORPH_CLOSE,  // operator code
element5);        // structuring element
```

Note that we used a 5x5 structuring element to make the effect of the filter more apparent. If we use the binary image of the preceding recipe as input, we will obtain the following image:

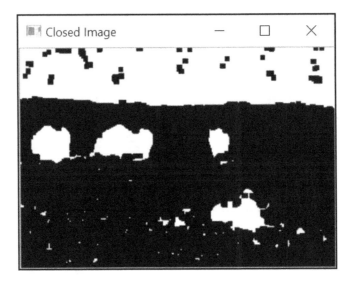

Similarly, applying the morphological opening operator will result in the following image:

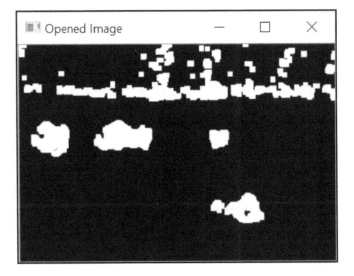

The preceding image is obtained from the following code:

```
cv::Mat opened;
cv::morphologyEx(image, opened, cv::MORPH_OPEN, element5);
```

How it works...

The opening and closing filters are simply defined in terms of the basic erosion and dilation operations. **Closing** is defined as the erosion of the dilation of an image. **Opening** is defined as the dilation of the erosion of an image.

Consequently, one can compute the closing of an image using the following calls:

```
// dilate original image
cv::dilate(image, result, cv::Mat());
// in-place erosion of the dilated image
cv::erode(result, result, cv::Mat());
```

The opening filter can be obtained by interchanging these two function calls.

While examining the result of the closing filter, it can be seen that the small holes of the white foreground objects have been filled. The filter also connects several adjacent objects together. Basically, any holes or gaps that are too small to completely contain the structuring element will be eliminated by the filter.

Reciprocally, the opening filter eliminated several small objects from the scene. All the objects that were too small to contain the structuring element have been removed.

These filters are often used in object detection. The closing filter connects the objects erroneously fragmented into smaller pieces together, while the opening filter removes the small blobs introduced by the image noise. Therefore, it is advantageous to use them in a sequence. You can then apply the opening filter before the closing filter if you wish to prioritize noise filtering, but this could be at the price of eliminating parts of fragmented objects.

The following image is the result of applying the opening filter before the closing filter:

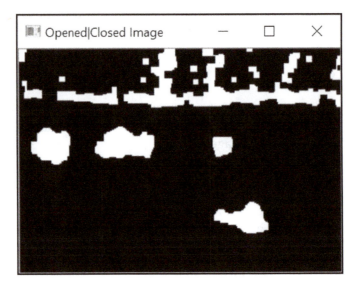

Note that applying the same opening (and similarly the closing) operator on an image several times has no effect. Indeed, as the holes have been filled by the first opening filter, an additional application of the same filter will not produce any other changes to the image. In mathematical terms, these operators are said to be **idempotent**.

See also

- The opening and closing operators are often used to clean up an image before extracting its connected components as explained in the *Extracting connected components* recipe of `Chapter 7`, *Extracting Lines, Contours, and Components*

Applying morphological operators on gray-level images

More advanced morphological operators can be composited by combining the different basic morphological filters introduced in this chapter. This recipe will present two morphological operators that, when applied to gray-level images, can lead to the detection of interesting image features.

How to do it...

One interesting morphological operator is the morphological gradient that allows extracting the edges of an image. This one can be accessed through the `cv::morphologyEx` function as follows:

```
// Get the gradient image using a 3x3 structuring element
cv::Mat result;
cv::morphologyEx(image, result,
                 cv::MORPH_GRADIENT, cv::Mat());
```

The following result shows the extracted contours of the image's elements (the resulting image has been inverted for better viewing):

Another useful morphological operator is the top-hat transform. This operator can be used to extract local small foreground objects in an image. The effect of this operator can be demonstrated by applying it on the book image of the last recipe of the previous chapter. This image shows an unevenly illuminated page of a book. A black top-hat transform will extract the characters of this page (considered here as the foreground objects). This operator is also called by using the `cv::morphologyEx` function with the appropriate flag:

```
// Apply the black top-hat transform using a 7x7 structuring element
cv::Mat element7(7, 7, CV_8U, cv::Scalar(1));
cv::morphologyEx(image, result, cv::MORPH_BLACKHAT, element7);
```

As it can be seen in the following image, this operator successfully extracted most of the characters of the original image:

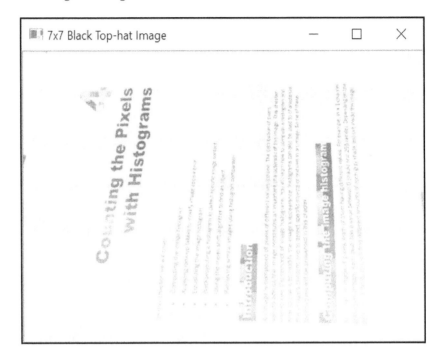

How it works...

A good way to understand the effect of morphological operators on a gray-level image is to consider an image as a topological relief in which the gray levels correspond to elevation (or altitude). Under this perspective, the bright regions correspond to mountains, while the dark areas correspond to the valleys of the terrain. Also, since edges correspond to a rapid transition between the dark and bright pixels, these can be pictured as abrupt cliffs. If an erosion operator is applied on such a terrain, the net result will be to replace each pixel by the lowest value in a certain neighborhood, thus reducing its height. As a result, cliffs will be eroded as the valleys expand. Dilation has the exact opposite effect; that is, cliffs will gain terrain over the valleys. However, in both cases, the plateau (that is, the area of constant intensity) will remain relatively unchanged.

These observations lead to a simple way to detect the edges (or cliffs) of an image. This can be done by computing the difference between the dilated and eroded images. Since these two transformed images differ mostly at the edge locations, the image edges will be emphasized by the subtraction. This is exactly what the `cv::morphologyEx` function does when the `cv::MORPH_GRADIENT` argument is inputted. Obviously, the larger the structuring element is, the thicker the detected edges will be. This edge detection operator is called the **Beucher gradient** (the next chapter will discuss the concept of an image gradient in more detail). Note that similar results can also be obtained by simply subtracting the original image from the dilated one or the eroded image from the original. The resulting edges would simply be thinner.

The top-hat operator is also based on image difference. This time, the operator uses opening and closing. When a gray-level image is morphologically opened, its local peaks are eliminated; this is due to the erosion operator that is applied first. The rest of the image is preserved. Consequently, the difference between the original image and the opened one is the set of local peaks. These local peaks are the foreground objects we want to extract. In the book example of this recipe, the objective was to extract the characters of the page. Since the foreground objects are, in this case, black over a white background, we used the complementary operator, called the black top-hat, which consists of subtracting the original image from its closing. We used a `7x7` structuring element in order to have the closing operation big enough to remove the characters.

See also

- The *Applying directional filters to detect edges* recipe in `Chapter 6`, *Filtering the Images*, describes the other filters that perform edge detection
- The article, *The Morphological gradients, J.-F. Rivest, P. Soille, and S. Beucher, ISET's symposium on electronic imaging science and technology, SPIE*, Feb. 1992, discusses the concept of morphological gradients in more detail
- The article *Morphological operator for corner detection, R. Laganière, Pattern Recognition*, volume 31, issue 11, 1998, presents an operator for the detection of corners using morphological filters

Segmenting images using watersheds

The watershed transformation is a popular image processing algorithm that is used to quickly segment an image into homogenous regions. It relies on the idea that when the image is seen as a topological relief, the homogeneous regions correspond to relatively flat basins delimited by steep edges. With the watershed algorithm, segmentation is achieved by flooding this relief by gradually increasing the level of water in this one. As a result of its simplicity, the original version of this algorithm tends to over-segment the image, which produces multiple small regions. This is why OpenCV proposes a variant of this algorithm that uses a set of predefined markers to guide the definition of the image segments.

How to do it…

The watershed segmentation is obtained through the use of the `cv::watershed` function. The input for this function is a 32-bit signed integer marker image in which each nonzero pixel represents a label. The idea is to mark some pixels of the image that are known to belong to a given region. From this initial labeling, the watershed algorithm will determine the regions to which the other pixels belong. In this recipe, we will first create the marker image as a gray-level image and then convert it into an image of integers. We have conveniently encapsulated this step into a `WatershedSegmenter` class containing a method to specify the marker image and a method to compute the watershed:

```
class WatershedSegmenter {

  private:
  cv::Mat markers;

  public:
  void setMarkers(const cv::Mat& markerImage) {

    // Convert to image of ints
    markerImage.convertTo(markers,CV_32S);
  }

  cv::Mat process(const cv::Mat &image) {

    // Apply watershed
    cv::watershed(image,markers);
    return markers;
  }
```

The way these markers are obtained depends on the application. For example, some preprocessing steps might have resulted in the identification of some pixels that belong to an object of interest. The watershed would then be used to delimitate the complete object from that initial detection. In this recipe, we will simply use the binary image used throughout this chapter in order to identify the animals of the corresponding original image (this is the image shown at the beginning of Chapter 4, *Counting the Pixels with Histograms*). Therefore, from our binary image, we need to identify pixels that belong to the foreground (the animals) and pixels that belong to the background (mainly the grass). Here, we will mark the foreground pixels with the label 255 and the background pixels with the label 128 (this choice is totally arbitrary; any label number other than 255 will work). The other pixels, that is, the ones for which the labeling is unknown, are assigned the value 0.

As of now, the binary image includes white pixels that belong to the various parts of the image. We will then severely erode this image in order to retain only the pixels that certainly belong to the foreground objects:

```
// Eliminate noise and smaller objects
cv::Mat fg;
cv::erode(binary,fg,cv::Mat(),cv::Point(-1,-1),4);
```

The result is the following image:

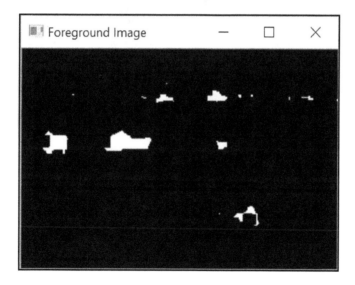

Note that a few pixels that belong to the background forest are still present. Let's keep them. Therefore, they will be considered to correspond to an object of interest. Similarly, we can select a few pixels of the background by a large dilation of the original binary image:

```
// Identify image pixels without objects
cv::Mat bg;
cv::dilate(binary,bg,cv::Mat(),cv::Point(-1,-1),4);
cv::threshold(bg,bg,1,128,cv::THRESH_BINARY_INV);
```

The resulting black pixels correspond to background pixels. This is why the thresholding operation assigns the value `128` to these pixels immediately after the dilation. The following image is obtained:

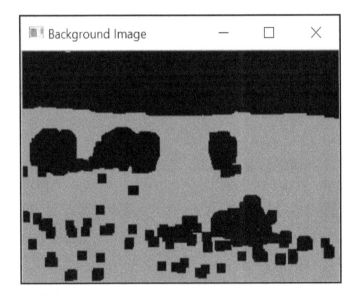

These images are combined to form the marker image as follows:

```
// Create markers image
cv::Mat markers(binary.size(),CV_8U,cv::Scalar(0));
markers= fg+bg;
```

Note how we used the overloaded `operator+` here in order to combine the images. The following image will be used as the input to the watershed algorithm:

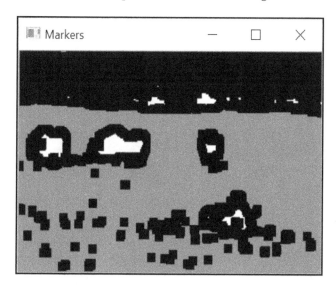

In this input image, the white areas belong, for sure, to the foreground objects, the gray areas are a part of the background, and the black areas have an unknown label. The role of the watershed segmentation is therefore to assign a label (background/foreground) to the black marked pixels by establishing the exact border delimitating the foreground objects from the background. This segmentation is then obtained as follows:

```
// Create watershed segmentation object
WatershedSegmenter segmenter;

// Set markers and process
segmenter.setMarkers(markers);
segmenter.process(image);
```

The marker image is then updated such that each zero pixel is assigned one of the input labels, while the pixels that belong to the found boundaries have a value −1. The resulting image of the labels is as follows:

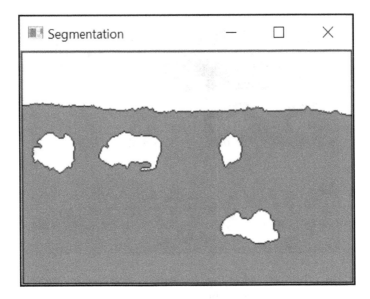

And the boundary image is as follows:

How it works...

As we did in the preceding recipes, we will use the topological map analogy in the description of the watershed algorithm. In order to create watershed segmentation, the idea is to progressively flood the image starting at level 0. As the level of water progressively increases (to levels 1, 2, 3, and so on), catchment basins are formed. The size of these basins also gradually increases and, consequently, the water of two different basins will eventually merge. When this happens, a watershed is created in order to keep the two basins separated. Once the level of water has reached its maximum level, the sets of these created basins and watersheds form the watershed segmentation.

As expected, the flooding process initially creates many small individual basins. When all of these are merged, many watershed lines are created, which results in an over-segmented image. To overcome this problem, a modification to this algorithm has been proposed in which the flooding process starts from a predefined set of marked pixels. The basins created from these markers are labeled in accordance with the values assigned to the initial marks. When two basins having the same label merge, no watershed is created, thus preventing over-segmentation. This is what happens when the cv::watershed function is called. The input marker image is updated to produce the final watershed segmentation. Users can input a marker image with any number of labels and pixels of unknown labeling left to value 0. The marker image is chosen to be an image of a 32-bit signed integer in order to be able to define more than 255 labels. It also allows the special value, -1, to be assigned to the pixels associated with a watershed.

To facilitate the display of the result, we have introduced two special methods. The first method returns an image of the labels (with watersheds at value 0). This is easily done through thresholding, as follows:

```cpp
// Return result in the form of an image
cv::Mat getSegmentation() {

  cv::Mat tmp;
  // all segment with label higher than 255
  // will be assigned value 255
  markers.convertTo(tmp,CV_8U);

  return tmp;
}
```

Similarly, the second method returns an image in which the watershed lines are assigned the value 0, and the rest of the image is at 255. This time, the `cv::convertTo` method is used to achieve this result, as follows:

```
// Return watershed in the form of an image
cv::Mat getWatersheds() {

  cv::Mat tmp;
  // Each pixel p is transformed into
  // 255p+255 before conversion
  markers.convertTo(tmp,CV_8U,255,255);

  return tmp;
}
```

The linear transformation that is applied before the conversion allows the -1 pixels to be converted into 0 (since -1*255+255=0).

Pixels with a value greater than 255 are assigned the value 255. This is due to the saturation operation that is applied when signed integers are converted into unsigned characters.

There's more...

Obviously, the marker image can be obtained in many different ways. For example, users can be interactively asked to mark the objects of an image by painting some areas on the objects and the background of a scene. Alternatively, in an attempt to identify an object located at the center of an image, one can also simply input an image with the central area marked with a certain label and the border of the image (where the background is assumed to be present) marked with another label. This marker image can be created by drawing thick rectangles on a marker image as follows:

```
// Identify background pixels
cv::Mat imageMask(image.size(),CV_8U,cv::Scalar(0));
cv::rectangle(imageMask, cv::Point(5,5),
            cv::Point(image.cols-5, image.rows-5),
            cv::Scalar(255), 3);
// Identify foreground pixels
// (in the middle of the image)
cv::rectangle(imageMask,
            cv::Point(image.cols/2-10,image.rows/2-10),
            cv::Point(image.cols/2+10,image.rows/2+10),
            cv::Scalar(1), 10);
```

If we superimpose this marker image on a test image, we will obtain the following image:

The following is the resulting watershed image:

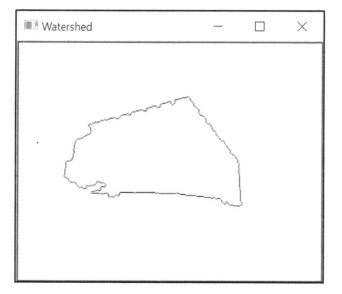

See also

- The article, *The viscous watershed transform*, C. Vachier and F. Meyer, *Journal of Mathematical Imaging and Vision*, volume 22, issue 2-3, May 2005, gives more information on the watershed transform

Extracting distinctive regions using MSER

In the previous recipe, you learned how an image can be segmented into regions by gradually flooding it and creating watersheds. The **Maximally Stable External Regions** (**MSER**) algorithm uses the same immersion analogy in order to extract meaningful regions in an image. These regions will also be created by flooding the image level by level, but this time, we will be interested in the basins that remain relatively stable for a period of time during the immersion process. It will be observed that these regions correspond to some distinctive parts of the scene objects pictured in the image.

How to do it...

The basic class to compute the MSER of an image is `cv::MSER`. This class is an abstract interface that inherits from the `cv::Feature2D` class; in fact, all feature detectors in OpenCV inherit from this super-class. An instance of the `cv::MSER` class can be created by using the `create` method. Here, we initialize it by specifying a minimum and maximum size for the detected regions in order to limit the number of detected features as follows:

```
// basic MSER detector
cv::Ptr<cv::MSER> ptrMSER=
  cv::MSER::create(5,     // delta value for local detection
                   200,   // min acceptable area
                   2000); // max acceptable area
```

Now, the MSER can be obtained by a call to the `detectRegions` method, specifying the input image and the appropriate output data structures, as follows:

```
// vector of point sets
std::vector<std::vector<cv::Point> > points;
// vector of rectangles
std::vector<cv::Rect> rects;
// detect MSER features
ptrMSER->detectRegions(image, points, rects);
```

The detection results are provided in the form of a vector of regions represented by the pixel points that compose each of them and by a vector of bounding boxes enclosing the regions. In order to visualize the results, we create a blank image on which we will display the detected regions in different colors (which are randomly chosen). This is done as follows:

```
// create white image
cv::Mat output(image.size(),CV_8UC3);
output= cv::Scalar(255,255,255);

// OpenCV random number generator
cv::RNG rng;

// Display the MSERs in color areas
// for each detected feature
// reverse order to display the larger MSER first
for (std::vector<std::vector<cv::Point> >::reverse_iterator
        it= points.rbegin();
        it!= points.rend(); ++it) {

    // generate a random color
    cv::Vec3b c(rng.uniform(0,254),
                rng.uniform(0,254), rng.uniform(0,254));

    // for each point in MSER set
    for (std::vector<cv::Point>::iterator itPts= it->begin();
            itPts!= it->end(); ++itPts) {

      // do not overwrite MSER pixels
      if (output.at<cv::Vec3b>(*itPts)[0]==255) {
        output.at<cv::Vec3b>(*itPts)= c;
      }
    }
  }
```

Note that the MSER form a hierarchy of regions. Therefore, to make all of these visible, we have chosen not to overwrite the larger regions when they include smaller ones. We can detect MSERs on the following image:

The resulting image will be as follows:

Not all regions are visible in this image. Nevertheless, it can be observed how this operator has been able to extract some meaningful regions (for example, the building's windows) from this image.

How it works...

MSER uses the same mechanism as the watershed algorithm; that is, it proceeds by gradually flooding the image from level 0 to level 255. Note that in image processing, the set of pixels above a certain threshold is often call a **level set**. As the level of water increases, you can observe that the sharply delimited darker areas form basins that have a relatively stable shape for a period of time (recall that under the immersion analogy, the water levels correspond to the intensity levels). These stable basins are the MSER. These are detected by considering the connected regions (the basins) at each level and measuring their stability. This is done by comparing the current area of a region with the area it previously had when the level was down by a value of delta. When this relative variation reaches a local minimum, the region is identified as a MSER. The delta value that is used to measure the relative stability is the first parameter in the constructor of the `cv::MSER` class; its default value is 5. In addition, to be considered, the size of a region must be within a certain predefined range. The acceptable minimum and maximum region sizes are the next two parameters of the constructor. We must also ensure that the MSER is stable (the fourth parameter), that is, the relative variation of its shape is small enough. Stable regions can be included in the larger regions (called parent regions).

To be valid, a parent MSER must be sufficiently different from its child; this is the diversity criterion, and it is specified by the fifth parameter of the `cv::MSER` constructor. In the example used in the previous section, the default values for these last two parameters were used. (The default values are 0.25 for the maximum allowable variation of a MSER and 0.2 for the minimum diversity of a parent MSER). As you see, the detection of MSERs requires the specification of several parameters which can make it difficult to work well in various contexts.

The first output of the MSER detector is a vector of point sets; each of these point sets constitutes a region. Since we are generally more interested in a region as a whole rather than its individual pixel locations, it is common to represent a MSER by a simple geometrical shape that enclosed the detected region. The second output of the detection is therefore a list of bounding boxes. We can therefore show the result of the detection by drawing all these rectangular bounding boxes. However, this may represent a large number of rectangles to be drawn which would make the results difficult to visualize (remember that we also have regions inside regions which makes the representation even more cluttered). In the case of our example, let's assume we are mainly interested in detecting the building's windows. We will therefore extract all regions that have an upright rectangular shape. This could be done by comparing the area of each bounding box with the area of the corresponding detected region. If both have the same value (here, we check if the ratio of these two areas is greater than 0.6), then we accept this MSER. The following code implements this test:

```
// Extract and display the rectangular MSERs
std::vector<cv::Rect>::iterator itr = rects.begin();
std::vector<std::vector<cv::Point> >::iterator itp = points.begin();
for (; itr != rects.end(); ++itr, ++itp) {
  // ratio test
  if (static_cast<double>(itp->size())/itr->area() > 0.6)
    cv::rectangle(image, *itr, cv::Scalar(255), 2);
}
```

The extracted MSERs are then as follows:

Other criteria and representation can also be adopted depending on the application. The following code tests if the detected region is not too elongated (based on the aspect ratio of its rotated bounding rectangle) and then displays them using properly oriented bounding ellipses.

```
// Extract and display the elliptic MSERs
for (std::vector<std::vector<cv::Point> >::iterator
        it = points.begin();
        it != points.end(); ++it) {
  // for each point in MSER set
  for (std::vector<cv::Point>::iterator itPts = it->begin();
        itPts != it->end(); ++itPts) {

    // Extract bouding rectangles
```

```
    cv::RotatedRect rr = cv::minAreaRect(*it);
    // check ellipse elongation
    if (rr.size.height / rr.size.height > 0.6 ||
        rr.size.height / rr.size.height < 1.6)
        cv::ellipse(image, rr, cv::Scalar(255), 2);
    }
  }
```

The result is the following image:

Note how the child and parent MSER are often represented by very similar ellipses. In some cases, it would then be interesting to apply a minimum variation criterion on these ellipses in order to eliminate these repeated representations.

See also

- The *Computing components' shape descriptors* recipe in Chapter 7, *Extracting Lines, Contours, and Components*, will show you how to compute other properties of connected point sets
- Chapter 8, *Detecting Interest Points*, will explain how to use MSER as an interest point detector

6
Filtering the Images

In this chapter, we will cover the following recipes:

- Filtering images using low-pass filters
- Downsampling images with filters
- Filtering images using a median filter
- Applying directional filters to detect edges
- Computing the Laplacian of an image

Introduction

Filtering is one of the fundamental tasks in signal and image processing. It is a process aimed at selectively extracting certain aspects of an image that are considered to convey important information in the context of a given application. Filtering removes noise in images, extracts interesting visual features, allows image resampling, and so on. It finds its roots in the general **Signals and Systems** theory. We will not cover this theory in detail here. However, this chapter will present some of the important concepts related to filtering and will show you how filters can be used in image-processing applications. But first, let's begin with a brief explanation of the concept of frequency domain analysis.

When we look at an image, we observe different gray-levels (or colors) patterns laid out over it. Images differ from each other because they have different gray-level distributions. However, there is another point of view under which an image can be analyzed. We can look at the gray-level variations that are present in an image. Some images contain large areas of almost constant intensity (for example, a blue sky), while in other images, the gray-level intensities vary rapidly over the image (for example, a busy scene crowded with many small objects).

Therefore, observing the frequency of these variations in an image constitutes another way of characterizing an image. This point of view is referred to as the **frequency domain**, while characterizing an image by observing its gray-level distribution is referred to as the **spatial domain**.

The frequency domain analysis decomposes an image into its frequency content from the lowest to the highest frequencies. Areas where the image intensities vary slowly contain only low frequencies, while high frequencies are generated by rapid changes in intensities. Several well-known transformations exist, such as the **Fourier transform** or the **Cosine transform**, which can be used to explicitly show the frequency content of an image. Note that since an image is a two-dimensional entity, it is made of both vertical frequencies (variations in the vertical directions) and horizontal frequencies (variations in the horizontal directions).

Under the frequency domain analysis framework, a **filter** is an operation that amplifies certain bands of frequencies of an image (or leaves them unchanged) while blocking (or reducing) other image frequency bands. A low-pass filter is, for instance, a filter that eliminates the high-frequency components of an image; and reciprocally, a high-pass filter eliminates the low-frequency components. This chapter will present some filters that are frequently used in image processing and will explain their effect when applied on an image.

Filtering images using low-pass filters

In this first recipe, we will present some very basic low-pass filters. In the introductory section of this chapter, we learned that the objective of such filters is to reduce the amplitude of the image variations. One simple way to achieve this goal is to replace each pixel with the average value of the pixels around it. By doing this, the rapid intensity variations will be smoothed out and thus replaced by more gradual transitions.

How to do it...

The objective of the `cv::blur` function is to smooth an image by replacing each pixel with the average pixel value computed over a rectangular neighborhood. This low-pass filter is applied as follows:

```
cv::blur(image,result, cv::Size(5,5)); // size of the filter
```

This kind of filter is also called a **box filter**. Here, we applied it by using a 5x5 filter in order to make the filter's effect more visible. Our original image is the following:

The result of the filter being applied on the preceding image is as follows:

In some cases, it might be desirable to give more importance to the closer pixels in the neighborhood of a pixel. Therefore, it is possible to compute a weighted average in which nearby pixels are assigned a larger weight than ones that are further away. This can be achieved by using a weighted scheme that follows a **Gaussian function** (a "bell-shaped" function). The `cv::GaussianBlur` function applies such a filter and it is called as follows:

```
cv::GaussianBlur(image, result,
                 cv::Size(5,5), // size of the filter
                 1.5);          // parameter controlling
                                // the shape of the Gaussian
```

The result is then the following image:

How it works...

A filter is said to be linear if its application corresponds to replacing a pixel with a weighted sum of neighboring pixels. This is the case of the mean filter in which a pixel is replaced by the sum of all pixels in a rectangular neighborhood divided by the size of this neighborhood (to get the average value). This is like multiplying each neighboring pixel by 1 over the total number of pixels and summing all of these values. The different weights of a filter can be represented using a matrix that shows the multiplying factors associated with each pixel position in the considered neighborhood.

The central element of the matrix corresponds to the pixel on which the filter is currently applied. Such a matrix is sometimes called a **kernel** or a **mask**. For a 3x3 mean filter, the corresponding kernel would be as follows:

1/9	1/9	1/9
1/9	1/9	1/9
1/9	1/9	1/9

The `cv::boxFilter` function filters an image with a square kernel made of many 1s only. It is similar to the mean filter but without dividing the result by the number of coefficients.

Applying a linear filter then corresponds to moving a kernel over each pixel of an image and multiplying each corresponding pixel by its associated weight. Mathematically, this operation is called a **convolution** and can formally be written as follows:

$$I_{out}(x,y) = \sum_i \sum_j I_{in}(x-i, y-j) K(i, j)$$

The preceding double summation aligns the current pixel at (x, y) with the center of the kernel, which is assumed to be at coordinate (0, 0).

Looking at the output images produced in this recipe, it can be observed that the net effect of a low-pass filter is to blur or smooth the image. This is not surprising since this filter attenuates the high-frequency components that correspond to the rapid variations visible on an object's edge.

In the case of a Gaussian filter, the weight associated with a pixel is proportional to its distance from the central pixel. Recall that the 1D Gaussian function has the following form:

$$G(x) = Ae^{-x^2/2\sigma^2}$$

The normalizing coefficient A is chosen so that the area under the Gaussian curve equals one. The σ (sigma) value controls the width of the resulting Gaussian function. The greater this value is, the flatter the function will be. For example, if we compute the coefficients of the 1D Gaussian filter for the interval `[-4, 0, 4]` with σ = 0.5, we obtain the following coefficients:

```
[0.0 0.0 0.00026 0.10645 0.78657 0.10645 0.00026 0.0 0.0]
```

For σ=1.5, these coefficients are as follows:

```
[0.0076 0.03608 0.1096 0.2135 0.2667 0.2135 0.1096 0.0361 0.0076 ]
```

Note that these values were obtained by calling the `cv::getGaussianKernel` function with the appropriate σ value:

```
cv::Mat gauss= cv::getGaussianKernel(9, sigma,CV_32F);
```

The shape of the Gaussian curve for these two σ values is shown in the following figure. The symmetrical bell shape of the Gaussian function makes it a good choice for filtering:

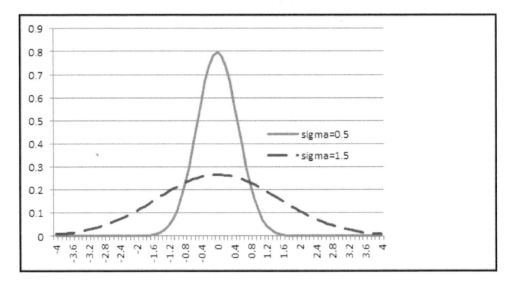

As it can be observed, pixels farther from the center have a lower weight, which makes the pixel-to-pixel transitions smoother. This contrasts with the flat mean filter where pixels far away can cause sudden changes in the current mean value. In terms of frequencies, this implies that the mean filter does not remove all the high frequency components.

To apply a 2D Gaussian filter on an image, one can simply apply a 1D Gaussian filter on the image lines first (to filter the horizontal frequencies), followed by the application of another 1D Gaussian filter on the image columns (to filter the vertical frequencies). This is possible because the Gaussian filter is a **separable filter** (that is, the 2D kernel can be decomposed into two 1D filters). The `cv::sepFilter2D` function can be used to apply a general separable filter. It is also possible to directly apply a 2D kernel using the `cv::filter2D` function. In general, separable filters are faster to compute than non-separable ones because they require less multiplication operations.

With OpenCV, the Gaussian filter to be applied to an image is specified by providing both the number of coefficients (the third parameter, which is an odd number) and the value of σ (the fourth parameter) to `cv::GaussianBlur`. You can also simply set the value of σ and let OpenCV determine the appropriate number of coefficients (you then input a value of 0 for the filter size). The opposite is also possible, where you input a size and a value of 0 for σ. The σ value that best fits the given size will be determined.

See also

- The *Downsampling images with filters* recipe explains how to reduce the size of an image using low-pass filters.
- The *There's more...* section of the *Scanning an image with neighbor access recipe* in Chapter 2, *Manipulating Pixels*, introduces the `cv::filter2D` function. This function lets you apply a linear filter to an image by inputting the kernel of your choice.

Downsampling images with filters

Images often need to be resized (resampled). The process of reducing the size of an image is often called **downsampling**, while increasing its size is **upsampling**. The challenge in performing these operations is to ensure that the visual quality of the image is preserved as much as possible. To accomplish this objective, low-pass filters are often used; this recipe explains why.

How to do it...

You might think that you can reduce the size of an image by simply eliminating some of the columns and rows of the image. Unfortunately, the resulting image will not look very nice. The following figure illustrates this fact by showing you a test image that is reduced by a factor of 4 with respect to its original size by simply keeping 1 of every 4 columns and rows.

Note that to make the defects in this image more apparent, we zoom in on the image by displaying it with pixels that are four times larger:

Clearly, one can see that the image quality has degraded. For example, the oblique edges of the castle's roof in the original image now appear as a staircase on the reduced image. Other jagged distortions are also visible on the textured parts of the image (the brick walls, for instance).

These undesirable artifacts are caused by a phenomenon called **spatial aliasing** that occurs when you try to include high-frequency components in an image that is too small to contain them. Indeed, smaller images (that is, images with fewer pixels) cannot represent fine textures and sharp edges as nicely as higher resolution images (think of the difference between high-definition TV versus older TV technology). Since fine details in an image correspond to high frequencies, we need to remove these higher frequency components in an image before reducing its size.

We learned in the previous recipe that this can be done through a low-pass filter. Consequently, to reduce the size of an image by four without adding annoying artifacts, you must first apply a low-pass filter to the original image before throwing away columns and rows. This is how you would do this using OpenCV:

```cpp
// first remove high frequency component
cv::GaussianBlur(image,image,cv::Size(11,11),2.0);
// keep only 1 of every 4 pixels
cv::Mat reduced(image.rows/4,image.cols/4,CV_8U);
for (int i=0; i<reduced.rows; i++)
  for (int j=0; j<reduced.cols; j++)
    reduced.at<uchar>(i,j)= image.at<uchar>(i*4,j*4);
```

The resulting image (also displayed with pixel of four times the normal size) is as follows:

Of course, some of the fine details of the image have been lost, but globally, the visual quality of the image is better preserved than in the previous case (looking at this image from far away should convince you of the relative good quality of the image).

How it works...

In order to avoid undesirable aliasing effect, an image must always be low-pass filtered before reducing its size. As we explained previously, the role of the low-pass filter is to eliminate the high-frequency components that cannot be represented in the reduced image. The formal theory demonstrating this fact is well established and is often referred to as the **Nyquist-Shannon theorem**. In substance, the theory tells us that if you downsample an image by two, then the bandwidth of the representable frequencies is also reduced by two.

A special OpenCV function performs image reduction using this principle. This is the `cv::pyrDown` function:

```
cv::Mat reducedImage;            // to contain reduced image
cv::pyrDown(image,reducedImage); // reduce image size by half
```

The preceding function uses a 5x5 Gaussian filter to low-pass the image before reducing it by a factor of two. The reciprocal `cv::pyrUp` function that doubles the size of an image also exists. It is interesting to note that in this case, the upsampling is done by inserting the 0 values between every two columns and rows and then by applying the same 5x5 Gaussian filter (but with the coefficients multiplied by four) on the expanded image. Obviously, if you downsize an image and then upsize it, you will not recover the exact original image. What was lost during the downsizing process cannot be recovered. These two functions are used to create image pyramids. This is a data structure made of stacked versions of an image at different sizes built for efficient multi-scale image analysis. The resulting image is as follows:

Here, each level is two times smaller than the previous level, but the reduction factor can be less, and not necessarily an integer (for example, `1.2`). For example, if you want to efficiently detect an object in an image, the detection can be first accomplished on the small image at the top of the pyramid, and as you locate the object of interest, you can refine the search by moving to the lower levels of the pyramid that contains the higher resolution versions of the image.

Note that there is also a more general `cv::resize` function that allows you to specify the size you want for the resulting image. You simply call it by specifying a new size that could be smaller or larger than the original image:

```
cv::Mat resizedImage;                      // to contain resized image
cv::resize(image, resizedImage,
           cv::Size(image.cols/4,image.rows/4)); // 1/4 resizing
```

It is also possible to specify resizing in terms of scale factors. In this case, an empty size instance is given as an argument followed by the desired scale factors:

```
cv::resize(image, resizedImage,
           cv::Size(), 1.0/4.0, 1.0/4.0); // 1/4 resizing
```

A final parameter allows you to select the interpolation method that is to be used in the resampling process. This is discussed in the following section.

There's more...

When an image is resized by a factional factor, it becomes necessary to perform some pixel interpolation in order to produce new pixel values at locations that fall in between the existing ones. General image remapping, as discussed in the *Remapping an image* recipe in `Chapter 2`, *Manipulating Pixels*, is another situation where pixel interpolation is required.

Interpolating pixel values

The most basic approach to perform interpolation is to use a nearest neighbor strategy. The new grid of pixels that must be produced is placed on top of the existing image, and each new pixel is assigned the value of its closest pixel in the original image. In the case of image upsampling (that is, when using a new grid denser than the original one), this implies that more than one pixel of the new grid will receive its value from the same original pixel. For example, resizing the reduced image of the previous section by four using nearest neighbor interpolation has been done as follows:

```
cv::resize(reduced, newImage, cv::Size(), 3, 3, cv::INTER_NEAREST);
```

In this case, the interpolation corresponds to simply increasing the size of each pixel by four. A better approach consists of interpolating a new pixel value by combining the values of several neighboring pixels. Hence, we can linearly interpolate a pixel value by considering the four pixels around it, as illustrated by the following figure:

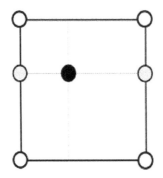

This is done by first vertically interpolating two pixel values to the left- and right-hand side of the added pixel. Then, these two interpolated pixels (drawn in gray in the preceding figure) are used to horizontally interpolate the pixel value at the desired location. This bilinear interpolation scheme is the default approach used by cv::resize (that can also be explicitly specified by the cv::INTER_LINEAR flag):

```
cv::resize(reduced, newImage, cv::Size(), 4, 4, cv::INTER_LINEAR);
```

The following is the result:

There are also other approaches that can produce superior results. With **bicubic interpolation**, a neighborhood of 4x4 pixels is considered to perform the interpolation. However, since the approach uses more pixels (16) and implies the computation of cubic terms, it is slower to compute than bilinear interpolation.

See also

- The *There's more...* section of the *Scanning an image with neighbor access* recipe in Chapter 2, *Manipulating Pixels*, introduces the cv::filter2D function. This function lets you apply a linear filter to an image by inputting the kernel of your choice.
- The *Detecting scale-invariant features* recipe in Chapter 8, *Detecting Interest Points*, uses image pyramids to detect interest points in an image.

Filtering images using a median filter

The first recipe of this chapter introduced the concept of linear filters. Non-linear filters also exist and can be advantageously used in image processing. One such filter is the median filter that we present in this recipe.

Since median filters are particularly useful in order to combat salt-and-pepper noise (or salt-only, in our case), we will use the image we created in the first recipe of Chapter 2, *Manipulating Pixels*, which is reproduced here:

How to do it...

The call to the median filtering function is done in a way that is similar to the other filters:

```
cv::medianBlur(image, result, 5);
// last parameter is size of the filter
```

The resulting image is as follows:

How it works...

Since the median filter is not a linear filter, it cannot be represented by a kernel matrix, it cannot be applied through a convolution operation (that is, using the double-summation equation introduced in the first recipe of this chapter). However, it also operates on a pixel's neighborhood in order to determine the output pixel value. The pixel and its neighborhood form a set of values and, as the name suggests, the median filter will simply compute the median value of this set (the median of a set is the value at the middle position when the set is sorted). The current pixel is then replaced with this median value.

This explains why the filter is so efficient in eliminating the salt-and-pepper noise. Indeed, when an outlier black or white pixel is present in a given pixel neighborhood, it is never selected as the median value (it is rather the maximal or minimal value), so it is always replaced by a neighboring value.

In contrast, a simple mean filter would be greatly affected by such noise, as can be observed in the following image, which represents the mean filtered version of our salt-and-pepper corrupted image:

Clearly, the noisy pixels shifted the mean value of neighboring pixels. As a result, the noise is still visible even if it has been blurred by the mean filter.

The median filter also has the advantage of preserving the sharpness of the edges. However, it washes out the textures in uniform regions (for example, the trees in the background). Because of the visual impact it has on images, the median filter is often used to create special effects in photo-editing software tools. You should test it on a color image to see how it can produce cartoon-like images.

Applying directional filters to detect edges

The first recipe of this chapter introduced the idea of linear filtering using kernel matrices. The filters that were used had the effect of blurring an image by removing or attenuating its high-frequency components. In this recipe, we will perform the opposite transformation, that is, amplifying the high-frequency content of an image. As a result, the high-pass filters introduced in this recipe will perform **edge detection**.

How to do it...

The filter that we will use here is called the **Sobel** filter. It is said to be a directional filter, because it only affects the vertical or the horizontal image frequencies depending on which kernel of the filter is used. OpenCV has a function that applies the Sobel operator on an image. The horizontal filter is called as follows:

```
cv::Sobel(image,      // input
          sobelX,     // output
          CV_8U,      // image type
          1, 0,       // kernel specification
          3,          // size of the square kernel
          0.4, 128);  // scale and offset
```

Vertical filtering is achieved by the following (and very similar to the horizontal filter) call:

```
cv::Sobel(image,      // input
          sobelY,     // output
          CV_8U,      // image type
          0, 1,       // kernel specification
          3,          // size of the square kernel
          0.4, 128);  // scale and offset
```

Several integer parameters are provided to the function, and these will be explained in the next section. Note that these have been chosen to produce an 8-bit image (CV_8U) representation of the output.

The result of the horizontal Sobel operator is as follows:

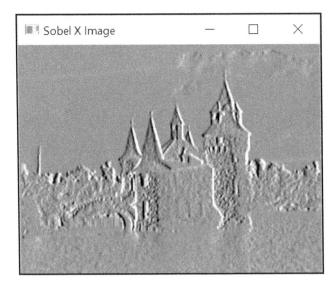

Since, as will be seen in the next section, the kernels of the `Sobel` operator contain both positive and negative values, the result of the `Sobel` filter is generally computed in a 16-bit signed integer image (`CV_16S`). To make the results displayable as an 8-bit image, as shown in the preceding figure, we used a representation in which a zero value corresponds to gray-level `128`. Negative values are represented by darker pixels, while positive values are represented by brighter pixels. The vertical Sobel image is as follows:

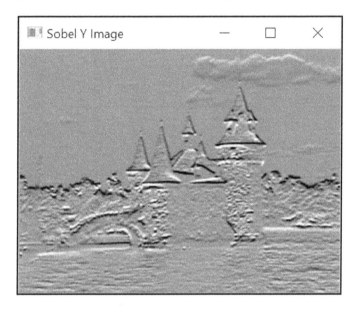

If you are familiar with photo-editing software, the preceding images might remind you of the image emboss effect, and indeed, this image transformation is generally based on the use of directional filters.

The two results (vertical and horizontal) can then be combined to obtain the norm of the `Sobel` filter:

```
// Compute norm of Sobel
cv::Sobel(image,sobelX,CV_16S,1,0);
cv::Sobel(image,sobelY,CV_16S,0,1);
cv::Mat sobel;
//compute the L1 norm
sobel= abs(sobelX)+abs(sobelY);
```

The Sobel norm can be conveniently displayed in an image using the optional rescaling parameter of the `convertTo` method in order to obtain an image in which zero values correspond to white, and higher values are assigned darker gray shades:

```
// Find Sobel max value
double sobmin, sobmax;
cv::minMaxLoc(sobel,&sobmin,&sobmax);
// Conversion to 8-bit image
// sobelImage = -alpha*sobel + 255
cv::Mat sobelImage;
sobel.convertTo(sobelImage,CV_8U,-255./sobmax,255);
```

The following image is then produced:

Looking at this image, it is now clear why this kind of operator is called an edge detector. It is then possible to threshold the image in order to obtain a binary map showing the image contours. The following snippet creates the image that follows it:

```
cv::threshold(sobelImage, sobelThresholded,
              threshold, 255, cv::THRESH_BINARY);
```

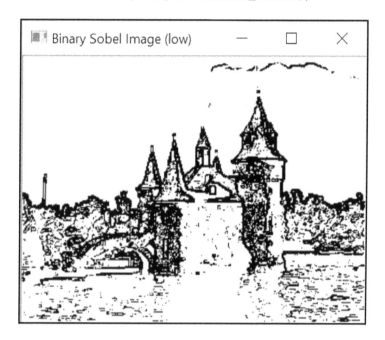

How it works...

The Sobel operator is a classic edge-detection linear filter that is based on two simple 3x3 kernels that have the following structure:

-1	0	1
-2	0	2
-1	0	1

-1	-2	-1
0	0	0
1	2	1

If we view the image as a two-dimensional function, the Sobel operator can then be seen as a measure of the variation of the image in the vertical and horizontal directions. In mathematical terms, this measure is called a **gradient**, and it is defined as a 2D vector that is made from the function's first derivatives in two orthogonal directions:

$$grad\left(I\right) = \left[\frac{\partial I}{\partial x}, \frac{\partial I}{\partial y}\right]^{T}$$

The Sobel operator gives you an approximation of the image gradient by differencing pixels in the horizontal and vertical directions. It operates on a window around the pixel of interest in order to reduce the influence of noise. The cv::Sobel function computes the result of the convolution of the image with a Sobel kernel. Its complete specification is as follows:

```
cv::Sobel(image,        // input
          sobel,        // output
          image_depth,  // image type
          xorder,yorder, // kernel specification
          kernel_size,  // size of the square kernel
          alpha, beta); // scale and offset
```

By using the appropriate arguments, you decide whether you wish to have the result written in an unsigned character, a signed integer, or a floating point image. Of course, if the result falls outside of the domain of the image pixel, saturation will be applied. This is where the last two parameters can be useful. Before storing the result in the image, the result can be scaled (multiplied) by alpha and an offset, beta, can be added.

This is how, in the previous section, we generated an image for which the Sobel value 0 was represented by the mid-gray level 128. Each Sobel mask corresponds to a derivative in one direction. Therefore, two parameters are used to specify the kernel that will be applied, the order of the derivative in the x, and the y directions. For instance, the horizontal Sobel kernel is obtained by specifying 1 and 0 for the xorder and yorder parameters, and the vertical kernel will be generated with 0 and 1. Other combinations are also possible, but these two are the ones that will be used most often (the case of second-order derivatives is discussed in the next recipe). Finally, it is also possible to use kernels of a size larger than 3x3. Values 1, 3, 5, and 7 are possible choices for the kernel size. A kernel of size 1 corresponds to a 1D Sobel filter (1x3 or 3x1). See the following *There's more...* section to learn why using a larger kernel might be useful.

Since the gradient is a 2D vector, it has a norm and a direction. The norm of the gradient vector tells you what the amplitude of the variation is, and it is normally computed as a Euclidean norm (also called **L2 norm**):

$$\left| grad\left(I \right) \right| = \sqrt{\left(\frac{\partial I}{\partial x} \right)^2 + \left(\frac{\partial I}{\partial y} \right)^2}$$

However, in image processing, this norm is often computed as the sum of the absolute values. This is called the **L1 norm**, and it gives values that are close to the L2 norm but at a lower computational cost. This is what we did in this recipe:

```
// compute the L1 norm
sobel= abs(sobelX)+abs(sobelY);
```

The gradient vector always points in the direction of the steepest variation. For an image, this means that the gradient direction will be orthogonal to the edge, pointing in the darker to brighter direction. Gradient angular direction is given by the following formula:

Most often, for edge detection, only the norm is computed. However, if you require both the norm and the orientation, then the following OpenCV function can be used:

```
// Sobel must be computed in floating points
cv::Sobel(image,sobelX,CV_32F,1,0);
cv::Sobel(image,sobelY,CV_32F,0,1);
// Compute the L2 norm and direction of the gradient
cv::Mat norm, dir;
// Cartesian to polar transformation to get magnitude and angle
cv::cartToPolar(sobelX,sobelY,norm,dir);
```

By default, the orientation is computed in radians. Just add `true` as an additional argument in order to have them computed in degrees.

A binary edge map has been obtained by applying a threshold on the gradient magnitude. Choosing the right threshold is not an obvious task. If the threshold value is too low, too many (thick) edges will be retained, while if we select a more severe (higher) threshold, then broken edges will be obtained. As an illustration of this trade-off situation, compare the preceding binary edge map with the following, which is obtained using a higher threshold value:

One way to get the best of both lower and higher thresholds is to use the concept of hysteresis thresholding. This will be explained in the next chapter, where we introduce the Canny operator.

There's more...

Other gradient operators also exist. We present some of them in this section. It is also possible to apply a Gaussian smoothing filter before applying a derivative filter. This makes it less sensitive to noise, as explained in this section.

Gradient operators

To estimate the gradient at a pixel location, the **Prewitt operator** defines the following kernels:

-1	0	1
-1	0	1
-1	0	1

-1	-1	-1
0	0	0
1	1	1

The **Roberts operator** is based on these simple 2x2 kernels:

1	0
0	-1

0	1
-1	0

The **Scharr operator** is preferred when more accurate estimates of the gradient orientation are required:

-3	0	3
-10	0	10
-3	0	3

-3	-10	-3
0	0	0
3	10	3

Note that it is possible to use the Scharr kernels with the `cv::Sobel` function by calling it with the `CV_SCHARR` argument:

```
cv::Sobel(image,sobelX,CV_16S,1,0, CV_SCHARR);
```

Or, equivalently, you can call the `cv::Scharr` function:

```
cv::Scharr(image,scharrX,CV_16S,1,0,3);
```

All of these directional filters try to estimate the first-order derivatives of the image function. Therefore, high values are obtained at areas where large intensity variations in the filter direction are present, while flat areas produce low values. This is why filters that compute image derivatives are high-pass filters.

Gaussian derivatives

Derivative filters are high-pass filters. As such, they tend to amplify noise and small highly-contrasted details in an image. In order to reduce the impact of these higher frequency elements, it is a good practice to first smooth the image before applying a derivative filter. You might think that this would be done in two steps, which are smoothing the image and then computing the derivative. However, a closer look at these operations reveals that it is possible to combine these two steps into one with a proper choice of the smoothing kernel. We learned previously that the convolution of an image with a filter can be expressed as a summation of terms. Interestingly, a well-known mathematical property is that the derivative of a summation of terms is equal to the summation of the terms' derivative.

Consequently, instead of applying the derivative on the result of the smoothing, it is possible to derive the kernel and then convolute it with the image; these two operations are then accomplished in a single pass over the pixels. Since the Gaussian kernel is continuously derivable, it represents a particularly appropriate choice. This is what is done when you call the `cv::sobel` function with different kernel sizes. The function will compute a Gaussian derivative kernel with different σ values. As an example, if we select the `7x7` Sobel filter (that is, `kernel_size=7`) in the x direction, the following result is obtained:

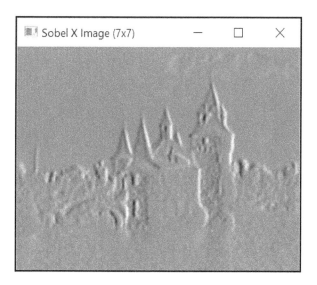

If you compare this image with the one shown earlier, it can be seen that many fine details have been removed, giving them more emphasis on the more significant edges. Note that we now have a band-pass filter, some higher frequencies being removed by the Gaussian filter and the lower frequencies being removed by the `Sobel` filter.

See also

- The *Detecting image contours with the Canny operator* recipe in Chapter 7, *Extracting Lines, Contours, and Components*, shows you how to obtain a binary edge map using two different threshold values

Computing the Laplacian of an image

The Laplacian is another high-pass linear filter that is based on the computation of the image derivatives. As it will be explained, it computes second-order derivatives to measure the curvature of the image function.

How to do it...

The OpenCV function, `cv::Laplacian`, computes the Laplacian of an image. It is very similar to the `cv::Sobel` function. In fact, it uses the same basic function, `cv::getDerivKernels`, in order to obtain its kernel matrix. The only difference is that there are no derivative order parameters since these ones are, by definition, second order derivatives.

For this operator, we will create a simple class that will encapsulate some useful operations related to the Laplacian. The basic attributes and methods are as follows:

```
class LaplacianZC {

  private:
  // laplacian
  cv::Mat laplace;
  // Aperture size of the laplacian kernel
  int aperture;

  public:

  LaplacianZC() : aperture(3) {}

  // Set the aperture size of the kernel
  void setAperture(int a) {
    aperture= a;
  }

  // Compute the floating point Laplacian
```

```
cv::Mat computeLaplacian(const cv::Mat& image) {

    // Compute Laplacian
    cv::Laplacian(image,laplace,CV_32F,aperture);
    return laplace;
}
```

The computation of the Laplacian is done here on a floating point image. To get an image of the result, we perform a rescaling, as shown in the previous recipe. This rescaling is based on the Laplacian maximum absolute value, where value 0 is assigned gray-level 128. A method of our class allows the following image representation to be obtained:

```
// Get the Laplacian result in 8-bit image
// zero corresponds to gray level 128
// if no scale is provided, then the max value will be
// scaled to intensity 255
// You must call computeLaplacian before calling this
cv::Mat getLaplacianImage(double scale=-1.0) {
    if (scale<0) {
        double lapmin, lapmax;
        // get min and max laplacian values
        cv::minMaxLoc(laplace,&lapmin,&lapmax);
        // scale the laplacian to 127
        scale= 127/ std::max(-lapmin,lapmax);
    }
    // produce gray-level image
    cv::Mat laplaceImage;
    laplace.convertTo(laplaceImage,CV_8U,scale,128);
    return laplaceImage;
}
```

Using this class, the Laplacian image computed from a 7x7 kernel is obtained as follows:

```
// Compute Laplacian using LaplacianZC class
LaplacianZC laplacian;
laplacian.setAperture(7); // 7x7 laplacian
cv::Mat flap= laplacian.computeLaplacian(image);
laplace= laplacian.getLaplacianImage();
```

The resulting image is shown here:

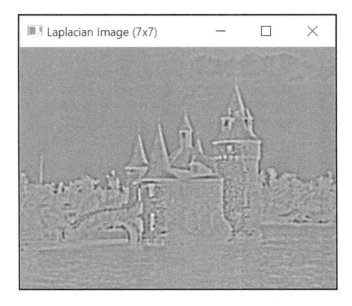

How it works...

Formally, the Laplacian of a 2D function is defined as the sum of its second derivatives:

$$laplacian(I) = \sqrt{\left(\frac{\partial I}{\partial x}\right)^2 + \left(\frac{\partial I}{\partial y}\right)^2}$$

In its simplest form, it can be approximated by the following 3x3 kernel:

0	1	0
1	-4	1
0	1	0

As for the Sobel operator, it is also possible to compute the Laplacian using larger kernels, and since this operator is even more sensitive to image noise, it is desirable to do so (unless computational efficiency is a concern). Since these larger kernels are computed using the second derivatives of the Gaussian function, the corresponding operator is often called **Laplacian of Gaussian** (**LoG**). Note that the kernel values of a Laplacian always sum up to 0. This guarantees that the Laplacian will be zero in areas of constant intensities. Indeed, since the Laplacian measures the curvature of the image function, it should be equal to 0 on flat areas.

At first glance, the effect of the Laplacian might be difficult to interpret. From the definition of the kernel, it is clear that any isolated pixel value (that is, a value that's very different from its neighbors) will be amplified by the operator. This is a consequence of the operator's high sensitivity to noise. However, it is more interesting to look at the Laplacian values around an image edge. The presence of an edge in an image is the result of a rapid transition between areas of different gray-level intensities. Following the evolution of the image function along an edge (for example, caused by a transition from dark to bright), one can observe that the gray-level ascension necessarily implies a gradual transition from a positive curvature (when the intensity values start to rise) to a negative curvature (when the intensity is about to reach its high plateau). Consequently, a transition between a positive and a negative Laplacian value (or reciprocally) constitutes a good indicator of the presence of an edge. Another way to express this fact is to say that edges will be located at the zero-crossings of the Laplacian function. We will illustrate this idea by looking at the values of a Laplacian inside a small window of our test image. We select one that corresponds to an edge created by the bottom part of the roof of one of the castle's tower. A white box has been drawn in the following image to show you the exact location of this region of interest:

The following figure shows the numerical values (divided by `100`) of the Laplacian image (`7x7` kernel) inside the selected window:

-142	-64	-24	-56	-141	-203	-179	-99	-35	-5	5	4
-225	-180	-85	-17	-33	-129	-205	-181	-97	-25	3	3
17	6	42	118	212	200	41	110	-123	-51	-4	0
188	176	185	246	397	474	297	23	-93	-59	-11	0
129	128	147	214	357	375	143	-76	-104	-48	-9	1
43	37	48	125	250	133	-203	-301	-140	-26	-1	1
-4	-9	-9	85	227	54	-327	-354	-114	-4	-1	0
-32	-47	-46	87	268	92	-292	-300	-70	6	-5	-3
-24	-59	-56	121	331	133	-274	-285	-59	14	3	2
8	-36	-24	172	382	162	-264	-279	-50	28	18	13
33	-10	18	205	380	150	-261	-268	-46	22	3	-7
32	-1	38	196	318	81	-288	-270	-53	-1	-32	-45

If, as illustrated, you carefully follow some of the zero-crossings of the Laplacian (located between pixels of different signs), you obtain a curve that corresponds some of the edges that is visible in the image window. In the preceding figure, we drew lines along the zero-crossings that correspond to the edge of the tower that is visible in the selected image window. This implies that, in principle, you can even detect the image edges at sub-pixel accuracy.

Following the zero-crossing curves in a Laplacian image is a delicate task. However, a simplified algorithm can be used to detect the approximate zero-crossing locations. This one proceeds by first thresholding the Laplacian at `0` so that a partition separating the positive and negative values is obtained. The limits between these two partitions then correspond to our zero-crossings. Therefore, we use a morphological operation to extract these contours, that is, we subtract the dilated image from the Laplacian image (this is the Beucher gradient presented in the *Applying morphological operators on gray-level images* recipe in `Chapter 5`, *Transforming Images with Morphological Operations*). This algorithm is implemented by the following method, which generates a binary image of zero-crossings:

```cpp
// Get a binary image of the zero-crossings
// laplacian image should be CV_32F
cv::Mat getZeroCrossings(cv::Mat laplace) {
   // threshold at 0
   // negative values in black
   // positive values in white
   cv::Mat signImage;
   cv::threshold(laplace,signImage,0,255,cv::THRESH_BINARY);

   // convert the +/- image into CV_8U
   cv::Mat binary;
```

```
signImage.convertTo(binary,CV_8U);
// dilate the binary image of +/- regions
cv::Mat dilated;
cv::dilate(binary,dilated,cv::Mat());

// return the zero-crossing contours
return dilated-binary;
}
```

The result is the following binary map:

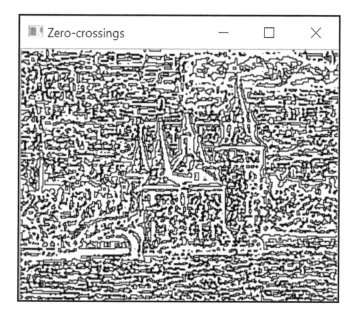

As you can see, the zero-crossings of the Laplacian detect all edges. No distinction is made between strong edges and weaker edges. We also mentioned that the Laplacian is very sensitive to noise. Also, it is interesting to note that some of the visible edges are due to compression artifacts. All these factors explain why so many edges are detected by the operator. In practice, the Laplacian is only used in conjunction with other operators to detect edges (for example, edges can be declared at zero-crossing locations of strong gradient magnitude). We will also learn in `Chapter 8`, *Detecting Interest Points*, that the Laplacian and other second-order operators are very useful in order to detect interest points at multiple scales.

There's more...

The Laplacian is a high-pass filter but, interestingly, it is possible to approximate it by using a combination of low-pass filters. But before exploring this aspect, let's have a word about image enhancement, which is a topic we have already discussed, in `Chapter 2`, *Manipulating Pixels*.

Enhancing the contrast of an image using the Laplacian

The contrast of an image can be enhanced by subtracting its Laplacian from it. This is what we did in the *Scanning an image with neighbor access* recipe of `Chapter 2`, *Manipulating Pixels*, where we introduced the kernel:

0	-1	0
-1	5	-1
0	-1	0

This is equal to 1 minus the Laplacian kernel (that is, the original image minus its Laplacian).

Difference of Gaussians

The Gaussian filter presented in the first recipe of this chapter extracts the low frequencies of an image. We learned that the range of frequencies that are filtered by a Gaussian filter depend on the parameter σ, which controls the width of the filter. Now, if we subtract the two images that result from the filtering of an image by two Gaussian filters of different bandwidths, then the resulting image will be composed of those higher frequencies that one filter has preserved, and not the other. This operation is called **Difference of Gaussians** (**DoG**) and is computed as follows:

```
cv::GaussianBlur(image,gauss20,cv::Size(),2.0);
cv::GaussianBlur(image,gauss22,cv::Size(),2.2);

// Compute a difference of Gaussians
cv::subtract(gauss22, gauss20, dog, cv::Mat(), CV_32F);

// Compute the zero-crossings of DoG
```

```
zeros= laplacian.getZeroCrossings(dog);
```

The last line of code computes the zero-crossings of the DoG operator. It results in the following image:

In fact, it can be demonstrated that with the proper choice of σ values, DoG operators can constitute a good approximation of LoG filters. Also, if you compute a series of difference of Gaussians from consecutive pair values in an increasing sequence of σ values, you obtain a scale-space representation of the image. This multiscale representation is useful, for example, for scale-invariant image feature detection, as will be explained in Chapter 8, *Detecting Interest Points*.

See also

- The *Detecting scale-invariant features* recipe in Chapter 8, *Detecting Interest Points*, uses the Laplacian and DoG for the detection of scale-invariant features

7

Extracting Lines, Contours, and Components

In this chapter, we will cover the following recipes:

- Detecting image contours with the Canny operator
- Detecting lines in images with the Hough transform
- Fitting a line to a set of points
- Extracting connected components
- Computing components' shape descriptors

Introduction

In order to perform content-based analysis of an image, it is necessary to extract meaningful features from the collection of pixels that constitute the image. Contours, lines, blobs, and so on, are fundamental image primitives that can be used to describe the elements contained in an image. This chapter will teach you how to extract some of these image primitives.

Detecting image contours with the Canny operator

In the previous chapter, we learned how it is possible to detect the edges of an image. In particular, we showed you that by applying a threshold to the gradient magnitude, a binary map of the main edges of an image can be obtained. Edges carry important visual information since they delineate the image elements. For this reason, they can be used, for example, in object recognition. However, simple binary edge maps suffer from two main drawbacks. First, the edges that are detected are unnecessarily thick; this makes the object's limits more difficult to identify. Second, and more importantly, it is often impossible to find a threshold that is sufficiently low in order to detect all important edges of an image and is, at the same time, sufficiently high in order to not include too many insignificant edges. This is a trade-off problem that the **Canny** algorithm tries to solve.

How to do it...

The Canny algorithm is implemented in OpenCV by the `cv::Canny` function. As will be explained, this algorithm requires the specification of two thresholds. The call to the function is, therefore, as follows:

```
//Apply Canny algorithm
cv::Mat contours;
cv::Canny(image,       // gray-level image
          contours,    // output contours
          125,         // low threshold
          350);        // high threshold
```

Let's consider the following image:

When the algorithm is applied on the preceding image, the result is as follows:

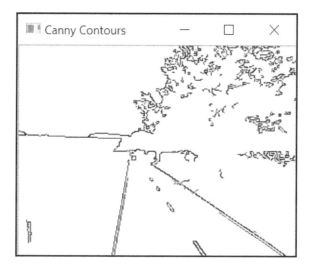

Note that here we have inverted the contour representation since the normal result represents contours by non-zero pixels. The displayed image is simply `255-contours`.

How it works...

The Canny operator is generally based on the Sobel operator that was presented in `Chapter 6`, *Filtering the Images*, although other gradient operators can also be used. The key idea here is to use two different thresholds in order to determine which point should belong to a contour: a low and a high threshold.

The low threshold should be chosen in a way that it includes all edge pixels that are considered to belong to a significant image contour. For example, using the low-threshold value specified in the example of the preceding section and applying it on the result of a Sobel operator, the following edge map is obtained:

As can be seen, the edges that delineate the road are very well defined. However, because a permissive threshold was used, more edges than what is ideally needed are also detected. The role of the second threshold, then, is to define the edges that belong to all important contours. It should exclude all edges considered as outliers. For example, the Sobel edge map that corresponds to the high threshold used in our example is as follows:

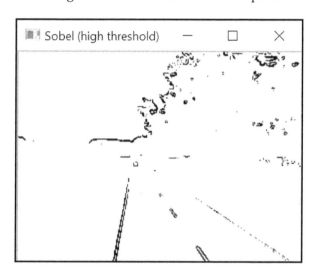

We now have an image that contains broken edges, but the ones that are visible certainly belong to the significant contours of the scene. The Canny algorithm combines these two edge maps in order to produce an optimal map of contours. It operates by keeping only the edge points of the low-threshold edge map for which a continuous path of edges exists, linking those edge points to an edge that belongs to the high-threshold edge map. Consequently, all edge points of the high-threshold map are kept, while all isolated chains of edge points in the low-threshold map are removed. The solution that is obtained constitutes a good compromise, allowing good quality contours to be obtained as long as appropriate threshold values are specified. This strategy, based on the use of two thresholds to obtain a binary map, is called **hysteresis thresholding,** and can be used in any context where a binary map needs to be obtained from a thresholding operation. However, this is done at the cost of higher computational complexity.

In addition, the Canny algorithm uses an extra strategy to improve the quality of the edge map. Prior to the application of the hysteresis thresholding, all edge points for which the gradient magnitude is not a maximum in the gradient direction are removed (recall that the gradient orientation is always perpendicular to the edge). Therefore, the local maximum of the gradient in this direction corresponds to the point of maximum strength of the contour. This is a contour thinning operation that creates edges having a width of 1 pixel. This explains why thin edges are obtained in the Canny contour maps.

See also

- The classic article by *J. Canny, A computational approach to edge detection, IEEE Transactions on Pattern Analysis and Image Understanding, vol. 18, issue 6, 1986*

Detecting lines in images with the Hough transform

In our human-made world, planar and linear structures abound. As a result, straight lines are frequently visible in images. These are meaningful features that play an important role in object recognition and image understanding. The **Hough transform** is a classic algorithm that is often used to detect these particular features in images. It was initially developed to detect lines in images and, as we will see, it can also be extended to detect other simple image structures.

Getting ready

With the Hough transform, lines are represented using the following equation:

$$\rho = x cos\theta + y sin\theta$$

The ρ parameter is the distance between the line and the image origin (the upper-left corner), and θ is the angle of the perpendicular to the line. In this representation, the lines visible in an image have a θ angle between 0 and π radians, while the ρ radius can have a maximum value that equals the length of the image diagonal. Consider, for example, the following set of lines:

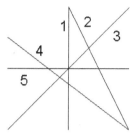

A vertical line such as line **1** has a θ angle value equal to zero, while a horizontal line (for example, line **5**) has its θ value equal to $\pi/2$. Therefore, line **3** has an angle θ equal to $\pi/4$, and line **4** is at 0.7π approximately. In order to be able to represent all possible lines with θ in the $[0,\ \pi]$ interval, the radius value can be made negative. This is the case with line **2**, which has a θ value equal to 0.8π with a negative value for ρ.

How to do it...

OpenCV offers two implementations of the Hough transform for line detection. The basic version is `cv::HoughLines`. Its input is a binary map that contains a set of points (represented by non-zero pixels), some of which are aligned to form lines. Usually, this is an edge map obtained, for example, from the Canny operator. The output of the `cv::HoughLines` function is a vector of `cv::Vec2f` elements, each of them being a pair of floating point values, representing the parameters of a detected line, (ρ, θ). The following is an example of using this function where we first apply the Canny operator to obtain the image contours and then detect the lines using the Hough transform:

```
// Apply Canny algorithm
cv::Mat contours;
cv::Canny(image,contours,125,350);
// Hough transform for line detection
std::vector<cv::Vec2f> lines;
cv::HoughLines(test, lines, 1,
               PI/180,  // step size
               60);     // minimum number of votes
```

Parameters 3 and 4 correspond to the step size for the line search. In our example, the function will search for lines of all possible radii by steps of 1 and all possible angles by steps of π/180. The role of the last parameter will be explained in the next section. With this particular choice of parameter values, several lines are detected on the road image of the preceding recipe. In order to visualize the result of the detection, it is interesting to draw these lines on the original image. However, it is important to note that this algorithm detects lines in an image and not line segments, since the endpoints of each line are not given. Consequently, we will draw lines that traverse the entire image. To do this, for a vertically oriented line, we calculate its intersection with the horizontal limits of the image (that is, the first and last rows) and draw a line between these two points. We proceed similarly with horizontally-oriented lines but using the first and last columns. Lines are drawn using the cv::line function. Note that this function works well even with point coordinates outside the image limits. Therefore, there is no need to check whether the computed intersection points fall within the image. Lines are then drawn by iterating over the line vector as follows:

```cpp
std::vector<cv::Vec2f>::const_iterator it= lines.begin();
while (it!=lines.end()) {

  float rho= (*it)[0];    // first element is distance rho
  float theta= (*it)[1]; // second element is angle theta

  if (theta < PI/4.|| theta > 3.*PI/4.) { //~vertical line

    // point of intersection of the line with first row
    cv::Point pt1(rho/cos(theta),0);
    // point of intersection of the line with last row
    cv::Point pt2((rho-result.rows*sin(theta))/
                  cos(theta),result.rows);
    //draw a white line
     cv::line( image, pt1, pt2, cv::Scalar(255), 1);
  } else { // ~horizontal line

    // point of intersection of the
    // line with first column
    cv::Point pt1(0,rho/sin(theta));
    //point of intersection of the line with last column
    cv::Point pt2(result.cols,
                  (rho-result.cols*cos(theta))/sin(theta));
    // draw a white line
    cv::line(image, pt1, pt2, cv::Scalar(255), 1);
  }
  ++it;
}
```

The following result is obtained:

As can be seen, the Hough transform simply looks for an alignment of edge pixels across the image. This can potentially create some false detections due to incidental pixel alignments or multiple detections when several lines with slightly different parameter values pass through the same alignment of pixels.

To overcome some of these problems, and to allow line segments to be detected (that is, with endpoints), a variant of the transform has been proposed. This is the Probabilistic Hough transform, and it is implemented in OpenCV as the cv::HoughLinesP function. We use it here to create our LineFinder class, which encapsulates the function parameters:

```
class LineFinder {

  private:

  // original image
  cv::Mat img;

  // vector containing the endpoints of the detected lines
  std::vector<cv::Vec4i> lines;

  // accumulator resolution parameters
  double deltaRho;
  double deltaTheta;

  // minimum number of votes that a line
  // must receive before being considered
  int minVote;
```

```
//min length for a line
double minLength;

//max allowed gap along the line
double maxGap;

public:
 // Default accumulator resolution is 1 pixel by 1 degree
 // no gap, no minimum length
 LineFinder() : deltaRho(1), deltaTheta(PI/180),
                minVote(10), minLength(0.), maxGap(0.) {}
```

Take a look at the corresponding setter methods:

```
// Set the resolution of the accumulator
void setAccResolution(double dRho, double dTheta) {

  deltaRho= dRho;
  deltaTheta= dTheta;
}

// Set the minimum number of votes
void setMinVote(int minv) {

  minVote= minv;
}

// Set line length and gap
void setLineLengthAndGap(double length, double gap) {

  minLength= length;
  maxGap= gap;
}
```

With the preceding method, the method that performs Hough line segment detection is as follows:

```
// Apply probabilistic Hough Transform
std::vector<cv::Vec4i> findLines(cv::Mat& binary) {

  lines.clear();
  cv::HoughLinesP(binary,lines,
                  deltaRho, deltaTheta, minVote,
                  minLength, maxGap);

  return lines;
}
```

This method returns a vector of `cv::Vec4i`, which contains the start and endpoint coordinates of each detected segment. The detected lines can then be drawn on an image with the following method:

```
// Draw the detected lines on an image
void drawDetectedLines(cv::Mat &image,
                      cv::Scalar color=cv::Scalar(255,255,255)) {

  // Draw the lines
  std::vector<cv::Vec4i>::const_iterator it2= lines.begin();

  while (it2!=lines.end()) {

    cv::Point pt1((*it2)[0],(*it2)[1]);
    cv::Point pt2((*it2)[2],(*it2)[3]);

    cv::line( image, pt1, pt2, color);

    ++it2;
  }
}
```

Now, using the same input image, lines can be detected with the following sequence:

```
// Create LineFinder instance
LineFinder finder;

// Set probabilistic Hough parameters
finder.setLineLengthAndGap(100,20);
finder.setMinVote(60);

// Detect lines and draw them on the image
std::vector<cv::Vec4i> lines= finder.findLines(contours);
finder.drawDetectedLines(image);
```

The preceding code gives the following result:

How it works...

The objective of the Hough transform is to find all lines in a binary image that pass through a sufficient number of points. It proceeds by considering each individual pixel point in the input binary map and identifying all possible lines that pass through it. When the same line passes through many points, it means that this line is significant enough to be considered.

The Hough transform uses a two-dimensional accumulator in order to count how many times a given line is identified. The size of this accumulator is defined by the specified step sizes (as mentioned in the preceding section) of the (ρ, θ) parameters of the adopted line representation. To illustrate the functioning of the transform, let's create a 180 by 200 matrix (corresponding to a step size of $\pi/180$ for θ and 1 for ρ):

```
// Create a Hough accumulator
// here a uchar image; in practice should be ints
cv::Mat acc(200,180,CV_8U,cv::Scalar(0));
```

This accumulator is a mapping of different (ρ, θ) values. Therefore, each entry of this matrix corresponds to one particular line. Now, if we consider one point, let's say one at $(50, 30)$, then it is possible to identify all lines that pass through this point by looping over all possible θ angles (with a step size of $\pi/180$) and computing the corresponding (rounded) ρ value:

```cpp
// Choose a point
int x=50, y=30;
// loop over all angles
for (int i=0; i<180; i++) {

    double theta= i*PI/180.;

    // find corresponding rho value
    double rho= x*std::cos(theta)+y*std::sin(theta);
    // j corresponds to rho from -100 to 100
    int j= static_cast<int>(rho+100.5);

    std::cout << i << "," << j << std::endl;

    // increment accumulator
    acc.at<uchar>(j,i)++;
}
```

The entries of the accumulator corresponding to the computed (ρ, θ) pairs are then incremented, signifying that all of these lines pass through one point of the image (or, to say it another way, each point votes for a set of possible candidate lines). If we display the accumulator as an image (inverted and multiplied by 100 to make the count of 1 visible), we obtain the following:

The preceding curve represents the set of all lines that pass through the specified point. Now, if we repeat the same exercise with, let's say, point (30,10), we now have the following accumulator:

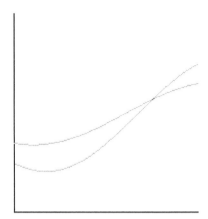

As can be seen, the two resulting curves intersect at one point: the point that corresponds to the line that passes through these two points. The corresponding entry of the accumulator receives two votes, indicating that two points pass through this line.

If the same process is repeated for all points of a binary map, then points aligned along a given line will increase a common entry of the accumulator many times. At the end, you just need to identify the local maxima in this accumulator that receives a significant number of votes in order to detect the lines (that is, point alignments) in the image. The last parameter specified in the cv::HoughLines function corresponds to the minimum number of votes that a line must receive to be considered as detected. This means that the lower this minimum number of votes is, then the higher the number of detected lines will be.

For example, if we lower this value to 50 in the case of our road example, then the following lines are now detected:

The Probabilistic Hough transform adds a few modifications to the basic algorithm. First, instead of systematically scanning the image row-by-row, points are chosen in random order in the binary map. Whenever an entry of the accumulator reaches the specified minimum value, the image is scanned along the corresponding line and all points that pass through it are removed (even if they have not voted yet). This scanning also determines the length of the segments that will be accepted. For this, the algorithm defines two additional parameters. One is the minimum length for a segment to be accepted, and the other is the maximum pixel gap that is permitted to form a continuous segment. This additional step increases the complexity of the algorithm, but this is partly compensated by the fact that fewer points will be involved in the voting process, as some of them are eliminated by the line-scanning process.

There's more...

The Hough transform can also be used to detect other geometrical entities. In fact, any entity that can be represented by a parametric equation is a good candidate for the Hough transform. There is also a Generalized Hough transform that can detect objects of any shape.

Detecting circles

In the case of circles, the corresponding parametric equation is as follows:

$$r^2 = (x - x_0)^2 + (y - y_0)^2$$

This equation includes three parameters (the circle radius and center coordinates), which means that a three-dimensional accumulator would be required. However, it is generally found that the Hough transform becomes more complex and less reliable as the dimensionality of its accumulator increases. Indeed, in this case, a large number of entries of the accumulator will be incremented for each point and, as a consequence, the accurate localization of local peaks becomes more difficult. Different strategies have been proposed in order to overcome this problem. The strategy used in the OpenCV implementation of the Hough circle detection uses two passes. During the first pass, a two-dimensional accumulator is used to find candidate circle locations. Since the gradient of points on the circumference of a circle should point in the direction of the radius, for each point, only the entries in the accumulator along the gradient direction are incremented (based on predefined minimum and maximum radius values). Once a possible circle center is detected (that is, has received a predefined number of votes), a 1D histogram of a possible radius is built during the second pass. The peak value in this histogram corresponds to the radius of the detected circles.

The `cv::HoughCircles` function that implements the preceding strategy integrates both the Canny detection and the Hough transform. It is called as follows:

```
cv::GaussianBlur(image,image,cv::Size(5,5),1.5);
std::vector<cv::Vec3f> circles;
    cv::HoughCircles(image, circles, cv::HOUGH_GRADIENT,
                    2,     //accumulator resolution (size of the image/2)
                    50,    // minimum distance between two circles
                    200,   // Canny high threshold
                    100,   // minimum number of votes
                    25,
                    100); // min and max radius
```

Note that it is always recommended that you smooth the image before calling the `cv::HoughCircles` function in order to reduce the image noise that could cause several false circle detections. The result of the detection is given in a vector of `cv::Vec3f` instances. The first two values are the circle center coordinates and the third is the radius.

The `cv::HOUGH_GRADIENT` argument was the only option available at the time of writing. It corresponds to the two-pass circle detection method. The fourth parameter defines the accumulator resolution. It is a divider factor; specifying a value of 2, for example, makes the accumulator half the size of the image. The next parameter is the minimum distance in pixels between two detected circles. The other parameter corresponds to the high threshold of the Canny edge detector. The low-threshold value is always set at half this value. The seventh parameter is the minimum number of votes that a center location must receive during the first pass to be considered as a candidate circle for the second pass. Finally, the last two parameters are the minimum and maximum radius values for the circles to be detected. As can be seen, the function includes many parameters that make it difficult to tune.

Once the vector of detected circles is obtained, these circles can be drawn on the image by iterating over the vector and calling the `cv::circle` drawing function with the obtained parameters:

```
std::vector<cv::Vec3f>::const_iterator itc= circles.begin();

while (itc!=circles.end()) {

   cv::circle(image,
              cv::Point((*itc)[0], (*itc)[1]), // circle centre
              (*itc)[2],           // circle radius
              cv::Scalar(255),     // color
              2);                  // thickness
   ++itc;
}
```

The following is the result obtained on a test image with the chosen arguments:

See also

- The following article, *Gradient-based Progressive Probabilistic Hough Transform* by C. Galambos, J. Kittler, and J. Matas, *IEE Vision Image and Signal Processing, vol. 148 no 3, pp. 158-165, 2002*, is one of the numerous references on the Hough transform and describes the probabilistic algorithm implemented in OpenCV.
- The following article, *Comparative Study of Hough Transform Methods for Circle Finding, Image and Vision Computing, vol. 8 no 1, pp. 71-77, 1990*, by H.K. Yuen, J. Princen, J. Illingworth, and J Kittler, describes different strategies for circle detection using the Hough transform.

Fitting a line to a set of points

In some applications, it could be important to not only detect lines in an image, but also to obtain an accurate estimate of the line's position and orientation. This recipe will show you how to estimate the exact line that best fits a given set of points.

How to do it...

The first thing to do is to identify points in an image that seem to be aligned along a straight line. Let's use one of the lines we detected in the preceding recipe. The lines detected using `cv::HoughLinesP` are contained in `std::vector<cv::Vec4i>` called `lines`. To extract the set of points that seem to belong to, let's say, the first of these lines, we can proceed as follows. We draw a white line on a black image and intersect it with the Canny image of `contours` used to detect our lines. This is simply achieved by the following statements:

```
int n=0;          // we select line 0
// black image
cv::Mat oneline(contours.size(),CV_8U,cv::Scalar(0));
// white line
cv::line(oneline, cv::Point(lines[n][0],lines[n][1]),
        cv::Point(lines[n] [2],
        lines[n][3]), cv::Scalar(255),
        3);       // line width
// contours AND white line
cv::bitwise_and(contours,oneline,oneline);
```

The result is an image that contains points that could be associated with the specified line. In order to introduce some tolerance, we draw a line of a certain thickness (here, 3). All points inside the defined neighborhood are, therefore, accepted.

The following is the image that is obtained (inverted for better viewing):

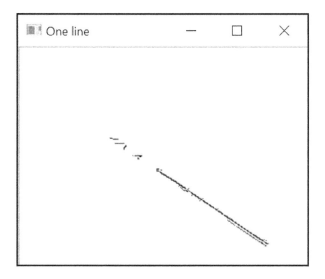

The coordinates of the points in this set can then be inserted in a std::vector of cv::Point objects (floating point coordinates, that is, cv::Point2f, can also be used) with the following double loop:

```
std::vector<cv::Point> points;

// Iterate over the pixels to obtain all point positions
for( int y = 0; y < oneline.rows; y++ ) {
  // row y

  uchar* rowPtr = oneline.ptr<uchar>(y);

  for( int x = 0; x < oneline.cols; x++ ) {
    // column x

    // if on a contour
    if (rowPtr[x]) {

      points.push_back(cv::Point(x,y));
    }
  }
}
```

We now have a list of points and we want to fit a line passing through these points. This best fitting line is easily found by calling the cv::fitLine OpenCV function:

```
cv::Vec4f line;
cv::fitLine(points,line,
            cv::DIST_L2, //distance type
            0,           //not used with L2 distance
            0.01,0.01);  //accuracy
```

The preceding code gives us the parameters of the line equation in the form of a unit-directional vector (the first two values of cv::Vec4f) and the coordinates of one point on the line (the last two values of cv::Vec4f). The last two parameters specify the requested accuracy for the line parameters.

In general, the line equation will be used in the calculation of some properties (calibration is a good example where precise parametric representation is required). As an illustration, and to make sure we calculated the right line, let's draw the estimated line on the image. Here, we simply draw an arbitrary black segment that has a length of 100 pixels and a thickness of 2 pixels (to make it visible):

```
int x0= line[2];         // a point on the line
int y0= line[3];
int x1= x0+100*line[0]; // add a vector of length 100
int y1= y0+100*line[1]; // using the unit vector
// draw the line
cv::line(image,cv::Point(x0,y0),cv::Point(x1,y1),
         0,2);            // color and thickness
```

The following image shows this line well aligned with one of the road's sides:

How it works...

Fitting lines to a set of points is a classic problem in mathematics. The OpenCV implementation proceeds by minimizing the sum of the distances from each point to the line. Several distance functions are proposed, and the fastest option is to use the Euclidean distance, which is specified by `cv::DIST_L2`. This choice corresponds to the standard least-squares line fitting. When outliers (that is, points that don't belong on the line) are included in the point set, other distance functions that give less influence to far points can be selected. The minimization is based on the M-estimator technique, which iteratively solves a weighted least-squares problem with weights that are inversely proportional to the distance from the line.

Using this function, it is also possible to fit a line to a 3D point set. The input is, in this case, a set of `cv::Point3i` or `cv::Point3f` objects, and the output is a `std::Vec6f` instance.

There's more...

The `cv::fitEllipse` function fits an ellipse to a set of 2D points. This returns a rotated rectangle (a `cv::RotatedRect` instance), inside which the ellipse is inscribed. In this case, you would write the following:

```
cv::RotatedRect rrect= cv::fitEllipse(cv::Mat(points));
cv::ellipse(image,rrect,cv::Scalar(0));
```

The `cv::ellipse` function is the one you would use to draw the computed ellipse.

Extracting connected components

Images generally contain representations of objects. One of the goals of image analysis is to identify and extract these objects. In object detection/recognition applications, the first step is often to produce a binary image that shows you where certain objects of interest could be located. No matter how this binary map is obtained (for example, from the histogram back projection we performed in Chapter 4, *Counting the Pixels with Histograms*, or from motion analysis as we will learn in Chapter 12, *Processing Video Sequences*), the next step is to extract the objects that are contained in this collection of 1s and 0s.

Consider, for example, the image of buffaloes in a binary form that we manipulated in Chapter 5, *Transforming Images with Morphological Operations*, as shown in the following figure:

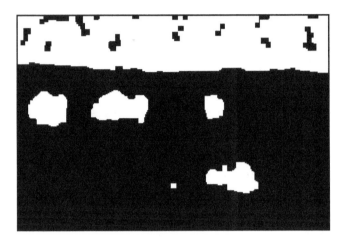

We obtained this image from a simple thresholding operation followed by the application of morphological filters. This recipe will show you how to extract the objects of such images. More specifically, we will extract the connected components, that is, shapes made of a set of connected pixels in a binary image.

How to do it...

OpenCV offers a simple function that extracts the contours of the connected components of an image. This is the cv::findContours function:

```
// the vector that will contain the contours
std::vector<std::vector<cv::Point>> contours;
cv::findContours(image,
            contours,            // a vector of contours
            cv::RETR_EXTERNAL,   // retrieve the external contours
            cv::CHAIN_APPROX_NONE);// all pixels of each contours
```

The input is obviously the binary image. The output is a vector of contours, each contour being represented by a vector of cv::Point objects. This explains why the output parameter is defined as a std::vector instance of the std::vector instances. In addition, two flags are specified. The first one indicates that only the external contours are required, that is, holes in an object will be ignored (the *There's more...* section will discuss the other options).

The second flag is there to specify the format of the contour. With the current option, the vector will list all of the points in the contour. With the `cv::CHAIN_APPROX_SIMPLE` flag, only the endpoints for horizontal, vertical, or diagonal contours will be included. Other flags would give a more sophisticated chain approximation of the contours in order to obtain a more compact representation. With the preceding image, nine connected components are obtained as given by `contours.size()`.

Fortunately, there is a very convenient function that can draw the contours of those components on an image (here, a white image):

```
//draw black contours on a white image
cv::Mat result(image.size(),CV_8U,cv::Scalar(255));
cv::drawContours(result,contours,
                -1, // draw all contours
                0,  // in black
                2); // with a thickness of 2
```

If the third parameter of this function is a negative value, then all contours are drawn. Otherwise, it is possible to specify the index of the contour to be drawn. The result is as follows:

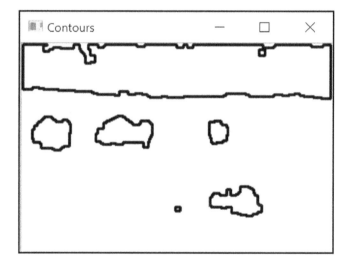

How it works…

The contours are extracted by a simple algorithm that consists of systematically scanning the image until a component is hit. From this starting point on the component, its contour is followed, marking the pixels on its border. When the contour is completed, the scanning resumes at the last position until a new component is found.

The identified connected components can then be individually analyzed. For example, if some prior knowledge is available about the expected size of the objects of interest, it becomes possible to eliminate some of the components. Let's then use a minimum and a maximum value for the perimeter of the components. This is done by iterating over the vector of contours and eliminating the invalid components:

```
// Eliminate too short or too long contours
int cmin= 50;    // minimum contour length
int cmax= 1000; // maximum contour length
std::vector<std::vector<cv::Point>>::
             iterator itc= contours.begin();
// for all contours
while (itc!=contours.end()) {
  // verify contour size
  if (itc->size() < cmin || itc->size() > cmax)
    itc= contours.erase(itc);
  else
    ++itc;
}
```

Note that this loop could have been made more efficient since each erasing operation in a `std::vector` instance is O(N). However, considering the small size of this vector, the overall cost is not too high.

This time, we draw the remaining contours on the original image and obtain the following result:

We were lucky enough to find a simple criterion that allowed us to identify all objects of interest in this image. In more complex situations, a more refined analysis of the components' properties is required. This is the object of the next recipe, *Computing components' shape descriptors*.

There's more...

With the `cv::findContours` function, it is also possible to include all closed contours in the binary map, including the ones formed by holes in the components. This is done by specifying another flag in the function call:

```
cv::findContours(image,
                contours,                 // a vector of contours
                cv::RETR_LIST,            // retrieve all contours
                cv::CHAIN_APPROX_NONE);   // all pixels
```

With this call, the following contours are obtained:

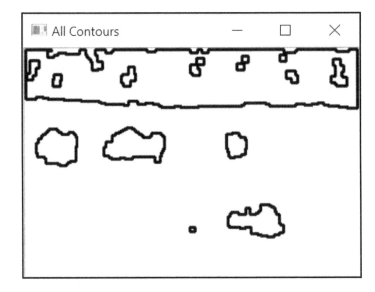

Notice the extra contours that were added in the background forest. It is also possible to have these contours organized into a hierarchy. The main component is the parent, holes in it are its children, and if there are components inside these holes, they become the children of the previous children, and so on. This hierarchy is obtained by using the cv::RETR_TREE flag, as follows:

```
std::vector<cv::Vec4i> hierarchy;
cv::findContours(image, contours, // a vector of contours
        hierarchy,                 // hierarchical representation
        cv::RETR_TREE,             // contours in tree format
        cv::CHAIN_APPROX_NONE);    //all pixels of each contours
```

In this case, each contour has a corresponding hierarchy element at the same index, made of four integers. The first two integers give you the index of the next and the previous contours of the same level, and the next two integers give you the index of the first child and the parent of this contour. A negative index indicates the end of a contour list. The cv::RETR_CCOMP flag is similar but limits the hierarchy at two levels.

Computing components' shape descriptors

A connected component often corresponds to the image of an object in a pictured scene. To identify this object, or to compare it with other image elements, it can be useful to perform some measurements on the component in order to extract some of its characteristics. In this recipe, we will look at some of the shape descriptors available in OpenCV that can be used to describe the shape of a connected component.

How to do it...

Many OpenCV functions are available when it comes to shape description. We will apply some of them on the components that we have extracted in the preceding recipe. In particular, we will use our vector of four contours corresponding to the four buffaloes we previously identified. In the following code snippets, we compute a shape descriptor on the contours (`contours[0]` to `contours[3]`) and draw the result (with a thickness of 2) over the image of the contours (with a thickness of 1). This image is shown at the end of this section.

The first one is the bounding box, which is applied to the bottom-right component:

```
// testing the bounding box
cv::Rect r0= cv::boundingRect(contours[0]);
// draw the rectangle
cv::rectangle(result,r0, 0, 2);
```

The minimum enclosing circle is similar. It is applied to the upper-right component:

```
// testing the enclosing circle
float radius;
cv::Point2f center;
cv::minEnclosingCircle(contours[1],center,radius);
// draw the circle
cv::circle(result,center,static_cast<int>(radius),
           cv::Scalar(0),2);
```

The polygonal approximation of a component's contour is computed as follows (on the left-hand component):

```
// testing the approximate polygon
std::vector<cv::Point> poly;
cv::approxPolyDP(contours[2],poly,5,true);
// draw the polygon
cv::polylines(result, poly, true, 0, 2);
```

Notice the polygon drawing function, `cv::polylines`. This operates similarly to the other drawing functions. The third Boolean parameter is used to indicate whether the contour is closed or not (if yes, the last point is linked to the first one).

The convex hull is another form of polygonal approximation (on the second component from the left):

```
// testing the convex hull
std::vector<cv::Point> hull;
cv::convexHull(contours[3],hull);
// draw the polygon
cv::polylines(result, hull, true, 0, 2);
```

Finally, the computation of the moments is another powerful descriptor (the center of mass is drawn inside all components):

```
// testing the moments
// iterate over all contours
itc= contours.begin();
while (itc!=contours.end()) {

    // compute all moments
    cv::Moments mom= cv::moments(cv::Mat(*itc++));
    // draw mass center
    cv::circle(result,
               // position of mass center converted to integer
               cv::Point(mom.m10/mom.m00,mom.m01/mom.m00),
               2, cv::Scalar(0),2); // draw black dot
}
```

The resulting image is as follows:

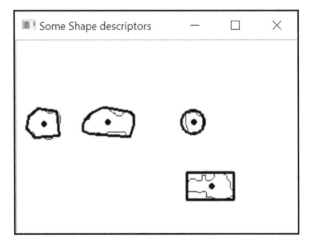

How it works...

The bounding box of a component is probably the most compact way to represent and localize a component in an image. It is defined as the upright rectangle of minimum size that completely contains the shape. Comparing the height and width of the box gives you an indication about the vertical or horizontal dimensions of the object (for example, one could use a height-to-width ratio in order to distinguish an image of a car from one of a pedestrian). The minimum enclosing circle is generally used when only the approximate component size and location is required.

The polygonal approximation of a component is useful when one wants to manipulate a more compact representation that resembles the component's shape. It is created by specifying an accuracy parameter, giving you the maximal acceptable distance between a shape and its simplified polygon. It is the fourth parameter in the `cv::approxPolyDP` function. The result is a vector of `cv::Point`, which corresponds to the vertices of the polygon. To draw this polygon, we need to iterate over the vector and link each point with the next one by drawing a line between them.

The convex hull, or convex envelope, of a shape is the minimal convex polygon that encompasses a shape. It can be visualized as the shape that an elastic band would take if placed around the component. As can be seen, the convex hull contour will deviate from the original one at the concave locations of the shape contour.

These locations are often designated as convexity defects, and a special OpenCV function is available to identify them: the `cv::convexityDefects` function. It is called as follows:

```
std::vector<cv::Vec4i> defects;
cv::convexityDefects(contour, hull, defects);
```

The `contour` and `hull` arguments are, respectively, the original and the convex hull contours (both represented with `std::vector<cv::Point>` instances). The output is a vector of four integer elements. The first two integers are the indices of the points on the contour, delimiting the defect; the third integer corresponds to the farthest point inside the concavity, and finally, the last integer corresponds to the distance between this farthest point and the convex hull.

Moments are commonly used mathematical entities in the structural analysis of shapes. OpenCV has defined a data structure that encapsulates all computed moments of a shape. It is the object returned by the `cv::moments` function. Together, the moments represent a compact description of the shape of an object. They are commonly used, for example, in character recognition. We simply use this structure to obtain the mass center of each component that is computed from the first three spatial moments here.

There's more...

Other structural properties can be computed using the available OpenCV functions. The `cv::minAreaRect` function computes the minimum enclosed rotated rectangle (this was used in Chapter 5, *Transforming Images with Morphological Operations*, in the *Extracting distinctive regions using MSER* recipe). The `cv::contourArea` function estimates the area of (the number of pixels inside) a contour. The `cv::pointPolygonTest` function determines whether a point is inside or outside a contour, and `cv::matchShapes` measures the resemblance between two contours. All these property measures can be advantageously combined in order to perform more advanced structural analysis.

Quadrilateral detection

The MSER features presented in Chapter 5, *Transforming Images with Morphological Operations*, constitutes an efficient tool to extract shapes in an image. Considering the MSER result obtained in the preceding chapter, we will now build an algorithm to detect quadrilateral components in an image. In the case of the current image, this detection will allow us to identify the building's windows. A binary version of the MSER image is easily obtained, as follows:

```
// create a binary version
components= components==255;
// open the image (white background)
cv::morphologyEx(components,components,
                cv::MORPH_OPEN,cv::Mat(),
                cv::Point(-1,-1),3);
```

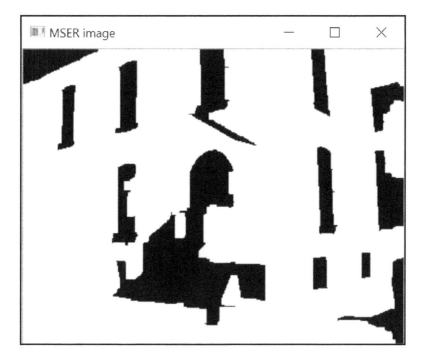

The next step is to obtain the contours:

```
//invert image (background must be black)
cv::Mat componentsInv= 255-components;
//Get the contours of the connected components
cv::findContours(componentsInv,
                contours,          // a vector of contours
                cv::RETR_EXTERNAL, // retrieve the external contours
                cv::CHAIN_APPROX_NONE);
```

Finally, we go over all the contours and roughly approximate them with a polygon:

```
// white image
cv::Mat quadri(components.size(),CV_8U,255);

// for all contours
std::vector<std::vector<cv::Point>>::iterator it= contours.begin();
while (it!= contours.end()) {
  poly.clear();
  // approximate contour by polygon
  cv::approxPolyDP(*it,poly,10,true);
    // do we have a quadrilateral?
```

```
if (poly.size()==4) {
  //draw it
  cv::polylines(quadri, poly, true, 0, 2);
}
++it;
}
```

The quadrilaterals are those polygons that have four edges. The detected ones are the following:

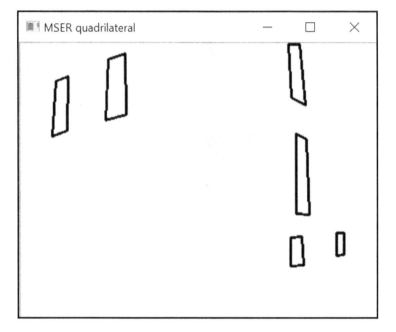

To detect rectangles, you can simply measure the angles between adjacent edges and reject the quadrilaterals that have angles that deviate too much from 90 degrees.

8
Detecting Interest Points

In this chapter, we will cover the following recipes:

- Detecting corners in an image
- Detecting features quickly
- Detecting scale-invariant features
- Detecting FAST features at multiple scales

Introduction

In computer vision, the concept of **interest points** also called **keypoints** or **feature points** has been largely used to solve many problems in object recognition, image registration, visual tracking, 3D reconstruction, and more. This concept relies on the idea that instead of looking at the image as a whole (that is, extracting global features), it could be advantageous to select some special points in the image and perform a local analysis on them (that is, extracting local features). This approach works well as long as a sufficient number of such points are detected in the images of interest, and these points are distinguishing and stable features, that can be accurately localized.

Because they are used for analyzing image content, feature points should ideally be detected at the same scene or object location, no matter from which viewpoint, scale, or orientation the image was taken. View invariance is a very desirable property in image analysis and has been the object of numerous studies. As we will see, different detectors have different invariance properties. This chapter focuses on the keypoint extraction process itself. The following chapters will then show you how interest points can be put to work in different contexts, such as image matching or image geometry estimation.

Detecting corners in an image

When searching for interesting feature points in images, corners come out as an interesting solution. They are indeed local features that can be easily localized in an image, and in addition, they should abound in scenes of man-made objects (where they are produced by walls, doors, windows, tables, and so on). Corners are also interesting because they are two-dimensional features that can be accurately detected (even at sub-pixel accuracy), as they are at the junction of two edges. This is in contrast to points located on a uniform area or on the contour of an object; these ones would be difficult to repeatedly localize precisely on other images of the same object. The Harris feature detector is a classical approach to detecting corners in an image. We will explore this operator in this recipe.

How to do it...

The basic OpenCV function that is used to detect Harris corners is called `cv::cornerHarris` and is straightforward to use. You call it on an input image, and the result is an image of floats that gives you the corner strength at each pixel location. A threshold is then applied on this output image in order to obtain a set of detected corners. This is accomplished with the following code:

```cpp
// Detect Harris Corners
cv::Mat cornerStrength;
cv::cornerHarris(image,            // input image
            cornerStrength,  // image of cornerness
            3,               // neighborhood size
            3,               // aperture size
            0.01);           // Harris parameter

// threshold the corner strengths
cv::Mat harrisCorners;
double threshold= 0.0001;
cv::threshold(cornerStrength,harrisCorners,
            threshold,255,cv::THRESH_BINARY);
```

Here is the original image:

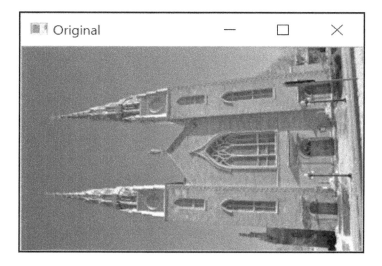

The result is a binary map image, shown in the following screenshot, which is inverted for better viewing (that is, we used `cv::THRESH_BINARY_INV` instead of `cv::THRESH_BINARY` to get the detected corners in black):

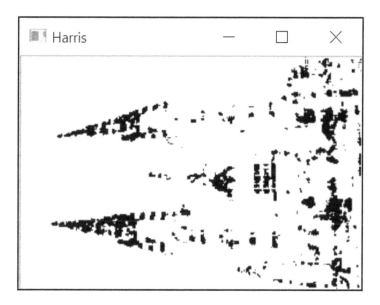

From the preceding function call, we observe that this interest point detector requires several parameters (these will be explained in the next section) that might make it difficult to tune. In addition, the corner map that is obtained contains many clusters of corner pixels that contradict the fact that we would like to detect well-localized points. Therefore, we will try to improve the corner detection method by defining our own class to detect Harris corners.

The class encapsulates the Harris parameters with their default values and corresponding getter and setter methods (which are not shown here):

```
class HarrisDetector {

  private:

    // 32-bit float image of corner strength
    cv::Mat cornerStrength;
    // 32-bit float image of thresholded corners
    cv::Mat cornerTh;
    // image of local maxima (internal)
    cv::Mat localMax;
    // size of neighborhood for derivatives smoothing
    int neighborhood;
    // aperture for gradient computation
    int aperture;
    // Harris parameter
    double k;
    // maximum strength for threshold computation
    double maxStrength;
    // calculated threshold (internal)
    double threshold;
    // size of neighborhood for non-max suppression
    int nonMaxSize;
    // kernel for non-max suppression
    cv::Mat kernel;

  public:

    HarrisDetector(): neighborhood(3), aperture(3),
                      k(0.01), maxStrength(0.0),
                      threshold(0.01), nonMaxSize(3) {

      // create kernel used in non-maxima suppression
      setLocalMaxWindowSize(nonMaxSize);
    }
```

To detect the Harris corners on an image, we proceed in two steps. First, the Harris values at each pixel are computed:

```
// Compute Harris corners
void detect(const cv::Mat& image) {

    // Harris computation
    cv::cornerHarris(image,cornerStrength,
                     neighbourhood,// neighborhood size
                     aperture,     // aperture size
                     k);           // Harris parameter
    // internal threshold computation
    cv::minMaxLoc(cornerStrength,0,&maxStrength);

    // local maxima detection
    cv::Mat dilated;   //temporary image
    cv::dilate(cornerStrength,dilated,cv::Mat());
    cv::compare(cornerStrength,dilated, localMax, cv::CMP_EQ);
}
```

Next, the feature points are obtained, based on a specified threshold value. Since the range of possible values for Harris depends on the particular choices of its parameters, the threshold is specified as a quality level that is defined as a fraction of the maximal Harris value computed in the image:

```
// Get the corner map from the computed Harris values
cv::Mat getCornerMap(double qualityLevel) {

    cv::Mat cornerMap;

    // thresholding the corner strength
    threshold= qualityLevel*maxStrength;
    cv::threshold(cornerStrength,cornerTh, threshold, 255,
                  cv::THRESH_BINARY);

    // convert to 8-bit image
    cornerTh.convertTo(cornerMap,CV_8U);

    // non-maxima suppression
    cv::bitwise_and(cornerMap,localMax,cornerMap);

    return cornerMap;
}
```

This method returns a binary corner map of the detected features. The fact that the detection of the Harris features has been split into two methods, allows us to test the detection with a different threshold (until an appropriate number of feature points are obtained) without the need to repeat costly computations. It is also possible to obtain the Harris features in the form of a `std::vector` of `cv::Point` instances:

```
// Get the feature points from the computed Harris values
void getCorners(std::vector<cv::Point> &points, double qualityLevel) {

  // Get the corner map
  cv::Mat cornerMap= getCornerMap(qualityLevel);
  // Get the corners
  getCorners(points, cornerMap);
}

// Get the feature points from the computed corner map
void getCorners(std::vector<cv::Point> &points,
                const cv::Mat& cornerMap) {

  // Iterate over the pixels to obtain all features
  for( int y = 0; y < cornerMap.rows; y++ ) {

    const uchar* rowPtr = cornerMap.ptr<uchar>(y);

    for( int x = 0; x < cornerMap.cols; x++ ) {

      // if it is a feature point
      if (rowPtr[x]) {

        points.push_back(cv::Point(x,y));
      }
    }
  }
}
```

This class also improves the detection of the Harris corners by adding a non-maxima suppression step, which will be explained in the next section. The detected points can now be drawn on an image using the `cv::circle` function, as demonstrated by the following method:

```
// Draw circles at feature point locations on an image
void drawOnImage(cv::Mat &image,
                 const std::vector<cv::Point> &points,
                 cv::Scalar color= cv::Scalar(255,255,255),
                 int radius=3, int thickness=1) {
  std::vector<cv::Point>::const_iterator it= points.begin();
  // for all corners
```

```
    while (it!=points.end()) {

        // draw a circle at each corner location
        cv::circle(image,*it,radius,color,thickness);
        ++it;
    }
}
```

Using this class, the detection of the Harris points is accomplished as follows:

```
// Create Harris detector instance
HarrisDetector harris;
// Compute Harris values
harris.detect(image);
// Detect Harris corners
std::vector<cv::Point> pts;
harris.getCorners(pts,0.02);
// Draw Harris corners
harris.drawOnImage(image,pts);
```

This results in the following image:

How it works...

To define the notion of corners in images, the Harris feature detector looks at the average directional change in intensity in a small window around a putative interest point. If we consider a displacement vector, `(u,v)`, the intensity change can be measured by a sum of squared difference:

$$R = \sum \left(I\left(x+u, y+v\right) - I(x,y)\right)^2$$

The summation is over a defined neighborhood around the considered pixel (the size of this neighborhood corresponds to the third parameter in the `cv::cornerHarris` function). This average intensity change can then be computed in all possible directions, which leads to the definition of a corner as a point for which the average change is high in more than one direction. From this definition, the Harris test is performed as follows: We first obtain the direction of the maximal average intensity change. Next, we check whether the average intensity change in the orthogonal direction is high as well. If this is the case, then we have a corner.

Mathematically, this condition can be tested by using an approximation of the preceding formula using the Taylor expansion:

$$R \approx \sum \left(I(x,y) + \frac{\partial I}{\partial x}u + \frac{\partial I}{\partial y}v - I(x,y)\right)^2 = \sum \left(\left(\frac{\partial I}{\partial x}u\right)^2 + \left(\frac{\partial I}{\partial y}v\right)^2 + 2\frac{\partial I}{\partial x}\frac{\partial I}{\partial y}uv\right)$$

This is then rewritten in matrix form:

$$R \approx [u\ v]\begin{bmatrix} \sum\left(\frac{\delta I}{\delta x}\right)^2 & \sum \frac{\delta I}{\delta x}\frac{\delta I}{\delta y} \\ \sum \frac{\delta I}{\delta x}\frac{\delta I}{\delta y} & \sum\left(\frac{\delta I}{\delta y}\right)^2 \end{bmatrix}\begin{bmatrix} u \\ v \end{bmatrix}$$

This matrix is a covariance matrix that characterizes the rate of intensity change in all directions. This definition involves the image's first derivatives that are often computed using the Sobel operator. This is the case with the OpenCV implementation, in which the fourth parameter of the function corresponds to the aperture used for the computation of the Sobel filters. It can be shown that the two eigenvalues of the covariance matrix give you the maximal average intensity change and the average intensity change for the orthogonal direction. Then, if these two eigenvalues are low, we are in a relatively homogenous region. If one eigenvalue is high and the other is low, we must be on an edge. Finally, if both eigenvalues are high, then we are at a corner location. Therefore, the condition for a point to be accepted as a corner is to have the smallest eigenvalue of its covariance matrix higher than a given threshold.

The original definition of the Harris corner algorithm uses some properties of the eigen decomposition theory in order to avoid the cost of explicitly computing the eigenvalues. These properties are as follows:

- The product of the eigenvalues of a matrix is equal to its determinant
- The sum of the eigenvalues of a matrix is equal to the sum of the diagonal of the matrix (also known as the trace of the matrix)

It then follows that we can verify whether the eigenvalues of a matrix are high by computing the following score:

$$Det(C) - kTrace^2(C)$$

One can easily verify that this score will indeed be high only if both eigenvalues are high too. This is the score that is computed by the `cv::cornerHarris` function at each pixel location. The value of `k` is specified as the fifth parameter of the function. It could be difficult to determine what value is best for this parameter. However, in practice, a value in the range of `0.05` and `0.5` generally gives good results.

To improve the result of the detection, the class described in the previous section adds an additional non-maxima suppression step. The goal here is to exclude Harris corners that are adjacent to others. Therefore, to be accepted, the Harris corner must not only have a score higher than the specified threshold, but it must also be a local maximum. This condition is tested by using a simple trick that consists of dilating the image of the Harris score in our `detect` method:

```
cv::dilate(cornerStrength, dilated,cv::Mat());
```

Since the dilation replaces each pixel value with the maximum in the defined neighborhood, the only points that will not be modified are the local maxima. This is what is verified by the following equality test:

```
cv::compare(cornerStrength, dilated, localMax,cv::CMP_EQ);
```

The `localMax` matrix will therefore be true (that is, non-zero) only at local maxima locations. We then use it in our `getCornerMap` method to suppress all non-maximal features (using the `cv::bitwise` function).

There's more...

Additional improvements can be made to the original Harris corner algorithm. This section describes another corner detector found in OpenCV, which expands the Harris detector to make its corners more uniformly distributed across the image. As we will see, this operator implements a generic interface defining the behavior of all feature detection operators. This interface allows easy testing of different interest point detectors within the same application.

Good features to track

With the advent of floating-point processors, the mathematical simplification introduced to avoid eigenvalue decomposition has become negligible, and consequently, the detection of Harris corners can be made based on the explicitly computed eigenvalues. In principle, this modification should not significantly affect the result of the detection, but it avoids the use of the arbitrary `k` parameter. Note that two functions exist that allow you to explicitly get the eigenvalues (and eigenvectors) of the Harris covariance matrix; these are `cv::cornerEigenValsAndVecs` and `cv::cornerMinEigenVal`.

A second modification addresses the problem of feature point clustering. Indeed, in spite of the introduction of the local maxima condition, interest points tend to be unevenly distributed across an image, showing concentrations at highly textured locations. A solution to this problem is to impose a minimum distance between two interest points. This can be achieved using the following algorithm. Starting from the point with the strongest Harris score (that is, with the largest minimum eigenvalue), only accept interest points if they are located at, at least, a given distance from the already accepted points. This solution is implemented in OpenCV by the **good-features-to-track** (**GFTT**) operator, which is thus named because the features it detects can be used as a good starting set in visual tracking applications. This operator is deployed as follows:

```
// Compute good features to track
```

```
std::vector<cv::KeyPoint> keypoints;
// GFTT detector
cv::Ptr<cv::GFTTDetector> ptrGFTT =
    cv::GFTTDetector::create(
                    500,    // maximum number of keypoints
                    0.01,   // quality level
                    10);    //minimum allowed distance between points
// detect the GFTT
ptrGFTT->detect(image,keypoints);
```

The first step is to create the feature detector using the appropriate static function (here, cv::GFTTDetector::create) and the initialization parameters. In addition to the quality-level threshold value, and the minimum tolerated distance between interest points, the function also uses a maximum number of points that can be returned (this is possible since points are accepted in the order of strength). Calling this function returns a OpenCV smart pointer to the detector instance. Once this object constructed, its detect method can be called. Note that the common interface also includes the definition of a cv::Keypoint class that encapsulates the properties of each detected feature point. For the Harris corners, only the position of the keypoints and its response strength is relevant. The *Detecting scale-invariant features* recipe of this chapter will discuss the other properties that can be associated with a keypoint.

The preceding code produces the following result:

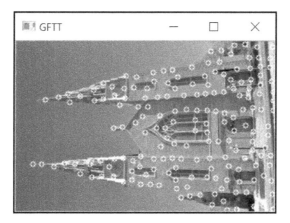

This approach increases the complexity of the detection, since it requires the interest points to be sorted by their Harris score, but it also clearly improves the distribution of the points across the image. Note that this function also includes an optional flag, that requests Harris corners to be detected using the classical corner score definition (using the covariance matrix determinant and trace).

The OpenCV common interface for the feature detector defines an abstract class called `cv::Feature2D` that basically imposes, among others, the existence of a `detect` operation with the following signatures:

```
void detect( cv::InputArray image,
             std::vector<KeyPoint>& keypoints,
             cv::InputArray mask );

void detect( cv::InputArrayOfArrays images,
             std::vector<std::vector<KeyPoint> >& keypoints,
             cv::InputArrayOfArrays masks );
```

The second method allows interest points to be detected in a vector of images. The class also includes other methods such as the ones to compute feature descriptors (to be discussed in the next chapter) and the ones can read and write the detected points in a file.

See also

- The classic article that describes the Harris operator by *C. Harris* and *M.J. Stephens, A combined corner and edge detector, Alvey Vision Conference,* pp. 147-152, 1988
- The article by *J. Shi* and *C. Tomasi, Good features to track, Int. Conference on Computer Vision and Pattern Recognition,* pp. 593-600, 1994, introduces this special feature
- The article by *K. Mikolajczyk* and *C. Schmid, Scale and Affine invariant interest point detectors, International Journal of Computer Vision, vol 60,* no 1, pp. 63-86, 2004, proposes a multi-scale and affine-invariant Harris operator

Detecting features quickly

-The Harris operator proposed a formal mathematical definition for corners (or more generally, interest points) based on the rate of intensity changes in two perpendicular directions. Although this constitutes a sound definition, it requires the computation of the image derivatives, which is a costly operation, especially considering the fact that interest point detection is often just the first step in a more complex algorithm.

In this recipe, we present another feature point operator, called **FAST (Features from Accelerated Segment Test)**. This one has been specifically designed to allow quick detection of interest points in an image, the decision to accept or not to accept a keypoint being based on only a few pixel comparisons.

How to do it...

As seen in the last section of the previous recipe, *Detecting corners in an image*, using the OpenCV common interface for feature point detection makes the deployment of any feature point detectors easy. The detector presented in this recipe is the FAST detector. As the name suggests, it has been designed to quickly detect interest points in an image:

```
// vector of keypoints
std::vector<cv::KeyPoint> keypoints;
// FAST detector with a threshold of 40
cv::Ptr<cv::FastFeatureDetector> ptrFAST =
        cv::FastFeatureDetector::create(40);
// detect the keypoints
ptrFAST->detect(image,keypoints);
```

Note that OpenCV also proposes a generic function to draw `keypoints` on an image:

```
cv::drawKeypoints(image,                         // original image
    keypoints,                                   // vector of keypoints
    image,                                       // the output image
    cv::Scalar(255,255,255),                     // keypoint color
    cv::DrawMatchesFlags::DRAW_OVER_OUTIMG);// drawing flag
```

By specifying the chosen drawing flag, the keypoints are drawn over the input image, thus producing the following output result:

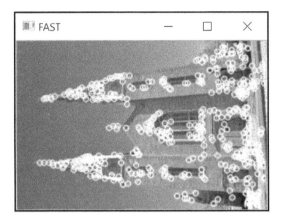

An interesting option is to specify a negative value for the keypoint color. In this case, a different random color will be selected for each drawn circle.

How it works...

As in the case with the Harris point detector, the FAST feature algorithm derives from the definition of what constitutes a corner. This time, this definition is based on the image intensity around a putative feature point. The decision to accept a keypoint is taken by examining a circle of pixels centered at a candidate point. If an arc of contiguous points of a length greater than three quarters of the circle perimeter in which all pixels significantly differ from the intensity of the center point (being all darker or all brighter) is found, then a keypoint is declared.

This is a simple test that can be computed quickly. Moreover, in its original formulation, the algorithm uses an additional trick to further speed up the process. Indeed, if we first test four points separated by 90 degrees on the circle (for example, top, bottom, right, and left points), it can be easily shown that in order to satisfy the condition expressed previously, at least three of these points must all be brighter or darker than the central pixel.

If this is not the case, the point can be rejected immediately, without inspecting additional points on the circumference. This is a very effective test, since in practice, most of the image points will be rejected by this simple 4-comparison test.

In principle, the radius of the circle of examined pixels could have been a parameter of the method. However, it has been found that in practice, a radius of 3 gives you both good results and high efficiency. There are, then, 16 pixels that need to be considered on the circumference of the circle, shown as follows:

		16	1	2	
	15				3
14					4
13			0		5
12					6
	11				7
		10	9	8	

The four points used for the pretest are pixels **1, 5, 9**, and **13**, and the required number of contiguous darker or brighter points is **9**. This specific setting is often designated as the FAST-9 corner detector, and this the one OpenCV uses by default. You can, in fact, specify which type of FAST detector you want to use when you construct the detector instance; there is also a `setType` method. The options are `cv::FastFeatureDetector::TYPE_5_8`, `cv::FastFeatureDetector::TYPE_7_12`, and `cv::FastFeatureDetector::TYPE_9_16`.

To be considered as being significantly darker or brighter, the intensity of a point must differ from the intensity of the central pixel by at least a given amount; this value corresponds to the threshold parameter specified when creating the detector instance. The larger this threshold is, the fewer corner points will be detected.

As for Harris features, it is often better to perform non-maxima suppression on the corners that have been found. Therefore, a corner strength measure needs to be defined. Several alternative measures to this can considered, and the one that has been retained is the following. The strength of a corner is given by the sum of the absolute difference between the central pixel and the pixels on the identified contiguous arc. You can read the corner strength from the `response` attribute of the `cv::KeyPoint` instances.

This algorithm results in very fast interest point detection and is therefore the feature of choice when speed is a concern. This is the case, for example, in real-time visual tracking or object-recognition applications where several points must be tracked or matched in a live video stream.

There's more...

Different strategies can be used to make feature detection more suitable for your application.

For example, it is sometimes desirable to dynamically adapt the feature detection such to obtain a predefined number of interest points. A simple strategy to achieve this goal consists in using a permissive detection threshold such that a large number of interest points is obtained. You then simply have to extract the nth strongest points in the set. A standard C++ function allows you to accomplish this:

```
if (numberOfPoints < keypoints.size())
   std::nth_element(keypoints.begin(),
                    keypoints.begin() + numberOfPoints,
                    keypoints.end(),
                    [](cv::KeyPoint& a, cv::KeyPoint& b) {
                    return a.response > b.response; });
```

Here, `keypoints` is your `std::vector` of detected interest points and `numberOfPoints` is the desirable quantity of interest points. The last parameter in this function is the lambda comparator used to extract the best interest points. Note that if the number of detected interest points is too low (that is, lower than the seek quantity), this means that you should have used a lower threshold for detection. However, using a very permissive threshold generally increases the computational load; there is therefore a trade-off value that has to be identified.

Another issue that often arises when detecting features, is the uneven distribution of the interest points over an image. Indeed, the `keypoints` tend to agglomerate at highly textured areas of the image. For example, here is the result obtained when detecting 100 interest points on our church image:

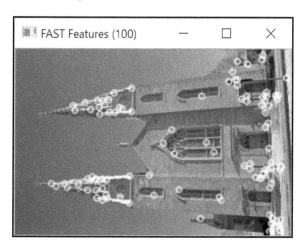

As you can see, most feature points are on the upper and bottom parts of the building. A common strategy used to obtain a better distribution of the interest points in an image consists in dividing this one into a grid of sub-images and perform an independent detection of each sub-image. The following code performs this grid adapted detection:

```
// The final vector of keypoints
keypoints.clear();
// detect on each grid
for (int i = 0; i < vstep; i++)
  for (int j = 0; j < hstep; j++) {
    // create ROI over current grid
    imageROI = image(cv::Rect(j*hsize, i*vsize, hsize, vsize));
    // detect the keypoints in grid
    gridpoints.clear();
    ptrFAST->detect(imageROI, gridpoints);

    // get the strongest FAST features
    auto itEnd(gridpoints.end());
    if (gridpoints.size() > subtotal) {
      // select the strongest features
      std::nth_element(gridpoints.begin(),
                       gridpoints.begin() + subtotal,
                       gridpoints.end(),
                       [](cv::KeyPoint& a,
                       cv::KeyPoint& b) {
```

```
            return a.response > b.response; });
        itEnd = gridpoints.begin() + subtotal;
    }

    // add them to the global keypoint vector
    for (auto it = gridpoints.begin(); it != itEnd; ++it) {
        // convert to image coordinates
        it->pt += cv::Point2f(j*hsize, i*vsize);
        keypoints.push_back(*it);
    }
  }
}
```

The key idea here is to use image ROIs in order to perform keypoint detection inside each sub-image of the grid. The resulting detection shows a more uniform keypoint distribution:

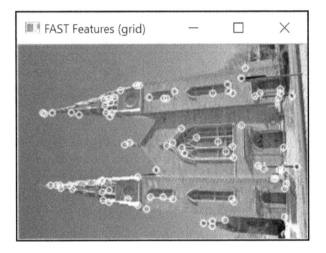

See also

- OpenCV2 includes specialized adapted feature detection wrapper classes; see, for example, `cv::DynamicAdaptedFeatureDetector` or `GridAdaptedFeatureDetector`
- The article by *E. Rosten* and *T. Drummond, Machine learning for high-speed corner detection, International European Conference on Computer Vision, pp. 430-443, 2006,* describes the FAST feature algorithm and its variants in detail

Detecting scale-invariant features

The view invariance of feature detection was presented as an important concept in the introduction of this chapter. While orientation invariance, which is the ability to detect the same points even if an image is rotated, has been relatively well handled by the simple feature point detectors that have been presented so far, the invariance to scale changes is more difficult to achieve. To address this problem, the concept of scale-invariant features has been introduced in computer vision. The idea here is to not only have a consistent detection of keypoints no matter at which scale an object is pictured, but to also have a scale factor associated with each of the detected feature points. Ideally, for the same object point featured at two different scales on two different images, the ratio of the two computed scale factors should correspond to the ratio of their respective scales. In recent years, several scale-invariant features have been proposed, and this recipe presents one of them, the **SURF** features. SURF stands for **Speeded Up Robust Features**, and as we will see, they are not only scale-invariant features, but they also offer the advantage of being computed efficiently.

How to do it...

The SURF feature detector is part of the `opencv_contrib` repository. To use it, you must then have built the OpenCV library together with these extra modules, as explained in `Chapter 1`, *Playing with Images*. In particular, we are interested here by the `cv::xfeatures2d` module that gives us access to the `cv::xfeatures2d::SurfFeatureDetector` class. As for the other detector, interest points are detected by first creating an instance of the detector and then calling its `detect` method:

```
// Construct the SURF feature detector object
cv::Ptr<cv::xfeatures2d::SurfFeatureDetector> ptrSURF =
            cv::xfeatures2d::SurfFeatureDetector::create(2000.0);
// detect the keypoints
ptrSURF->detect(image, keypoints);
```

To draw these features, we again use the `cv::drawKeypoints` OpenCV function but now with the `cv::DrawMatchesFlags::DRAW_RICH_KEYPOINTS` flag so that we can visualize the associated scale factor:

```
// Draw the keypoints with scale and orientation information
cv::drawKeypoints(image,                        // original image
        keypoints,                              // vector of keypoints
        featureImage,                           // the resulting image
        cv::Scalar(255,255,255),                // color of the points
        cv::DrawMatchesFlags::DRAW_RICH_KEYPOINTS);
```

The resulting image with the detected features is then as follows:

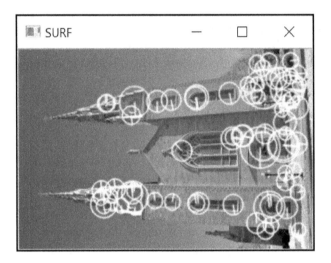

Here, the size of the keypoint circles resulting from the use of the `cv::DrawMatchesFlags::DRAW_RICH_KEYPOINTS` flag is proportional to the computed scale of each feature. The SURF algorithm also associates an orientation with each feature to make them invariant to rotations. This orientation is illustrated by a radial line inside each drawn circle.

If we take another picture of the same object but at a different scale, the feature-detection result is as follows:

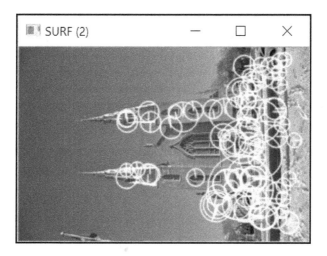

By carefully observing the detected keypoints on the two images, it can be seen that the change in the size of corresponding circles is often proportional to the change in scale. As an example, consider the two windows on the right part of the church; in both images, a SURF feature has been detected at that location, and the two corresponding circles (of different sizes) contain the same visual elements. Of course, this is not the case for all features, but as we will discover in the next chapter, the repeatability rate is sufficiently high to allow good matching between the two images.

How it works...

In Chapter 6, *Filtering the Images*, we learned that the derivatives of an image can be estimated using Gaussian filters. These filters make use of a σ parameter, which defines the aperture (size) of the kernel. As we saw, this σ parameter corresponds to the variance of the Gaussian function used to construct the filter, and it then implicitly defines a scale at which the derivative is evaluated. Indeed, a filter that has a larger σ value smooths out the finer details of the image. This is why we can say that it operates at a coarser scale.

Now, if we compute, for instance, the Laplacian of a given image point using Gaussian filters at different scales, then different values are obtained. Looking at the evolution of the filter response for different scale factors, we obtain a curve that eventually reaches a maximum value at a given σ value. If we extract this maximum value for two images of the same object taken at two different scales, the ratio of these two σ maxima should correspond to the ratio of the scales at which the images were taken. This important observation is at the core of the scale-invariant feature extraction process. That is, scale-invariant features should be detected as the local maxima in both the spatial space (in the image) and the scale space (as obtained from the derivative filters applied at different scales).

SURF implements this idea by proceeding as follows. First, to detect the features, the Hessian matrix is computed at each pixel. This matrix measures the local curvature of a function and is defined as follows:

$$H(x, y) = \begin{bmatrix} \dfrac{\delta^2 I}{\delta x^2} & \dfrac{\delta^2 I}{\delta x \delta y} \\ \dfrac{\delta^2 I}{\delta x \delta y} & \dfrac{\delta^2 I}{\delta y^2} \end{bmatrix}$$

The determinant of this matrix gives you the strength of this curvature. The idea, therefore, is to define corners as image points with high local curvature (that is, high variation in more than one direction). Since it is composed of second-order derivatives, this matrix can be computed using Laplacian of Gaussian kernels of a different scale, that is, for different values of σ. This Hessian then becomes a function of three variables, $H(x, y, \sigma)$. Therefore, a scale-invariant feature is declared when the determinant of this Hessian reaches a local maximum in both spatial and scale space (that is, 3x3x3 non-maxima suppression needs to be performed). Note that in order to be considered as a valid point, this determinant must have a minimum value as specified by the first parameter of the `create` method of the `cv::xfeatures2d::SurfFeatureDetector` class.

However, the calculation of all of these derivatives at different scales is computationally costly. The objective of the SURF algorithm is to make this process as efficient as possible. This is achieved by using approximated Gaussian kernels that involve only few integer additions. These have the following structure:

The kernel on the left-hand side is used to estimate the mixed second derivatives, while the one on the right-hand side estimates the second derivative in the vertical direction. A rotated version of this second kernel estimates the second derivative in the horizontal direction. The smallest kernels have a size of 9x9 pixels, corresponding to σ≈1.2. To obtain a scale-space representation, kernels of increasing size are successively applied. The exact number of filters that are applied can be specified by additional parameters of the `cv::xfeatures2d::SurfFeatureDetector::create` method. By default, 12 different sizes of kernels are used (going up to size 99x99). Note that, as explained in Chapter 4, *Counting the Pixels with Histograms*, the use of integral images guarantees that the sum inside each lobe of each filter can be computed by using only three additions independent of the size of the filter.

Once the local maxima are identified, the precise position of each detected interest point is obtained through interpolation in both scale and image space. The result is then a set of feature points that are localized at sub-pixel accuracy and to which a scale value is associated.

There's more...

The SURF algorithm has been developed as an efficient variant of another well-known scale-invariant feature detector called **SIFT** (**Scale-Invariant Feature Transform**).

The SIFT feature-detection algorithm

SIFT also detects features as local maxima in the image and scale space, but uses the Laplacian filter response instead of the Hessian determinant. This Laplacian is computed at different scales (that is, increasing values of σ) using the Difference of Gaussian filters, as explained in Chapter 6, *Filtering the Images*. To improve efficiency, each time the value of σ is doubled, the size of the image is reduced by two. Each pyramid level corresponds to an octave, and each scale is a *layer*. There are typically three layers per octave.

The following figure illustrates a pyramid of two octaves in which the four Gaussian-filtered images of the first octave produce three DoG layers:

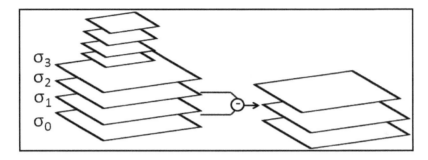

The detection of the SIFT features proceeds in a way very similar to SURF:

```
// Construct the SIFT feature detector object
cv::Ptr<cv::xfeatures2d::SiftFeatureDetector> ptrSIFT =
                    cv::xfeatures2d::SiftFeatureDetector::create();
// detect the keypoints
ptrSIFT->detect(image, keypoints);
```

Here, we use all the default arguments to construct the detector, but you can specify the number of desired SIFT points (the strongest ones are kept), the number of layers per octave, and the initial value for σ. As you can see in the following image, using three octaves for the detection (default value) leads to a quite broad range of scales:

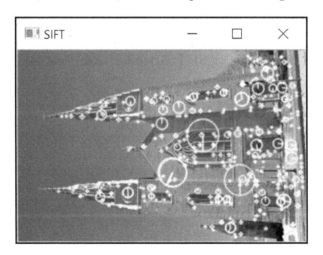

Since the computation of the feature point is based on floating-point kernels, SIFT is generally considered to be more accurate in terms of feature localization in regards to space and scale. For the same reason, it is also more computationally expensive, although this relative efficiency depends on each particular implementation.

Note that in this recipe we used the `cv::xfeatures2d::SurfFeatureDetector` and the `cv::xfeatures2d::SiftFeatureDetector` classes to make explicit the fact that we are using them as interest point detectors. Equivalently, we could have used the `cv::xfeatures2d::SURF` and `cv::xfeatures2d::SIFT` classes (they are type equivalent). Indeed, the SURF and SIFT operators cover both the detection and the description of interest points. Interest point description is the object of the next chapter.

As a final remark, it is important to mention the SURF and SIFT operators have been patented, and as such, their use in commercial applications might be subject to licensing agreements. This restriction is one of the reasons why these feature detectors are found in the `cv::xfeatures2d` package.

See also

- The *Computing the Laplacian of an image* recipe in `Chapter 6`, *Filtering the Images*, gives you more details on the Laplacian-of-Gaussian operator and the use of the difference of Gaussians
- The *Counting pixels with integral images* recipe in `Chapter 4`, *Counting the Pixels with Histograms* explains how integral images accelerate the computation of sums of pixels
- The *Describing and matching local intensity patterns* recipe in `Chapter 9`, *Describing and Matching Interest Points*, explains how these scale-invariant features can be described for robust image matching
- The article *SURF: Speeded Up Robust Features* by *H. Bay, A. Ess, T. Tuytelaars* and *L. Van Gool* in *Computer Vision and Image Understanding, vol. 110,* No. 3, pp. 346-359, 2008, describes the SURF feature algorithm
- The pioneering work by *D. Lowe, Distinctive Image Features from Scale Invariant Features* in *International Journal of Computer Vision, Vol. 60,* No. 2, 2004, pp. 91-110, describes the SIFT algorithm

Detecting FAST features at multiple scales

FAST has been introduced as a quick way to detect keypoints in an image. With SURF and SIFT, the emphasis was on designing scale-invariant features. More recently, new interest point detectors have been proposed with the objective of achieving both fast detection and invariance to scale changes. This recipe presents the **Binary Robust Invariant Scalable Keypoints** (BRISK) detector. It is based on the FAST feature detector that we described in a previous recipe of this chapter. Another detector, called **ORB** (**Oriented FAST and Rotated BRIEF**), will also be discussed at the end of this recipe. These two feature point detectors constitute an excellent solution when fast and reliable image matching is required. They are especially efficient when they are used in conjunction with their associated binary descriptors, as will be discussed in Chapter 9, *Describing and Matching Interest Points*.

How to do it...

Following what we did in the previous recipes, we first create an instance of the detector, and then the detect method is called on an image:

```
// Construct the BRISK feature detector object
cv::Ptr<cv::BRISK> ptrBRISK = cv::BRISK::create();
// detect the keypoints
ptrBRISK->detect(image, keypoints);
```

The image result shows the BRISK keypoints detected at multiple scales:

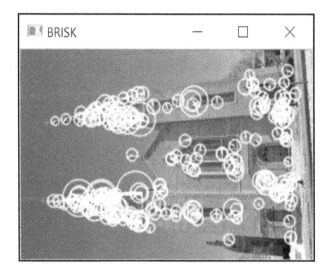

How it works...

BRISK is not only a feature point detector; the method also includes a procedure that describes the neighborhood of each detected keypoint. This second aspect will be the subject of the next chapter. We describe here how the quick detection of keypoints at multiple scales is performed using BRISK.

In order to detect interest points at different scales, the method first builds an image pyramid through two down-sampling processes. The first process starts from the original image size and downscales it by half at each layer (or octave). Secondly, in-between layers are created by down-sampling the original image by a factor of 1.5, and from this reduced image, additional layers are generated through successive half-sampling.

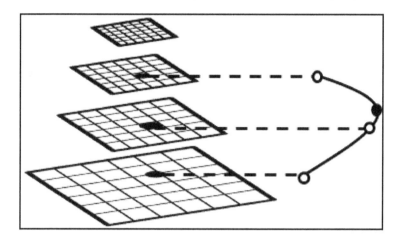

The FAST feature detector is then applied on all the images of this pyramid. Keypoint extraction is based on a criterion that is similar to the one used by SIFT. First, an acceptable interest point must be a local maximum, when comparing its strength with one of its eight spatial neighbors. If this is the case, the point is then compared with the scores of the neighboring points in the layers above and below; if its score is higher in scale as well, then it is accepted as an interest point. A key aspect of BRISK resides in the fact that the different layers of the pyramid have different resolutions. The method requires interpolation in both scale and space in order to locate each keypoint precisely. This interpolation is based on the FAST keypoint scores. In space, the interpolation is performed on a 3x3 neighborhood. In scale, it is computed by fitting a 1D parabola along the scale axis through the current point and its two neighboring local keypoints in the layers above and below; this keypoint localization in scale is illustrated in the preceding figure. As a result, even if the FAST keypoint detection is performed at discrete image scales, the resulting detected scales associated with each keypoint are continuous values.

The `cv::BRISK` detector has two main parameters. The first one is a threshold value for FAST keypoints to be accepted, and the second parameter is the number of octaves that will be generated in the image pyramid; in our example, we used 5 octaves, which explains the large number of scales in the detected keypoints.

There's more...

BRISK is not the only multiscale, fast detector that is proposed in OpenCV. Another one is the ORB feature detector that can also perform efficient keypoint detection.

The ORB feature-detection algorithm

ORB stands for Oriented FAST and Rotated BRIEF. The first part of this acronym refers to the keypoint detection part, while the second part refers to the descriptor that is proposed by ORB. Here, we focus on the detection method; the descriptor will be presented in the next chapter.

As with BRISK, ORB first creates an image pyramid. This one is made of a number of layers each of which being a down-sampled version of the previous one by a certain scale factor (typically, 8 scales and 1.2 scale factor reduction; these are the default parameter values when creating a `cv::ORB` detector). The strongest N keypoints are then accepted where the keypoint score is defined by the Harris cornerness measure, as defined in the first recipe of this chapter (the authors of this method found the Harris score to be a more reliable measure than the usual FAST corner strength).

An original aspect of the ORB detector resides in the fact that an orientation is associated with each detected interest point. As we will see in the next chapter, this information will be useful to align the descriptors of keypoints detected in different images. In the *Computing components' shape descriptors* recipe of `Chapter 7`, *Extracting Lines, Contours, and Components*, we introduced the concept of image moments and in particular, we showed you how the centroid of a component can be computed from its first three moments. ORB proposes to use the orientation of the centroid of a circular neighborhood around the keypoint. Since, FAST keypoints, by definition, always have a decentered centroid, the angle of the line that joins the central point and the centroid will always be well defined.

The ORB features are detected as follows:

```cpp
// Construct the ORB feature detector object
cv::Ptr<cv::ORB> ptrORB =
  cv::ORB::create(75,  // total number of keypoints
                  1.2, // scale factor between layers
                  8);  // number of layers in pyramid
// detect the keypoints
ptrORB->detect(image, keypoints);
```

This call produces the following result:

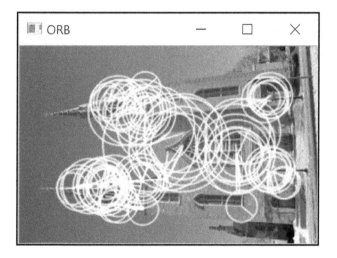

As can be seen, since the keypoints are independently detected on each pyramid layer, the detector tends to repeatedly detect the same feature point at different scales.

See also

- The *Matching keypoints with binary descriptors* recipe in `Chapter 9`, *Describing and Matching Interest Points*, explains how simple binary descriptors can be used for efficient robust matching of these features
- The article *BRISK: Binary Robust Invariant Scalable Keypoint* by *S. Leutenegger, M. Chli* and *R. Y. Siegwart* in *IEEE International Conference on Computer Vision*, pp. 2448–2555, 2011, describes the BRISK feature algorithm
- The article *ORB: an efficient alternative to SIFT or SURF* by *E. Rublee, V. Rabaud, K. Konolige* and *G. Bradski* in *IEEE International Conference on Computer Vision*, pp.2564-2571, 2011, describes the ORB feature algorithm

9
Describing and Matching Interest Points

In this chapter, we will cover the following recipes:

- Matching local templates
- Describing and matching local intensity patterns
- Matching keypoints with binary descriptors

Introduction

In the previous chapter, we learned how to detect special points in an image with the objective of subsequently performing local image analysis. These keypoints are chosen to be distinctive enough so that if a keypoint is detected on the image of an object, then the same point is expected to be detected in other images depicting the same object. We also described some more sophisticated interest point detectors that can assign a representative scale factor and/or an orientation to a keypoint. As we will see in this chapter, this additional information can be useful to normalize scene representations with respect to viewpoint variations.

In order to perform image analysis based on interest points, we now need to build rich representations that uniquely describe each of these keypoints. This chapter looks at different approaches that have been proposed to extract descriptors from interest points. These descriptors are generally 1D or 2D vectors of binary, integer, or floating-point numbers that describe a keypoint and its neighborhood. A good descriptor should be distinctive enough to uniquely represent each keypoint of an image; it should be robust enough to have the same points represented similarly in spite of possible illumination changes or viewpoint variations. Ideally, it should also be compact to reduce memory load and improve computational efficiency.

One of the most common operations accomplished with keypoints is image matching. This task could be performed, for example, to relate two images of the same scene or to detect the occurrence of a target object in an image. Here, we will study some basic matching strategies, a subject that will be further discussed in the next chapter.

Matching local templates

Feature point matching is the operation by which one can put in correspondence points from one image to points from another image (or points from an image set). Image points should match when they correspond to the image of the same scene element in the real world.

A single pixel is certainly not sufficient to make a decision on the similarity of two keypoints. This is why an image patch around each keypoint must be considered during the matching process. If two patches correspond to the same scene element, then one might expect their pixels to exhibit similar values. A direct pixel-by-pixel comparison of pixel patches is the solution presented in this recipe. This is probably the simplest approach to feature point matching, but as we will see, it is not the most reliable one. Nevertheless, in several situations, it can give good results.

How to do it...

Most often, patches are defined as squares of odd sizes centered at the keypoint position. The similarity between two square patches can then be measured by comparing the corresponding pixel intensity values inside the patches. A simple **Sum of Squared Differences (SSD)** is a popular solution. The feature matching strategy then works as follows. First, the keypoints are detected in each image. Here, we use the FAST detector:

```
// Define feature detector
cv::Ptr<cv::FeatureDetector> ptrDetector;    // generic detector
ptrDetector= // we select the FAST detector
            cv::FastFeatureDetector::create(80);

// Keypoint detection
ptrDetector->detect(image1,keypoints1);
ptrDetector->detect(image2,keypoints2);
```

Note how we used the generic `cv::Ptr<cv::FeatureDetector>` pointer type, which can refer to any feature detector. One can then test this code on different interest point detectors just by changing the detector to be used when calling the `detect` function.

The second step is to define a rectangle of, for example, size `11x11` that will be used to define patches around each keypoint:

```
// Define a square neighborhood
const int nsize(11);                          // size of the neighborhood
cv::Rect neighborhood(0, 0, nsize, nsize); // 11x11
cv::Mat patch1;
cv::Mat patch2;
```

The keypoints in one image are compared with all the keypoints in the other image. For each keypoint of the first image, the most similar patch in the second image is identified. This process is implemented using two nested loops, as shown in the following code:

```
// For all keypoints in first image
// find best match in second image
cv::Mat result;
std::vector<cv::DMatch> matches;

// for all keypoints in image 1
for (int i=0; i<keypoints1.size(); i++) {

  // define image patch
  neighborhood.x = keypoints1[i].pt.x-nsize/2;
  neighborhood.y = keypoints1[i].pt.y-nsize/2;
```

```
    // if neighborhood of points outside image,
    // then continue with next point
    if (neighborhood.x<0 || neighborhood.y<0 ||
        neighborhood.x+nsize >= image1.cols ||
        neighborhood.y+nsize >= image1.rows)
      continue;

    // patch in image 1
    patch1 = image1(neighborhood);

    // to contain best correlation value;
    cv::DMatch bestMatch;

    // for all keypoints in image 2
    for (int j=0; j<keypoints2.size(); j++) {

      // define image patch
      neighborhood.x = keypoints2[j].pt.x-nsize/2;
      neighborhood.y = keypoints2[j].pt.y-nsize/2;

      // if neighborhood of points outside image,
      // then continue with next point
      if (neighborhood.x<0 || neighborhood.y<0 ||
          neighborhood.x + nsize >= image2.cols ||
          neighborhood.y + nsize >= image2.rows)
        continue;

      // patch in image 2
      patch2 = image2(neighborhood);

      // match the two patches
      cv::matchTemplate(patch1,patch2,result, cv::TM_SQDIFF);

      // check if it is a best match
      if (result.at<float>(0,0) < bestMatch.distance) {

        bestMatch.distance= result.at<float>(0,0);
        bestMatch.queryIdx= i;
        bestMatch.trainIdx= j;
      }
    }

    // add the best match
    matches.push_back(bestMatch);
  }
```

Note the use of the `cv::matchTemplate` function, which we will describe in the next section and that computes the patch similarity score. When a potential match is identified, this match is represented through the use of a `cv::DMatch` object. This utility class stores the index of the two matching `keypoints` as well as their similarity score.

The more similar the two image patches are, the higher the probability that these patches correspond to the same scene point. This is why it is a good idea to sort the resulting match points by their similarity scores:

```
// extract the 25 best matches
std::nth_element(matches.begin(),
                 matches.begin() + 25,matches.end());
matches.erase(matches.begin() + 25,matches.end());
```

You can then simply retain the matches that pass a given similarity threshold. Here, we chose to keep only the N best matching points (we use N=25 to facilitate the visualization of the matching results).

Interestingly, there is an OpenCV function that can display the matching results by concatenating the two images and joining each corresponding point by a line. The function is used as follows:

```
//Draw the matching results
cv::Mat matchImage;
cv::drawMatches(image1,keypoints1,        // first image
                image2,keypoints2,        // second image
                matches,                  // vector of matches
                cv::Scalar(255,255,255),  // color of lines
                cv::Scalar(255,255,255)); // color of points
```

Here are the match results:

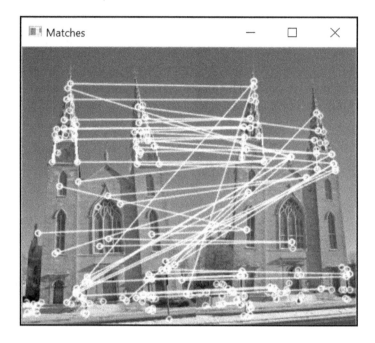

How it works...

The results obtained are certainly not perfect, but a visual inspection of the matched image points shows a number of successful matches. It can also be observed that the symmetry of the two towers of the church causes some confusion. Also, since we tried to match all the points in the left image with the ones in the right image, we obtained cases where a point in the right image was matched with multiple points in the left image. This is an asymmetrical matching situation that can be corrected by, for example, keeping only the match with the best score for each point in the right image.

To compare the image patches from each image, here we used a simple criterion, that is, a pixel-per-pixel sum of the squared difference specified using the `cv::TM_SQDIFF` flag. If we compare the point `(x,y)` of image `I1` with a putative match at `(x',y')` in image `I2`, then the similarity measure is as follows:

$$\sum_{i,j}\left(I_1\left(x+i,y+j\right)-I_2\left(x'+i,y'+j\right)\right)^2$$

Here, the sum of the `(i,j)` point provides the offset to cover the square template centered at each point. Since the difference between adjacent pixels in similar patches should be small, the best-matching patches should be the ones with the smallest sum. This is what is done in the main loop of the matching function; that is, for each keypoint in one image, we identify the keypoint in the other image that gives the lowest sum of the squared difference. We can also reject matches for which this sum is over a certain threshold value. In our case, we simply sort them from the most similar to the least similar ones.

In our example, the matching was done with square patches of size `11x11`. A larger neighborhood creates more distinctive patches, but it also makes them more sensitive to local scene variations.

Comparing two image windows from a simple sum of square differences will work relatively well as long as the two images show the scene from similar points of views and similar illumination. Indeed, a simple lighting change will increase or decrease all the pixel intensities of a patch, resulting in a large square difference. To make matching more invariant to lighting changes, other formulae could be used to measure the similarity between two image windows. OpenCV offers a number of these. A very useful formula is the normalized sum of square differences (the `cv::TM_SQDIFF_NORMED` flag):

$$\frac{\sum_{i,j}\left(I_1\left(x+i,y+j\right)-I_2\left(x'+i,y'+j\right)\right)^2}{\sqrt{\sum_{i,j}I_1\left(x+i,y+j\right)^2}\sqrt{\sum_{i,j}I_2\left(x'+i,y'+j\right)^2}}$$

Other similarity measures are based on the concept of correlation, defined in the signal processing theory, as follows (with the `cv::TM_CCORR` flag):

$$\sum_{i,j}I_1\left(x+i,y+j\right)I_2\left(x'+i,y'+j\right)$$

This value will be maximal when two patches are similar.

The identified matches are stored in a vector of `cv::DMatch` instances. Essentially, the `cv::DMatch` data structure contains a first index that refers to an element in the first vector of keypoints and a second index that refers to the matching feature in the second vector of keypoints. It also contains a real value that represents the distance between the two matched descriptors. This distance value is used in the definition of `operator<` when comparing two `cv::DMatch` instances.

When we drew the matches in the previous section, we wanted to limit the number of lines to make the results more readable. Therefore, we only displayed the 25 matches that had the lowest distance. To do this, we used the `std::nth_element` function, which positions the Nth element at the Nth position, with all smaller elements placed before this element. Once this is done, the vector is simply purged of its remaining elements.

There's more...

The `cv::matchTemplate` function is at the heart of our feature matching method. We used it here in a very specific way, which is to compare two image patches. However, this function has been designed to be used in a more generic way.

Template matching

A common task in image analysis is to detect the occurrence of a specific pattern or object in an image. This can be done by defining a small image of the object, a template, and searching for a similar occurrence in a given image. In general, the search is limited to a region of interest inside which we think the object can be found. The template is then slid over this region, and a similarity measure is computed at each pixel location. This is the operation performed by the `cv::matchTemplate` function. The input is a template image of a small size and an image over which the search is performed.

The result is a `cv::Mat` function of floating-point values that correspond to the similarity score at each pixel location. If the template is of size MxN and the image is of size WxH, then the resulting matrix will have a size of `(W-M+1)x(H-N+1)`. In general, you will be interested in the location of the highest similarity; so, the typical template-matching code will look as follows (assuming that the target variable is our template):

```
// define search region
cv::Mat roi(image2, // here top half of the image
cv::Rect(0,0,image2.cols,image2.rows/2));

// perform template matching
cv::matchTemplate(roi,              // search region
```

```
                target,         // template
                result,         // result
                cv::TM_SQDIFF); // similarity measure

// find most similar location
double minVal, maxVal;
cv::Point minPt, maxPt;
cv::minMaxLoc(result, &minVal, &maxVal, &minPt, &maxPt);

// draw rectangle at most similar location
// at minPt in this case
cv::rectangle(roi, cv::Rect(minPt.x, minPt.y,
                    target.cols, target.rows), 255);
```

Remember that this is a costly operation, so you should limit the search area and use a template having a size of only a few pixels.

See also

- The next recipe, *Describing and matching local intensity patterns*, describes the cv::BFMatcher class, which implements the matching strategy that was used in this recipe

Describing and matching local intensity patterns

The SURF and SIFT keypoint detection algorithms, discussed in Chapter 8, *Detecting Interest Points*, define a location, an orientation, and a scale for each of the detected features. The scale factor information is useful for defining the size of a window of analysis around each feature point. Thus, the defined neighborhood would include the same visual information no matter at what scale of the object to which the feature belongs has been pictured. This recipe will show you how to describe an interest point's neighborhood using feature descriptors. In image analysis, the visual information included in this neighborhood can be used to characterize each feature point in order to make each point distinguishable from the others. Feature descriptors are usually N-dimensional vectors that describe a feature point in a way that is invariant to change in lighting and to small perspective deformations. Generally, descriptors can be compared using simple distance metrics, for example, the Euclidean distance. Therefore, they constitute a powerful tool that can be used in object matching applications.

How to do it...

The cv::Feature2D abstract class defines a number of member functions that are used to compute the descriptors of a list of keypoints. As most feature-based methods include both a detector and a descriptor component, the associated classes include both a detect function (to detect the interest points) and a compute function (to compute their descriptors). This is the case of the cv::SURF and cv::SIFT classes. Here is, for example, how you can detect and describe feature points in two images using one instance of cv::SURF:

```
// Define keypoints vector
std::vector<cv::KeyPoint> keypoints1;
std::vector<cv::KeyPoint> keypoints2;

// Define feature detector
cv::Ptr<cv::Feature2D> ptrFeature2D =
                    cv::xfeatures2d::SURF::create(2000.0);

// Keypoint detection
ptrFeature2D->detect(image1,keypoints1);
ptrFeature2D->detect(image2,keypoints2);

// Extract the descriptor
cv::Mat descriptors1;
cv::Mat descriptors2;
ptrFeature2D->compute(image1,keypoints1,descriptors1);
ptrFeature2D->compute(image2,keypoints2,descriptors2);
```

For SIFT, you simply call the cv::SIFT::create function. The result of the computation of the interest point descriptors is a matrix (that is, a cv::Mat instance) that will contain as many rows as the number of elements in the keypoint vector. Each of these rows is an N-dimensional descriptor vector. In the case of the SURF descriptor, it has a default size of 64, and for SIFT, the default dimension is 128. This vector characterizes the intensity pattern surrounding a feature point. The more similar the two feature points, the closer their descriptor vectors should be. Note that you do not have to necessarily use the SURF (SIFT) descriptor with SURF (SIFT) points; detectors and descriptors can be used in any combination.

These descriptors will now be used to match our keypoints. Exactly as we did in the previous recipe, each feature descriptor vector in the first image is compared to all the feature descriptors in the second image. The pair that obtains the best score (that is, the pair with the lowest distance between the two descriptor vectors) is then kept as the best match for that feature. This process is repeated for all the features in the first image. Very conveniently, this process is implemented in OpenCV in the `cv::BFMatcher` class, so we do not need to re-implement the double loops that we previously built. This class is used as follows:

```
// Construction of the matcher
cv::BFMatcher matcher(cv::NORM_L2);
// Match the two image descriptors
std::vector<cv::DMatch> matches;
matcher.match(descriptors1,descriptors2, matches);
```

This class is a subclass of the `cv::DescriptorMatcher` class that defines the common interface for different matching strategies. The result is a vector of the `cv::DMatch` instances.

With the current Hessian threshold for SURF, we obtained 74 keypoints for the first image and 71 for the second. The brute-force approach will then produce 74 matches. Using the `cv::drawMatches` class as in the previous recipe produces the following image:

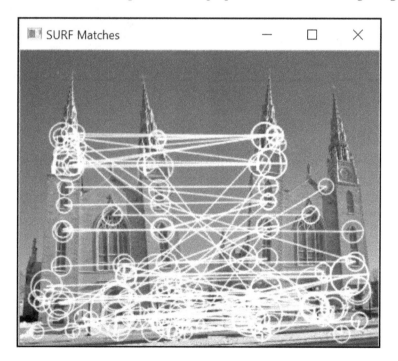

As it can be seen, several of these matches correctly link a point on the left-hand side with its corresponding point on the right-hand side. You might notice some errors; some of these are due to the fact that the observed building has a symmetrical facade, which makes some of the local matches ambiguous. For SIFT, with the same number of keypoints, we obtained the following match result:

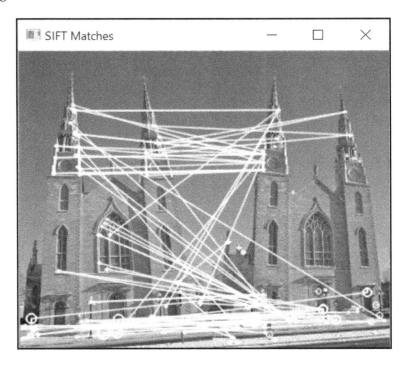

How it works...

Good feature descriptors must be invariant to small changes in illumination and viewpoint and to the presence of image noise. Therefore, they are often based on local intensity differences. This is the case for the SURF descriptors, which locally apply the following simple kernels around a keypoint:

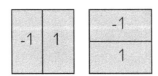

The first kernel simply measures the local intensity difference in the horizontal direction (designated as dx), and the second measures this difference in the vertical direction (designated as dy). The size of the neighborhood used to extract the descriptor vector is generally defined as 20 times the scale factor of the feature (that is, 20σ). This square region is then split into 4x4 smaller square subregions. For each subregion, the kernel responses (dx and dy) are computed at 5x5 regularly-spaced locations (with the kernel size being 2σ). All of these responses are summed up as follows in order to extract four descriptor values for each subregion:

$$\left[\sum dx \quad \sum dy \quad \sum |dx| \quad \sum |dy| \right]$$

Since there are 4x4=16 subregions, we have a total of 64 descriptor values. Note that in order to give more importance to the neighboring pixels, that is, values closer to the keypoint, the kernel responses are weighted by a Gaussian centered at the keypoint location (with $\sigma=3.3$).

The dx and dy responses are also used to estimate the orientation of the feature. These values are computed (with a kernel size of 4σ) within a circular neighborhood of radius 6σ at locations regularly spaced by intervals of σ. For a given orientation, the responses inside a certain angular interval ($\pi/3$) are summed, and the orientation giving the longest vector is defined as the dominant orientation.

SIFT is a richer descriptor that uses an image gradient instead of simple intensity differences. It also splits the square neighborhood around each keypoint into 4x4 subregions (it is also possible to use 8x8 or 2x2 subregions). Inside each of these regions, a histogram of gradient orientations is built. The orientations are discretized into 8 bins, and each gradient orientation entry is incremented by a value proportional to the gradient magnitude.

This is illustrated by the following figure, inside which each star-shaped arrow set represents a local histogram of gradient orientations:

These 16 histograms of 8 bins each concatenated together then produce a descriptor of 128 dimensions. Note that as for SURF, the gradient values are weighted by a Gaussian filter centered at the keypoint location in order to make the descriptor less sensitive to sudden changes in gradient orientations at the perimeter of the defined neighborhood. The final descriptor is then normalized to make the distance measurement more consistent.

With SURF and SIFT features and descriptors, scale-invariant matching can be achieved. Here is an example that shows the SURF match result for two images at different scales (here, the 50 best matches have been displayed):

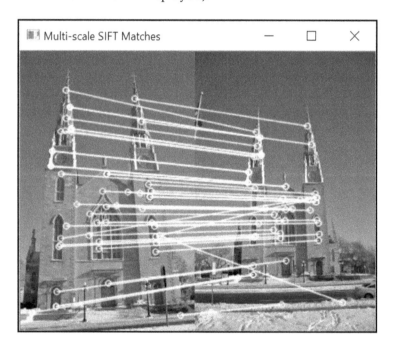

Note that the cv::Feature2D class includes a convenient member function that detects the interest points and compute their descriptors at the same time, for example:

```
ptrFeature2D->detectAndCompute(image, cv::noArray(),
                               keypoints, descriptors);
```

There's more...

The match result produced by any matching algorithm always contains a significant number of incorrect matches. In order to improve the quality of the match set, there exist a number of strategies. Three of them are discussed here.

Cross-checking matches

A simple approach to validating the matches obtained is to repeat the same procedure a second time, but this time, each keypoint of the second image is compared with all the keypoints of the first image. A match is considered valid only if we obtain the same pair of keypoints in both directions (that is, each keypoint is the best match of the other). The cv::BFMatcher function gives the option to use this strategy. It is indeed included as a flag; when set to true, it forces the function to perform the reciprocal match cross-check:

```
cv::BFMatcher matcher2(cv::NORM_L2,    // distance measure
                       true);          // cross-check flag
```

The improved match results are as shown in the following image (in the case of SURF):

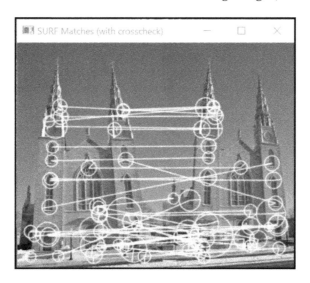

The ratio test

We have already noted that repetitive elements in scene objects create unreliable results because of the ambiguity in matching visually similar structures. What happens in such cases is that a keypoint will match well with more than one other keypoint. Since the probability of selecting the wrong correspondence is high, it might be preferable to reject a match in these ambiguous cases.

To use this strategy, we then need to find the best two matching points of each keypoint. This can be done by using the knnMatch method of the cv::DescriptorMatcher class. Since we want only two best matches, we specify k=2:

```
// find the best two matches of each keypoint
std::vector<std::vector<cv::DMatch>> matches;
matcher.knnMatch(descriptors1,descriptors2,
                matches, 2);  // find the k best matches
```

The next step is to reject all the best matches with a matching distance similar to that of their second best match. Since knnMatch produces a std::vector class of std::vector (this second vector is of size k), we do this by looping over each keypoint match and perform a ratio test, that is, computing the ratio of the second best distance over the best distance (this ratio will be one if the two best distances are equal). All matches that have a high ratio are judged ambiguous and are therefore rejected. Here is how we can do it:

```
//perform ratio test
double ratio= 0.85;
std::vector<std::vector<cv::DMatch>>::iterator it;
for (it= matches.begin(); it!= matches.end(); ++it) {

  // first best match/second best match
  if ((*it)[0].distance/(*it)[1].distance < ratio) {
    // it is an acceptable match
    newMatches.push_back((*it)[0]);
  }
}
// newMatches is the updated match set
```

The initial match set made up of 74 pairs is now reduced to 23 pairs:

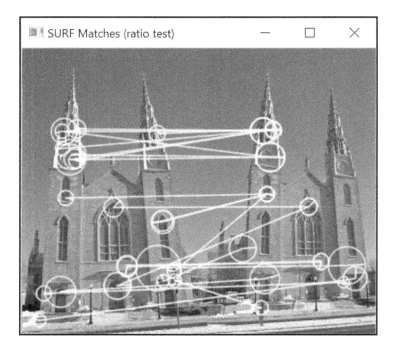

Distance thresholding

An even simpler strategy consists of rejecting matches for which the distance between their descriptors is too high. This is done using the `radiusMatch` method of the `cv::DescriptorMatcher` class:

```
// radius match
float maxDist= 0.4;
std::vector<std::vector<cv::DMatch>> matches2;
matcher.radiusMatch(descriptors1, descriptors2, matches2, maxDist);
                    // maximum acceptable distance
                    // between the 2 descriptors
```

The result is again a std::vector instance of std::vector because the method will retain all the matches with a distance smaller than the specified threshold. This means that a given keypoint might have more than one matching point in the other image. Conversely, other keypoints will not have any matches associated with them (the corresponding inner std::vector class will then have a size of 0). For our example, the result is a match set of 50 pairs:

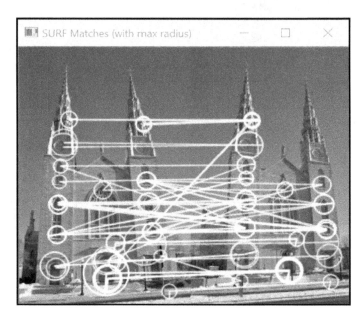

Obviously, you can combine all these strategies in order to improve your matching results.

See also

- The *Detecting scale-invariant features* recipe in Chapter 8, *Detecting Interest Points*, presents the associated SURF and SIFT feature detectors and provides more references on the subject
- The *Matching images using random sample consensus* recipe in Chapter 10, *Estimating Projective Relations in Images*, explains how to use the image and the scene geometry in order to obtain a match set of even better quality

- The *Detecting objects and peoples with Support Vector Machines and histograms of oriented gradients* recipe in `Chapter 14`, *Learning from Examples*, describes the HOG, another descriptor similar to SIFT
- The article *Matching feature points in stereo pairs: A comparative study of some matching strategies* by *E. Vincent* and *R. Laganière* in *Machine, Graphics and Vision*, pp. 237-260, 2001, describes other simple matching strategies that could be used to improve the quality of the match set

Matching keypoints with binary descriptors

In the previous recipe, we learned how to describe a keypoint using rich descriptors extracted from the image intensity gradient. These descriptors are floating-point vectors that have a dimension of 64, 128, or sometimes even longer. This makes them costly to manipulate. In order to reduce the memory and computational load associated with these descriptors, the idea of using descriptors composed of a simple sequence of bits (0s and 1s) has been introduced. The challenge here is to make them easy to compute and yet keep them robust to scene and viewpoint changes. This recipe describes some of these binary descriptors. In particular, we will look at the ORB and BRISK descriptors for which we presented their associated feature point detectors in `Chapter 8`, *Detecting Interest Points*.

How to do it...

Thanks to the common interface of the OpenCV detectors and descriptors, using a binary descriptor such as ORB is no different from using descriptors such as SURF and SIFT. The complete feature-based image matching sequence is then as follows:

```
// Define keypoint vectors and descriptors
std::vector<cv::KeyPoint> keypoints1;
std::vector<cv::KeyPoint> keypoints2;
cv::Mat descriptors1;
cv::Mat descriptors2;

// Define feature detector/descriptor
// Construct the ORB feature object
cv::Ptr<cv::Feature2D> feature = cv::ORB::create(60);
                    // approx. 60 feature points

// Keypoint detection and description
// Detect the ORB features
feature->detectAndCompute(image1, cv::noArray(),
                    keypoints1, descriptors1);
```

```
feature->detectAndCompute(image2, cv::noArray(),
                             keypoints2, descriptors2);

// Construction of the matcher
cv::BFMatcher matcher(cv::NORM_HAMMING); // always use hamming norm
// for binary descriptors
// Match the two image descriptors
std::vector<cv::DMatch> matches;
matcher.match(descriptors1, descriptors2, matches);
```

The only difference resides in the use of the Hamming norm (the `cv::NORM_HAMMING` flag), which measures the distance between two binary descriptors by counting the number of bits that are dissimilar. On many processors, this operation is efficiently implemented by using an exclusive OR operation, followed by a simple bit count. The matching results are the following:

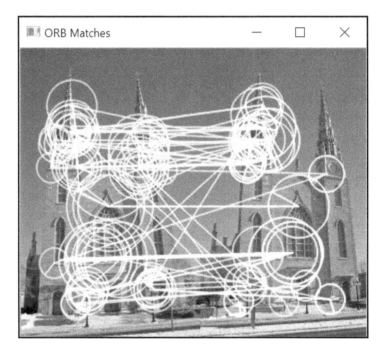

Similar results will be obtained with another popular binary feature detector/descriptor: BRISK. In this case, the `cv::Feature2D` instance is created by the `cv::BRISK::create` call. As we learned in the previous chapter, its first parameter is a threshold that controls the number of detected points.

How it works...

The ORB algorithm detects oriented feature points at multiple scales. Based on this result, the ORB descriptor extracts a representation of each keypoint by using simple intensity comparisons. In fact, ORB builds on a previously proposed descriptor called BRIEF. This later creates a binary descriptor by simply selecting a random pair of points inside a defined neighborhood around the keypoint. The intensity values of the two pixel points are then compared, and if the first point has a higher intensity, then the value `1` is assigned to the corresponding descriptor bit value. Otherwise, the value `0` is assigned. Repeating this test on a number of random pairs generates a descriptor that is made up of several bits; typically, `128` to `512` bits (pairwise tests) are used.

This is the scheme used by ORB. Then, the decision to be made is which set of point pairs should be used to build the descriptor. Indeed, even if the point pairs are randomly chosen, once they have been selected, the same set of binary tests must be performed to build the descriptor of all the keypoints in order to ensure consistency of the results. To make the descriptor more distinctive, intuition tells us that some choices must be better than others. Also, the fact that the orientation of each keypoint is known introduces some bias in the intensity pattern distribution when this one is normalized with respect to this orientation (that is, when the point coordinates are given relative to this keypoint orientation). From these considerations and the experimental validation, ORB has identified a set of `256` point pairs with high variance and minimal pairwise correlation. In other words, the selected binary tests are the ones that have an equal chance of being `0` or `1` over a variety of keypoints and also those that are as independent from each other as possible.

The descriptor of BRISK is very similar. It is also based on pairwise intensity comparisons with two differences. First, instead of randomly selecting the points from the `31x31` points of the neighborhood, the chosen points are selected from a sampling pattern of a set of concentric circles (made up of `60` points) with locations that are equally spaced. Second, the intensity at each of these sample points is a Gaussian-smoothed value with a σ value proportional to the distance from the central keypoint. From these points, BRISK selects `512` point pairs.

There's more...

Several other binary descriptors exist, and interested readers should take a look at the scientific literature to learn more on this subject. Since it is also available in the OpenCV contrib module, we will describe one additional descriptor here.

FREAK

FREAK stands for **Fast Retina Keypoint**. This is also a binary descriptor, but it does not have an associated detector. It can be applied on any set of keypoints detected, for example, SIFT, SURF, or ORB.

Like BRISK, the FREAK descriptor is also based on a sampling pattern defined on concentric circles. However, to design their descriptor, the authors used an analogy of the human eye. They observed that on the retina, the density of the ganglion cells decreases as the distance to the fovea increase. Consequently, they built a sampling pattern made of 43 points in which the density of a point is much greater near the central point. To obtain its intensity, each point is filtered with a Gaussian kernel that has a size that also increases with the distance to the center.

In order to identify the pairwise comparisons that should be performed, an experimental validation has been performed by following a strategy similar to the one used for ORB. By analyzing several thousands of keypoints, the binary tests with the highest variance and lowest correlation are retained, resulting in 512 pairs.

FREAK also introduced the idea of performing the descriptor comparisons in cascade. That is, the first 128 bits representing coarser information (corresponding to the tests performed at the periphery on larger Gaussian kernels) are performed first. Only if the compared descriptors pass this initial step will the remaining tests be performed.

Using the keypoints detected with ORB, we extract the FREAK descriptors by simply creating the cv::DescriptorExtractor instance, as follows:

```
// to describe with FREAK
feature = cv::xfeatures2d::FREAK::create();
```

The match result is as follows:

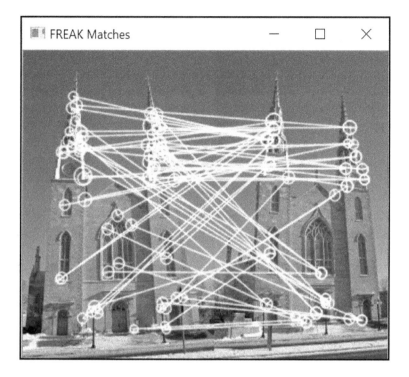

The following figure illustrates the sampling pattern used for the three descriptors presented in this recipe:

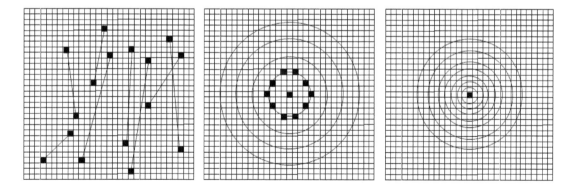

The first square is the ORB/BRIEF descriptor in which point pairs are randomly selected on a square grid. Each pair of points linked by a line represents a possible test to compare the two pixel intensities. Here, we show only eight such pairs; the default ORB uses 256 pairs. The middle square corresponds to the BRISK sampling pattern. Points are uniformly sampled on the circles shown (for clarity, we only identify the points on the first circle here). Finally, the third square shows the log-polar sampling grid of FREAK. While BRISK has a uniform distribution of points, FREAK has a higher density of points closer to the center. For example, in BRISK, you find 20 points on the outer circle, while in the case of FREAK, its outer circle includes only six points.

See also

- The *Detecting FAST features at multiple scales* recipe in `Chapter 8`, *Detecting Interest Points*, presents the associated BRISK and ORB feature detectors and provides more references on the subject
- The *BRIEF: Computing a Local Binary Descriptor Very Fast* article by *E. M. Calonder, V. Lepetit, M. Ozuysal, T. Trzcinski, C. Strecha,* and *P. Fua* in *IEEE Transactions on Pattern Analysis and Machine Intelligence,* 2012, describes the BRIEF feature descriptor that inspires the presented binary descriptors
- The *FREAK: Fast Retina Keypoint* article by *A. Alahi, R. Ortiz,* and *P. Vandergheynst* in *IEEE Conference on Computer Vision and Pattern Recognition,* 2012, describes the FREAK feature descriptor

10
Estimating Projective Relations in Images

In this chapter, we will cover the following recipes:

- Computing the fundamental matrix of an image pair
- Matching images using random sample consensus
- Computing a homography between two images
- Detecting a planar target in images

Introduction

Images are generally produced using a digital camera, which captures a scene by projecting light going through its lens onto an image sensor. The fact that an image is formed by the projection of a 3D scene onto a 2D plane implies the existence of important relationships both between a scene and its image and between different images of the same scene. Projective geometry is the tool that is used to describe and characterize, in mathematical terms, the process of image formation. In this chapter, we will introduce you to some of the fundamental projective relations that exist in multi-view imagery and explain how these can be used in computer vision programming. But, before we start the recipes, let's explore the basic concepts related to scene projection and image formation.

Image formation

Fundamentally, the process used to produce images has not changed since the beginning of photography. The light coming from an observed scene is captured by a camera through a frontal aperture, and the captured light rays hit an image plane (or an image sensor) located at the back of the camera. Additionally, a lens is used to concentrate the rays coming from the different scene elements. This process is illustrated by the following figure:

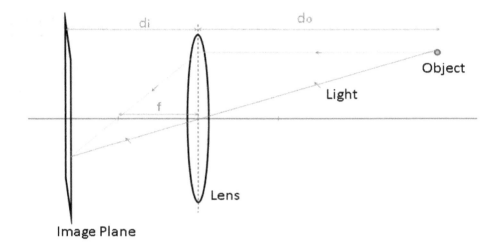

Here, do is the distance from the lens to the observed object, di is the distance from the lens to the image plane, and f is the focal length of the lens. These quantities are related by the so-called **thin lens equation**:

$$\frac{1}{f} = \frac{1}{do} + \frac{1}{di}$$

In computer vision, this camera model can be simplified in a number of ways. Firstly, we can neglect the effect of the lens by considering that we have a camera with an infinitesimal aperture since, in theory, this does not change the image appearance. (However, by doing so, we ignore the focusing effect by creating an image with an infinite depth of field.) In this case, therefore, only the central ray is considered. Secondly, since most of the time we have do>>di, we can assume that the image plane is located at the focal distance. Finally, we can note from the geometry of the system that the image on the plane is inverted. We can obtain an identical but upright image by simply positioning the image plane in front of the lens. Obviously, this is not physically feasible, but from a mathematical point of view, this is completely equivalent. This simplified model is often referred to as the **pinhole camera model**, and it is represented as follows:

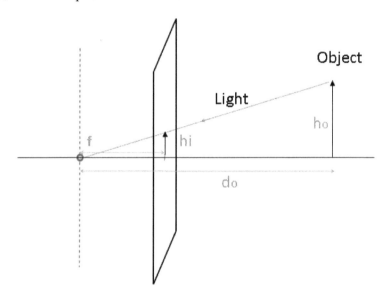

From this model, and using the law of similar triangles, we can easily derive the basic projective equation that relates a photographed object with its image:

$$hi = f \frac{ho}{do}$$

The size (hi) of the image of an object (of physical height ho) is therefore inversely proportional to its distance (do) from the camera, which is naturally true. In general, this relation describes where a 3D scene point will be projected on the image plane given the geometry of the camera. More specifically, if we assume that the reference frame is positioned at the focal point, then a 3D scene point located at position (X,Y,Z) will be projected onto the image plane at (x,y)=(fX/Z,fY/Z). Here, the Z coordinate corresponds with the depth of the point (or distance to camera, denoted by do in the previous equation). This relation can be rewritten in a simple matrix form through the introduction of homogeneous coordinates, in which 2D points are represented by 3-vectors, and 3D points are represented by 4-vectors (the extra coordinate is simply an arbitrary scale factor s that needs to be removed when a 2D coordinate needs to be extracted from a homogeneous 3-vector):

$$s\begin{bmatrix} x \\ y \\ 1 \end{bmatrix} = \begin{bmatrix} f & 0 & 0 & 0 \\ 0 & f & 0 & 0 \\ 0 & 0 & 1 & 0 \end{bmatrix} \begin{bmatrix} X \\ Y \\ Z \\ 1 \end{bmatrix}$$

This 3x4 matrix is called the projection matrix. In cases where the reference frame is not aligned with the focal point, then rotation r and translation t matrices must be introduced. The role of these ones is simply to express the projected 3D point into a camera-centric reference frame, which is as follows:

$$s\begin{bmatrix} x \\ y \\ 1 \end{bmatrix} = \begin{bmatrix} f & 0 & 0 \\ 0 & f & 0 \\ 0 & 0 & 1 \end{bmatrix} \begin{bmatrix} r1 & r2 & r3 & t1 \\ r4 & r5 & r6 & t2 \\ r7 & r8 & r9 & t3 \end{bmatrix} \begin{bmatrix} X \\ Y \\ Z \\ 1 \end{bmatrix}$$

The first matrix of this equation is said to contain the intrinsic parameters of the camera (here, only the focal length, but the next chapter will introduce a few more intrinsic parameters). The second matrix contains the extrinsic parameters that are the parameters that relate the camera to the exterior world. It should be noted that, in practice, image coordinates are expressed in pixels while 3D coordinates are expressed in world measurements (for example, meters). This aspect will be explored in Chapter 11, *Reconstructing 3D Scenes*.

Computing the fundamental matrix of an image pair

The introductory section of this chapter presented the projective equation, describing how a scene point projects onto the image plane of a single camera. In this recipe, we will explore the projective relationship that exists between two images that display the same scene. These two images could have been obtained by moving a camera to two different locations to take pictures from two viewpoints, or by using two cameras, each of them taking a different picture of the scene. When those two cameras are separated by a rigid baseline, we use the term **stereovision**.

Getting ready

Let's now consider two pinhole cameras observing a given scene point, as shown in the following figure:

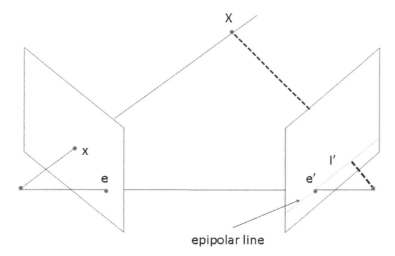

We learned that we can find the image x of a 3D point X by tracing a line joining this 3D point with the camera's center. Conversely, the scene point that has its image at position **x** on the image plane can be located anywhere on this line in the 3D space. This implies that, if we want to find the corresponding point of a given image point in another image, we need to search along the projection of this line onto the second image plane. This imaginary line is called the **epipolar line** of point x. It defines a fundamental constraint that must satisfy two corresponding points; that is, the match of a given point must lie on the epipolar line of this point in the other view, and the exact orientation of this epipolar line depends on the respective position of the two cameras. In fact, the configuration of the set of possible epipolar lines characterizes the geometry of a two-view system.

Another observation that can be made from the geometry of this two-view system is that all the epipolar lines pass through the same point. This point corresponds to the projection of one camera's center onto the other camera (points e and e' in the above figure). This special point is called an **epipole**.

Mathematically, the relationship between an image point and its corresponding epipolar line can be expressed using a 3x3 matrix, as follows:

$$\begin{bmatrix} l_1' \\ l_2' \\ l_3' \end{bmatrix} = F \begin{bmatrix} x \\ y \\ 1 \end{bmatrix}$$

In projective geometry, a 2D line is also represented by a 3-vector. It corresponds to the set of 2D points (x',y'), that satisfy the equation 11'x'+ 12'y'+ 13'= 0 (the prime superscript denotes that this line belongs to the second image). Consequently, the matrix F, called the fundamental matrix, maps a 2D image point in one view to an epipolar line in the other view.

How to do it...

The fundamental matrix of an image pair can be estimated by solving a set of equations that involve a certain number of known matched points between the two images. The minimum number of such matches is seven. In order to illustrate the fundamental matrix estimation process, we selected seven good matches from the matching results of SIFT features, as presented in the previous chapter.

These matches will be used to compute the fundamental matrix using the cv::findFundamentalMat OpenCV function. The image pair with its selected matches is shown here:

These matches are stored in a cv::DMatch vector pointing to indexes of cv::keypoint instances. These keypoints first need to be converted into cv::Point2f in order to be used with cv::findFundamentalMat. An OpenCV function can be used to this end:

```
// Convert keypoints into Point2f
std::vector<cv::Point2f> selPoints1, selPoints2;
std::vector<int> pointIndexes1, pointIndexes2;
cv::KeyPoint::convert(keypoints1,selPoints1,pointIndexes1);
cv::KeyPoint::convert(keypoints2,selPoints2,pointIndexes2);
```

The two resulting vectors `selPoints1` and `selPoints2` contain the corresponding point coordinates in the two images. The `pointIndexes1` and `pointIndexes2` vectors contain the indexes of the keypoints to be converted. The call to the `cv::findFundamentalMat` function is then as follows:

```
// Compute F matrix from 7 matches
cv::Mat fundamental= cv::findFundamentalMat(
                    selPoints1,      // 7 points in first image
                    selPoints2,      // 7 points in second image
                    cv::FM_7POINT);  // 7-point method
```

One way to visually verify the validity of the fundamental matrix is to draw the epipolar lines of some selected points. Another OpenCV function allows the epipolar lines of a given set of points to be computed. Once these have been computed, they can be drawn using the `cv::line` function. The following lines of code accomplish these two steps (that is, computing and drawing epipolar lines on the image on the right from the points in the image on the left):

```
// draw the left points corresponding epipolar
// lines in right image
std::vector<cv::Vec3f> lines1;
cv::computeCorrespondEpilines(
                selPoints1,  // image points
                1,           // in image 1 (can also be 2)
                fundamental, // F matrix
                lines1);     // vector of epipolar lines
// for all epipolar lines
for (vector<cv::Vec3f>::const_iterator it= lines1.begin();
            it!=lines1.end(); ++it) {
   // draw the line between first and last column
   cv::line(image2, cv::Point(0,-(*it)[2]/(*it)[1]),
            cv::Point(image2.cols,
                    -((*it)[2]+(*it)[0]*image2.cols)/(*it)[1]),
                    cv::Scalar(255,255,255));
}
```

The epipolar lines of the left image are obtained in a similar way. The following image shows these lines:

Remember that the epipole of one image is at the intersection of all its epipolar lines. This one is the projection of the other camera's center. Note that the epipolar lines can intersect (and often do) outside of the image boundaries. In the case of our example, the epipole of the second image is at the location where the first camera would be visible if the two images were taken at the same instant. Note also that the results can be quite unstable when the fundamental matrix is computed from only seven matches. Indeed, substituting one match for another could lead to a significantly different set of epipolar lines.

How it works...

We previously explained that, for a point in one image, the fundamental matrix gives the equation of the line on which its corresponding point in the other view should be found. If the corresponding point of a point `(x,y)` is `(x',y')`, suppose we have `F`, the fundamental matrix, between the two views. Since `(x',y')` lies on the epipolar line given by multiplying `F` by `(x,y)` expressed in homogenous coordinates, we must then have the following equation:

$$\begin{bmatrix} x' \\ y' \\ 1 \end{bmatrix}^{T} F \begin{bmatrix} x \\ y \\ 1 \end{bmatrix} = 0$$

This equation expresses the relationship between two corresponding points and is known as the **epipolar constraint**. Using this equation, it becomes possible to estimate the entries of the matrix using known matches. Since the entries of the `F` matrix are given up to a scale factor, there are only eight entries to be estimated (the ninth one can be arbitrarily set to 1). Each match contributes to one equation. Therefore, with eight known matches, the matrix can be fully estimated by solving the resulting set of linear equations. This is what is done when you use the `cv::FM_8POINT` flag with the `cv::findFundamentalMat` function. Note that, in this case, it is possible (and preferable) to input more than eight matches. The obtained over-determined system of linear equations can then be solved in a mean-square sense.

To estimate the fundamental matrix, an additional constraint can also be exploited. Mathematically, the `F` matrix maps a 2D point to a 1D pencil of lines (that is, lines that intersect at a common point). The fact that all these epipolar lines pass through this unique point (that is, the epipole) imposes a constraint on the matrix. This constraint reduces the number of matches required to estimate the fundamental matrix to seven. In mathematical terms, we say that the fundamental matrix has 7 degrees of freedom and is therefore of rank-2. Unfortunately, in this case, the set of equations becomes nonlinear, with up to three possible solutions (in this case, `cv::findFundamentalMat` will return a fundamental matrix of the size 9x3, that is, three 3x3 matrices stacked up). The seven-match solution of the `F` matrix estimation can be invoked in OpenCV by using the `cv::FM_7POINT` flag. This is what we did in the example in the preceding section.

Lastly, it should be mentioned that the choice of an appropriate set of matches in the image is important to obtain an accurate estimation of the fundamental matrix. In general, the matches should be well distributed across the images and include points at different depths in the scene. Otherwise, the solution will become unstable. In particular, the selected scene points should not be coplanar, as the fundamental matrix (in this case) becomes degenerated.

See also

- *Multiple View Geometry in Computer Vision*, Cambridge University Press, 2004, *R. Hartley* and *A. Zisserman*, is the most complete reference on projective geometry in computer vision
- The *Matching images using random sample consensus* recipe explains how a fundamental matrix can be robustly estimated from a larger match set
- The *Computing a homography between two images* recipe explains why a fundamental matrix cannot be computed when the matched points are coplanar, or are the result of a pure rotation

Matching images using random sample consensus

When two cameras observe the same scene, they see the same elements but under different viewpoints. We have already studied the feature point matching problem in the previous chapter. In this recipe, we come back to this problem, and we will learn how to exploit the epipolar constraint introduced in the previous recipe to match image features more reliably.

The principle that we will follow is simple: when we match feature points between two images, we only accept those matches that fall on corresponding epipolar lines. However, to be able to check this condition, the fundamental matrix must be known, but we need good matches to estimate this matrix. This seems to be a chicken-and-egg problem. However, in this recipe, we propose a solution in which the fundamental matrix and a set of good matches will be jointly computed.

How to do it...

The objective is to be able to compute a fundamental matrix and a set of good matches between two views. To do so, all the found feature point correspondences will be validated using the epipolar constraint introduced in the previous recipe. To this end, we have created a class that encapsulates the different steps of the proposed robust matching process:

```
class RobustMatcher {
 private:
  // pointer to the feature point detector object
  cv::Ptr<cv::FeatureDetector> detector;
  // pointer to the feature descriptor extractor object
  cv::Ptr<cv::DescriptorExtractor> descriptor;
  int normType;
  float ratio;          // max ratio between 1st and 2nd NN
  bool refineF;         // if true will refine the F matrix
  bool refineM;         // if true will refine the matches
  double distance;      // min distance to epipolar
  double confidence;    // confidence level (probability)

 public:

  RobustMatcher(const cv::Ptr<cv::FeatureDetector> &detector,
            const cv::Ptr<cv::DescriptorExtractor> &descriptor=
                  cv::Ptr<cv::DescriptorExtractor>()):
            detector(detector), descriptor(descriptor),
            normType(cv::NORM_L2), ratio(0.8f),
            refineF(true), refineM(true),
            confidence(0.98), distance(1.0) {

      // in this case use the associated descriptor
      if (!this->descriptor) {
        this->descriptor = this->detector;
      }
  }
}
```

Users of this class simply supply the feature detector and descriptor instances of their choice. These ones can also be specified using the defined setFeatureDetector and setDescriptorExtractor setter methods.

The main method is the match method, which returns matches, detected keypoints, and the estimated fundamental matrix. The method proceeds in four distinct steps (explicitly identified in the comments of the following code), which we will now explore:

```
// Match feature points using RANSAC
// returns fundamental matrix and output match set
cv::Mat match(cv::Mat& image1, cv::Mat& image2,      // input images
              std::vector<cv::DMatch>& matches,       // output matches
              std::vector<cv::KeyPoint>& keypoints1,//output keypoints
              std::vector<cv::KeyPoint>& keypoints2) {

  // 1. Detection of the feature points
  detector->detect(image1,keypoints1);
  detector->detect(image2,keypoints2);

  // 2. Extraction of the feature descriptors
  cv::Mat descriptors1, descriptors2;
  descriptor->compute(image1,keypoints1,descriptors1);
  descriptor->compute(image2,keypoints2,descriptors2);

  // 3. Match the two image descriptors
  // (optionally apply some checking method)
  // Construction of the matcher with crosscheck
  cv::BFMatcher matcher(normType,     //distance measure
                        true);        //crosscheck flag
  // match descriptors
  std::vector<cv::DMatch> outputMatches;
  matcher.match(descriptors1,descriptors2,outputMatches);

  // 4. Validate matches using RANSAC
  cv::Mat fundamental= ransacTest(outputMatches,
                                  keypoints1, keypoints2,
                                  matches);
  // return the found fundamental matrix
  return fundamental;
}
```

The first two steps simply detect the feature points and compute their descriptors. Next, we proceed to feature matching using the cv::BFMatcher class, as we did in the previous chapter. We use the crosscheck flag to obtain matches of better quality.

The fourth step is the new concept introduced in this recipe. It consists of an additional filtering test that will this time use the fundamental matrix in order to reject matches that do not obey the epipolar constraint. This test is based on the RANSAC method that can compute the fundamental matrix even when outliers are present in the match set (this method will be explained in the next section).

Using our `RobustMatcher` class, the robust matching of an image pair is then easily accomplished by the following calls:

```
// Prepare the matcher (with default parameters)
// SIFT detector and descriptor
RobustMatcher rmatcher(cv::xfeatures2d::SIFT::create(250));

// Match the two images
std::vector<cv::DMatch> matches;

std::vector<cv::KeyPoint> keypoints1, keypoints2;
cv::Mat fundamental = rmatcher.match(image1, image2,
                                     matches,
                                     keypoints1, keypoints2);
```

This results in 54 matches that are shown in the following screenshot:

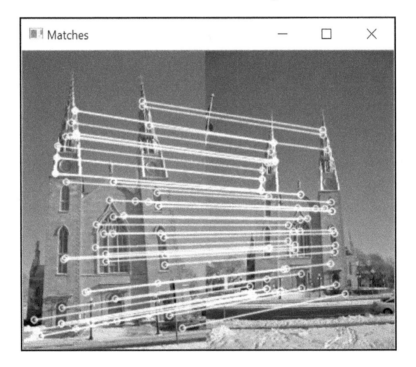

Most of the time, the resulting matches will be good matches. However, a few false matches might remain; these are ones that accidently fell on the corresponding epipolar lines of the computed fundamental matrix.

How it works...

In the preceding recipe, we learned that it is possible to estimate the fundamental matrix associated with an image pair from a number of feature point matches. Obviously, to be exact, this match set must be made up of only good matches. However, in a real context, it is not possible to guarantee that a match set obtained by comparing the descriptors of the detected feature points will be completely exact. This is why a fundamental matrix estimation method based on the **RANSAC (RANdom SAmpling Consensus)** strategy has been introduced.

The RANSAC algorithm aims to estimate a given mathematical entity from a data set that may contain a number of outliers. The idea is to randomly select some data points from the set and perform the estimation with only those. The number of selected points should be the minimum number of points required to estimate the mathematical entity. In the case of the fundamental matrix, eight matched pairs is the minimum number (in fact, the real minimum is seven matches, but the 8-point linear algorithm is faster to compute). Once the fundamental matrix is estimated from these eight random matches, all the other matches in the match set are tested against the epipolar constraint that derives from this matrix. All the matches that fulfill this constraint (that is, matches for which the corresponding feature is at a short distance from its epipolar line) are identified. These matches form the support set of the computed fundamental matrix.

The central idea behind the RANSAC algorithm is that, the larger the support set, the higher the probability that the computed matrix is the right one. Conversely, if one (or more) of the randomly selected matches is an incorrect match, then the computed fundamental matrix will also be incorrect, and its support set will be expected to be small. This process is repeated a number of times and, in the end, the matrix with the largest support will be retained as the most probable one.

Therefore, our objective is to pick eight random matches several times so that eventually we select eight good ones, which should give us a large support set. Depending on the proportion of incorrect matches in the entire data set, the probability of selecting a set of eight correct matches will differ. However, we know that, the more selections we make, the higher our confidence will be that we have at least one good match set among those selections. More precisely, if we assume that the match set is made of $w\%$ inliers (good matches), then the probability that we select eight good matches is w^8. Consequently, the probability that a selection contains at least one incorrect match is $(1-w^8)$. If we make k selections, the probability of having one random set that contains good matches only is $1-(1-w^8)^k$.

This is the confidence probability `c`, and we want this probability to be as high as possible, since we need at least one good set of matches in order to obtain the correct fundamental matrix. Therefore, when running the RANSAC algorithm, one needs to determine the number of `k` selections that need to be made in order to obtain a given confidence level.

The use of the RANSAC method to estimate the fundamental matrix is done inside the `ransacTest` method of our `RobustMatcher` class:

```
// Identify good matches using RANSAC
// Return fundamental matrix and output matches
cv::Mat ransacTest(const std::vector<cv::DMatch>& matches,
                   std::vector<cv::KeyPoint>& keypoints1,
                   std::vector<cv::KeyPoint>& keypoints2,
                   std::vector<cv::DMatch>& outMatches) {

  // Convert keypoints into Point2f
  std::vector<cv::Point2f> points1, points2;
  for (std::vector<cv::DMatch>::const_iterator it= matches.begin();
       it!= matches.end(); ++it) {

    // Get the position of left keypoints
    points1.push_back(keypoints1[it->queryIdx].pt);
    // Get the position of right keypoints
    points2.push_back(keypoints2[it->trainIdx].pt);
  }

  // Compute F matrix using RANSAC
  std::vector<uchar> inliers(points1.size(),0);
  cv::Mat fundamental=
     cv::findFundamentalMat( points1,
                      points2,       // matching points
                      inliers,       // match status (inlier or outlier)
                      cv::FM_RANSAC, // RANSAC method
                      distance,      // distance to epipolar line
                      confidence);   // confidence probability
  // extract the surviving (inliers) matches
  std::vector<uchar>::const_iterator itIn= inliers.begin();
  std::vector<cv::DMatch>::const_iterator itM= matches.begin();
  // for all matches
  for ( ;itIn!= inliers.end(); ++itIn, ++itM) {
    if (*itIn) { // it is a valid match
    outMatches.push_back(*itM);
  }
 }
}
 return fundamental;
}
```

This code is a bit long because the keypoints need to be converted into `cv::Point2f` before the F matrix computation. When using the `cv::findFundamentalMat` function with the `cv::FM_RANSAC` method, two extra parameters are provided. One of these extra parameters is the confidence level, which determines the number of iterations to be made (by default, it is `0.99`). The other parameter is the maximum distance to the epipolar line for a point to be considered as an inlier. All of the matched pairs in which a point is at a greater distance from its epipolar line than the distance specified will be reported as an outlier. The function also returns `std::vector` of the character value, indicating that the corresponding match in the input set has been identified either as an outlier (0) or as an inlier (1). This explains the last loop of our method that extracts the good matches from the original match set.

The more good matches you have in your initial match set, the higher the probability that RANSAC will give you the correct fundamental matrix. This is why we applied the crosscheck filter when matching the feature points. You could have also used the ratio test presented in the previous recipe in order to further improve the quality of the final match set. It is just a question of balancing the computational complexity, the final number of matches, and the required level of confidence that the obtained match set will contain only exact matches.

There's more…

The result of the robust matching process presented in this recipe is: 1) an estimate of the fundamental matrix computed using the eight selected matches that have the largest support and 2) the match set included in this support set. Using this information, it is possible to refine these results in two ways.

Refining the fundamental matrix

Since we now have a match set of good quality, as a last step, it might be a good idea to use all of them to re-estimate the fundamental matrix. We already mentioned that a linear 8-point algorithm to estimate this matrix exists. We can, therefore, obtain an over-determined system of equations that will solve the fundamental matrix in a least-squares sense. This step can be added the end of our `ransacTest` function:

```
// Convert the keypoints in support set into Point2f
points1.clear();
points2.clear();
for (std::vector<cv::DMatch>::const_iterator it=
                                 outMatches.begin();
    it!= outMatches.end(); ++it) {
  // Get the position of left keypoints
```

```
        points1.push_back(keypoints1[it->queryIdx].pt);
        // Get the position of right keypoints
        points2.push_back(keypoints2[it->trainIdx].pt);
}

// Compute 8-point F from all accepted matches
fundamental= cv::findFundamentalMat(
                points1,points2, // matching points
                cv::FM_8POINT);   // 8-point method solved using SVD
```

The `cv::findFundamentalMat` function does indeed accept more than 8 matches by solving the linear system of equations using singular value decomposition.

Refining the matches

We learned that in a two-view system, every point must lie on the epipolar line of its corresponding point. This is the epipolar constraint expressed by the fundamental matrix. Consequently, if you have a good estimate of a fundamental matrix, you can use this epipolar constraint to correct the obtained matches by forcing them to lie on their epipolar lines. This can be easily done by using the `cv::correctMatches` OpenCV function:

```
std::vector<cv::Point2f> newPoints1, newPoints2;
// refine the matches
correctMatches(fundamental,           // F matrix
            points1, points2,         // original position
            newPoints1, newPoints2);  // new position
```

This function proceeds by modifying the position of each corresponding point so that it satisfies the epipolar constraint while minimizing the cumulative (squared) displacement.

Computing a homography between two images

The first recipe of this chapter showed you how to compute the fundamental matrix of an image pair from a set of matches. In projective geometry, another very useful mathematical entity also exists. This one can be computed from multi-view imagery and, as we will see, is a matrix with special properties.

Getting ready

Again, let's consider the projective relation between a 3D point and its image on a camera, which we presented in the introduction section of this chapter. Basically, we learned that this equation relates a 3D point to its image using the intrinsic properties of the camera and the position of that camera (specified with a rotation and a translation component). If we now carefully examine this equation, we realize that there are two special situations of particular interest. The first situation is when two views of a scene are separated by a pure rotation. We can then observe that the fourth column of the extrinsic matrix will be made up of 0s (that is, the translation is null):

$$
s \begin{bmatrix} x \\ y \\ 1 \end{bmatrix} = \begin{bmatrix} f & 0 & 0 \\ 0 & f & 0 \\ 0 & 0 & 1 \end{bmatrix} \begin{bmatrix} r1 & r2 & r3 & 0 \\ r4 & r5 & r6 & 0 \\ r7 & r8 & r9 & 0 \end{bmatrix} \begin{bmatrix} X \\ Y \\ Z \\ 1 \end{bmatrix}
$$

As a result, the projective relation in this special case becomes a 3x3 matrix. A similarly interesting situation also occurs when the object we observe is a plane. In this specific case, we can assume without loss of generality that the points on this plane will be located at Z=0. As a result, we obtain the following equation:

$$
s \begin{bmatrix} x \\ y \\ 1 \end{bmatrix} = \begin{bmatrix} f & 0 & 0 \\ 0 & f & 0 \\ 0 & 0 & 1 \end{bmatrix} \begin{bmatrix} r1 & r2 & r3 & t1 \\ r4 & r5 & r6 & t2 \\ r7 & r8 & r9 & t3 \end{bmatrix} \begin{bmatrix} X \\ Y \\ 0 \\ 1 \end{bmatrix}
$$

This zero coordinate of the scene points will then cancel the third column of the projective matrix, which will then again become a 3x3 matrix. This special matrix is called a **homography**, and it implies that, under special circumstances (here, a pure rotation or a planar object), a world point can be related to its image by a linear relation. In addition, because this matrix is invertible, you can also relate an image point on one view directly to its corresponding point on the other view, given that these two views are separated by a pure rotation, or are imaging a planar object. The homographic relation is then of the following form:

$$
s \begin{bmatrix} x' \\ y' \\ 1 \end{bmatrix} = H \begin{bmatrix} x \\ y \\ 1 \end{bmatrix}
$$

Here, H is a 3x3 matrix. This relation holds up to a scale factor represented here by the s scalar value. Once this matrix is estimated, all the points in one view can be transferred to a second view using this relation. This is the property that will be exploited in this recipe and the next one. Note that, as a side effect of the homography relation, the fundamental matrix becomes undefined in these cases.

How to do it...

Suppose that we have two images separated by a pure rotation. This happens, for example, when you take pictures of a building or a landscape by rotating yourself; as you are sufficiently far away from your subject, the translational component is, in this case, negligible. These two images can be matched using the features of your choice and the cv::BFMatcher function.

The result is something like this:

Then, as we did in the previous recipe, we will apply a RANSAC step that will this time involve the estimation of a homography based on a match set (which obviously contains a good number of outliers). This is done by using the cv::findHomography function, which is very similar to the cv::findFundamentalMat function:

```
// Find the homography between image 1 and image 2
std::vector<char> inliers;
cv::Mat homography= cv::findHomography(
                    points1,
                    points2,     // corresponding points
                    inliers,     // outputed inliers matches
                    cv::RANSAC, // RANSAC method
                    1.);        //max distance to reprojection point
```

Recall that a homography exists (instead of a fundamental matrix) because our two images are separated by a pure rotation. We display here the inlier keypoints as identified by the inliers argument of the function:

The homography is a 3x3 invertible matrix. Therefore, once it has been computed, you can transfer image points from one image to the other. In fact, you can do this for every pixel of an image. Consequently, you can transfer a complete image to the point of view of a second image. This process is called image **mosaicing** or image **stitching** and is often used to build a large panorama from multiple images. An OpenCV function that does exactly this is as follows:

```
// Warp image 1 to image 2
cv::Mat result;
cv::warpPerspective(image1,       // input image
                    result,       // output image
                    homography,   // homography
                    cv::Size(2*image1.cols,image1.rows));
                    // size of output image
```

Once this new image is obtained, it can be appended to the other image in order to expand the view (since the two images are now from the same point of view):

```
// Copy image 1 on the first half of full image
cv::Mat half(result,cv::Rect(0,0,image2.cols,image2.rows));
image2.copyTo(half);    // copy image2 to image1 roi
```

The following image is the result:

How it works...

When two views are related by a homography, it becomes possible to determine where a given scene point on one image is found on the other image. This property becomes particularly interesting for the points in one image that fall outside the image boundaries of the other. Indeed, since the second view shows a portion of the scene that is not visible in the first image, you can use the homography in order to expand the image by reading the color value of the additional pixels in the other image. That's how we were able to create a new image that is an expansion of our second image in which extra columns were added to the right-hand side.

The homography computed by `cv::findHomography` is the one that maps the points in the first image to the points in the second image. This homography can be computed from a minimum of four matches and the RANSAC algorithm is again used here. Once the homography with the best support is found, the `cv::findHomography` method refines it using all the identified inliers.

Now, in order to transfer the points of image 1 to image 2, what we need is, in fact, the inverse homography. This is exactly what the `cv::warpPerspective` function is doing by default; that is, it uses the inverse of the homography provided as the input to get the color value of each point of the output image (this is what we called backward mapping in `Chapter 2`, *Manipulating Pixels*). When an output pixel is transferred to a point outside the input image, a black value (0) is simply assigned to this pixel. Note that a `cv::WARP_INVERSE_MAP` flag can be specified as the optional fifth argument in `cv::warpPerspective` if you want to use direct homography instead of the inverted one during the pixel transfer process.

There's more...

The `contrib` package of OpenCV offers a complete stitching solution that can produce high-quality panoramas from multiple images.

Generating image panoramas with the cv::Stitcher module

The mosaic we obtained in this recipe is good but still contains some defects. The alignment of the images is not perfect and we can clearly see the cut between the two images because the brightness and contrast in the two images are not the same. Fortunately, there is now a stitching solution in OpenCV that looks at all these aspects and tries to produce a panorama of optimal quality. This solution is quite complex and elaborated but, at its core, it relies on the principles learned in this recipe. That is, matching feature points in images and robustly estimating a homography. In addition, the solution estimates the intrinsic and extrinsic camera parameters to ensure a better alignment. It also nicely blends the images together by compensating for the difference in exposure conditions. The high-level call of this function is as follows:

```
// Read input images
std::vector<cv::Mat> images;
images.push_back(cv::imread("parliament1.jpg"));
images.push_back(cv::imread("parliament2.jpg"));

cv::Mat panorama;    // output panorama
// create the stitcher
cv::Stitcher stitcher = cv::Stitcher::createDefault();
// stitch the images
cv::Stitcher::Status status = stitcher.stitch(images, panorama);
```

Numerous parameters in the instance can be adjusted to obtain high-quality results. Interested readers should explore this package in more depth in order to learn more about it. In our case, the result obtained is as follows:

Obviously, in general, an arbitrary number of input images can be used to compose a large panorama.

See also

- The *Remapping an image* recipe in `Chapter 2`, *Manipulating Pixels*, discusses the concept of backward mapping
- The *Automatic panoramic image stitching using invariant* features article by *M. Brown* and *D. Lowe* in *International Journal of Computer Vision*,74, 1, 2007, describes a complete method for building panoramas from multiple images

Detecting a planar target in images

In the previous recipe, we explained how homographies can be used to stitch together images separated by a pure rotation to create a panorama. In this recipe, we also learned that different images of a plane also generate homographies between views. We will now see how we can make use of this fact to recognize a planar object in an image.

How to do it...

Suppose you want to detect the occurrence of a planar object in an image. This object could be a poster, painting, logo, signage, and so on. Based on what we have learned in this chapter, the strategy would consist of detecting feature points on this planar object and to try to match them with the feature points in the image. These matches would then be validated using a robust matching scheme similar to the one we used previously, but this time based on a homography. If the number of valid matches is high, then this must mean that our planar object is visible in the current image.

In this recipe, our mission is to detect the occurrence of the first edition of our book in an image, more specifically, the following image:

Let's define a `TargetMatcher` class that is very similar to our `RobustMatcher` class:

```
class TargetMatcher {
  private:
  // pointer to the feature point detector object
  cv::Ptr<cv::FeatureDetector> detector;
  // pointer to the feature descriptor extractor object
  cv::Ptr<cv::DescriptorExtractor> descriptor;
  cv::Mat target;            // target image
  int normType;              // to compare descriptor vectors
  double distance;           // min reprojection error
  int numberOfLevels;        // pyramid size
  double scaleFactor;        // scale between levels
  // the pyramid of target images and its keypoints
  std::vector<cv::Mat> pyramid;
  std::vector<std::vector<cv::KeyPoint>> pyrKeypoints;
  std::vector<cv::Mat> pyrDescriptors;
```

The reference image of the planar object to be matched is held by the `target` attribute. As it will be explained in the next section, feature points will be detected in a pyramid of images of the target successively down-sampled. The matching methods are similar to the ones of the `RobustMatcher` class, except that they include `cv::findHomography` instead of `cv::findFundamentalMat` in the `ransacTest` method.

To use the `TargetMatcher` class, a specific feature point detector and descriptor must be instantiated and passed to the constructor:

```
// Prepare the matcher
TargetMatcher tmatcher(cv::FastFeatureDetector::create(10),
                       cv::BRISK::create());
tmatcher.setNormType(cv::NORM_HAMMING);
```

Here, we selected the FAST detector in conjunction with the BRISK descriptor because they are quick to compute. Then, you must specify the target to be detected:

```
// set the target image
tmatcher.setTarget(target);
```

In our case, this is the following image:

You can detect this target in an image by calling the `detectTarget` method:

```
// match image with target
tmatcher.detectTarget(image, corners);
```

This method returns the position of the four corners of the target in the image (if found). Lines can then be drawn to visually validate the detection:

```
// draw the target corners on the image
if (corners.size() == 4) { // we have a detection

    cv::line(image, cv::Point(corners[0]),
             cv::Point(corners[1]),
             cv::Scalar(255, 255, 255), 3);
    cv::line(image, cv::Point(corners[1]),
```

```
                    cv::Point(corners[2]),
                    cv::Scalar(255, 255, 255), 3);
        cv::line(image, cv::Point(corners[2]),
                    cv::Point(corners[3]),
                    cv::Scalar(255, 255, 255), 3);
        cv::line(image, cv::Point(corners[3]),
                    cv::Point(corners[0]),
                    cv::Scalar(255, 255, 255), 3);
    }
```

The result is as follows:

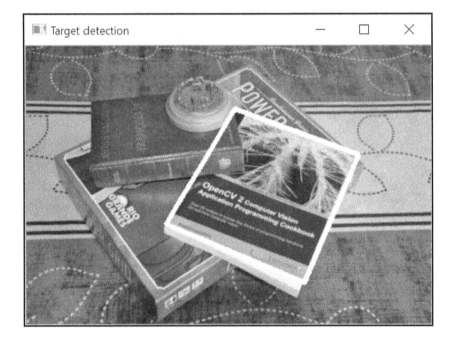

How it works...

Since we do not know what the size of the target in the image is, we have decided to build a pyramid made of the target image in different sizes. Another option would have been to use scale-invariant features. At each level of our pyramid, the size of the target image is reduced by a certain factor (attribute `scaleFactor`, `0.9` by default) and the pyramid is made of a number of levels (attribute `numberOfLevels`, 8 by default). Feature points are detected for each level of the pyramid:

```cpp
// Set the target image
void setTarget(const cv::Mat t) {

  target= t;
  createPyramid();
}
// create a pyramid of target images
void createPyramid() {

  // create the pyramid of target images
  pyramid.clear();
  cv::Mat layer(target);
  for (int i = 0;
       i < numberOfLevels; i++) { // reduce size at each layer
    pyramid.push_back(target.clone());
    resize(target, target, cv::Size(), scaleFactor, scaleFactor);
  }

  pyrKeypoints.clear();
  pyrDescriptors.clear();
  // keypoint detection and description in pyramid
  for (int i = 0; i < numberOfLevels; i++) {
    // detect target keypoints at level i
    pyrKeypoints.push_back(std::vector<cv::KeyPoint>());
    detector->detect(pyramid[i], pyrKeypoints[i]);
    // compute descriptor at level i
    pyrDescriptors.push_back(cv::Mat());
    descriptor->compute(pyramid[i],
                        pyrKeypoints[i],
                        pyrDescriptors[i]);
  }
}
```

The `detectTarget` method then proceeds onto three steps. Firstly, interest points are detected in the input image. Secondly, this image is robustly matched with each image of the target pyramid. The level with the highest number of inliers is retained. If this one has a sufficiently high number of surviving matches, then we have found the target. The third step consists of reprojecting the four corners of the target to the correct scale onto the input image using the found homography and the `cv::getPerspectiveTransform` function:

```cpp
// detect the defined planar target in an image
// returns the homography and
// the 4 corners of the detected target
cv::Mat detectTarget(
            const cv::Mat& image, // position of the
                                  // target corners (clock-wise)
            std::vector<cv::Point2f>& detectedCorners) {

  // 1. detect image keypoints
  std::vector<cv::KeyPoint> keypoints;
  detector->detect(image, keypoints);
  // compute descriptors
  cv::Mat descriptors;
  descriptor->compute(image, keypoints, descriptors);

  std::vector<cv::DMatch> matches;
  cv::Mat bestHomography;
  cv::Size bestSize;
  int maxInliers = 0;
  cv::Mat homography;

  // Construction of the matcher
  cv::BFMatcher matcher(normType);

  // 2. robustly find homography for each pyramid level
  for (int i = 0; i < numberOfLevels; i++) {
    // find a RANSAC homography between target and image
    matches.clear();
    // match descriptors
    matcher.match(pyrDescriptors[i], descriptors, matches);
    // validate matches using RANSAC
    std::vector<cv::DMatch> inliers;
    homography = ransacTest(matches, pyrKeypoints[i],
                            keypoints, inliers);

    if (inliers.size() > maxInliers) { // we have a better H
      maxInliers = inliers.size();
      bestHomography = homography;
      bestSize = pyramid[i].size();
    }
```

```
  }

  // 3. find the corner position on the image using best homography
  if (maxInliers > 8) { // the estimate is valid

    //target corners at best size
    std::vector<cv::Point2f> corners;
    corners.push_back(cv::Point2f(0, 0));
    corners.push_back(cv::Point2f(bestSize.width - 1, 0));
    corners.push_back(cv::Point2f(bestSize.width - 1,
                                  bestSize.height - 1));
    corners.push_back(cv::Point2f(0, bestSize.height - 1));

    // reproject the target corners
    cv::perspectiveTransform(corners, detectedCorners, bestHomography);
  }

  return bestHomography;
}
```

The following image shows the matching results obtained in the case of our example:

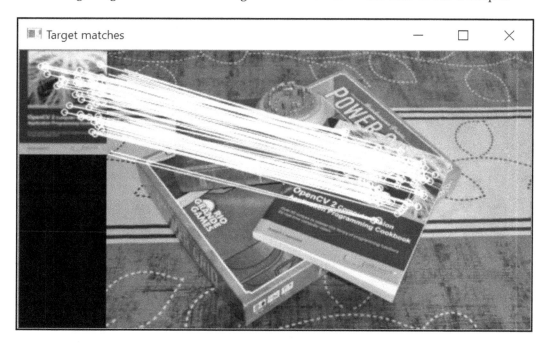

See also

- The *Fast and robust homography scheme for real-time planar target detection* article by *H. Bazargani, O. Bilaniuk* and *R. Laganière* in *Journal of Real-Time Image Processing,* May 2015, describes a method to detecting a planar target in real-time. It also describes the `cv::RHO` method for the `cv::findHomography` function.

11
Reconstructing 3D Scenes

In this chapter, we will cover the following recipes:

- Calibrating a camera
- Recovering camera pose
- Reconstructing a 3D scene from calibrated cameras
- Computing depth from stereo image

Introduction

We learned in the previous chapter how a camera captures a 3D scene by projecting light rays on a 2D sensor plane. The image produced is an accurate representation of what the scene looks like from a particular point of view, at the instant the image was captured. However, by its nature, the process of image formation eliminates all information concerning the depth of the represented scene elements. This chapter will teach how, under specific conditions, the 3D structure of the scene and the 3D pose of the cameras that captured it, can be recovered. We will see how a good understanding of projective geometry concepts allows us to devise methods that enable 3D reconstruction. We will therefore revisit the principle of image formation introduced in the previous chapter; in particular, we will now take into consideration that our image is composed of pixels.

Digital image formation

Let's now redraw a new version of the figure shown in `Chapter 10`, *Estimating Projective Relations in Images*, describing the pin-hole camera model. More specifically, we want to demonstrate the relation between a point in 3D at position (X, Y, Z) and its image (x, y) on a camera specified in pixel coordinates:

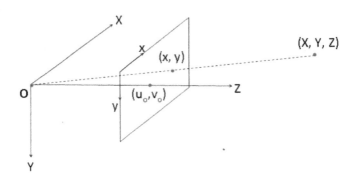

Notice the changes that have been made to the original figure. First, we added a reference frame that we positioned at the center of the projection. Second, we have the Y-axis pointing downward to get a coordinate system compatible with the usual convention that places the image origin in the upper-left corner of the image. Finally, we also identified a special point on the image plane: considering the line coming from the focal point that is orthogonal to the image plane, the point (u0, v0) is the pixel position at which this line pierces the image plane. This point is called the **principal point**. It could be logical to assume that this principal point is at the center of the image plane, but in practice, this one might be off by a few pixels, depending on the precision with which the camera has been manufactured.

In the previous chapter, we learned that the essential parameters of a camera in the pin-hole model are its focal length and the size of the image plane (which defines the field of view of the camera). In addition, since we are dealing with digital images, the number of pixels on the image plane (its resolution) is another important characteristic of a camera. We also learned previously that a 3D point (X, Y, Z) will be projected onto the image plane at (fX/Z, fY/Z).

Now, if we want to translate this coordinate into pixels, we need to divide the 2D image position by the pixel width (px) and height (py), respectively. We notice that by dividing the focal length given in world units (generally given in millimeters) by px, we obtain the focal length expressed in (horizontal) pixels. Let's define this term, then, as fx. Similarly, fy =f/py is defined as the focal length expressed in vertical pixel units. The complete projective equation is therefore as follows:

$$x = \frac{f_x X}{Z} + u_0$$

$$y = \frac{f_y Y}{Z} + v_0$$

Recall that (u0, v0) is the principal point that is added to the result in order to move the origin to the upper-left corner of the image. Note also that the physical size of a pixel can be obtained by dividing the size of the image sensor (generally in millimeters) by the number of pixels (horizontally or vertically). In modern sensors, pixels are generally square, that is, they have the same horizontal and vertical size.

The preceding equations can be rewritten in matrix form as we did in Chapter 10, *Estimating Projective Relations in Images*. Here is the complete projective equation in its most general form:

$$s \begin{bmatrix} x \\ y \\ 1 \end{bmatrix} = \begin{bmatrix} f_x & 0 & u_0 \\ 0 & f_y & v_0 \\ 0 & 0 & 1 \end{bmatrix} \begin{bmatrix} r1 & r2 & r3 & t1 \\ r4 & r5 & r6 & t2 \\ r7 & r8 & r9 & t3 \end{bmatrix} \begin{bmatrix} X \\ Y \\ Z \\ 1 \end{bmatrix}$$

Calibrating a camera

Camera calibration is the process by which the different camera parameters (that is, the ones appearing in the projective equation) are obtained. One can obviously use the specifications provided by the camera manufacturer, but for some tasks, such as 3D reconstruction, these specifications are not accurate enough. By undertaking an appropriate camera calibration step, accurate calibration information can be obtained.

An active camera calibration procedure will proceed by showing known patterns to the camera and analyzing the obtained images. An optimization process will then determine the optimal parameter values that explain the observations. This is a complex process that has been made easy by the availability of OpenCV calibration functions.

How to do it...

To calibrate a camera, the idea is to show it a set of scene points for which their 3D positions are known. Then, you need to observe where these points project on the image. With the knowledge of a sufficient number of 3D points and associated 2D image points, the exact camera parameters can be inferred from the projective equation. Obviously, for accurate results, we need to observe as many points as possible. One way to achieve this would be to take one picture of a scene with many known 3D points, but in practice, this is rarely feasible. A more convenient way is to take several images of a set of some 3D points from different viewpoints. This approach is simpler but requires you to compute the position of each camera view in addition to the computation of the internal camera parameters, which, fortunately, is feasible.

OpenCV proposes that you use a chessboard pattern to generate the set of 3D scene points required for calibration. This pattern creates points at the corners of each square, and since this pattern is flat, we can freely assume that the board is located at Z=0, with the X and Y axes well-aligned with the grid.

In this case, the calibration process simply consists of showing the chessboard pattern to the camera from different viewpoints. Here is one example of a calibration pattern image made of 7x5 inner corners as captured during the calibration step:

The good thing is that OpenCV has a function that automatically detects the corners of this chessboard pattern. You simply provide an image and the size of the chessboard used (the number of horizontal and vertical inner corner points). The function will return the position of these chessboard corners on the image. If the function fails to find the pattern, then it simply returns `false`:

```
// output vectors of image points
std::vector<cv::Point2f> imageCorners;
// number of inner corners on the chessboard
cv::Size boardSize(7,5);
// Get the chessboard corners
bool found = cv::findChessboardCorners(
                    image,          // image of chessboard pattern
                    boardSize,      // size of pattern
                    imageCorners);  // list of detected corners
```

The output parameter, `imageCorners`, will simply contain the pixel coordinates of the detected inner corners of the shown pattern. Note that this function accepts additional parameters if you need to tune the algorithm, which is not discussed here. There is also a special function that draws the detected corners on the chessboard image, with lines connecting them in a sequence:

```
// Draw the corners
cv::drawChessboardCorners(image, boardSize,
                imageCorners, found); // corners have been found
```

The following image is obtained:

The lines that connect the points show the order in which the points are listed in the vector of detected image points. To perform a calibration, we now need to specify the corresponding 3D points. You can specify these points in the units of your choice (for example, in centimeters or in inches); however, the simplest thing to do is to assume that each square represents one unit. In that case, the coordinates of the first point would be (0,0,0) (assuming that the board is located at a depth of Z=0), the coordinates of the second point would be (1,0,0), and so on, the last point being located at (6,4,0). There is a total of 35 points in this pattern, which is too small to obtain an accurate calibration. To get more points, you need to show more images of the same calibration pattern from various points of view. To do so, you can either move the pattern in front of the camera or move the camera around the board; from a mathematical point of view, this is completely equivalent. The OpenCV calibration function assumes that the reference frame is fixed on the calibration pattern and will calculate the rotation and translation of the camera with respect to the reference frame.

Let's now encapsulate the calibration process in a `CameraCalibrator` class. The attributes of this class are as follows:

```
class CameraCalibrator {

    // input points:
    // the points in world coordinates
    // (each square is one unit)
    std::vector<std::vector<cv::Point3f>> objectPoints;
    // the image point positions in pixels
    std::vector<std::vector<cv::Point2f>> imagePoints;
    // output Matrices
    cv::Mat cameraMatrix;
    cv::Mat distCoeffs;
    // flag to specify how calibration is done
    int flag;
```

Note that the input vectors of the scene and image points are in fact made of `std::vector` of point instances; each vector element is a vector of the points from one view. Here, we decided to add the calibration points by specifying a vector of the chessboard image filename as input; the method will take care of extracting the point coordinates from these images:

```
// Open chessboard images and extract corner points
int CameraCalibrator::addChessboardPoints(
    const std::vector<std::string> & filelist, // list of filenames
    cv::Size & boardSize) {   // calibration board size

    // the points on the chessboard
    std::vector<cv::Point2f> imageCorners;
```

```
std::vector<cv::Point3f> objectCorners;

// 3D Scene Points:
// Initialize the chessboard corners
// in the chessboard reference frame
// The corners are at 3D location (X,Y,Z)= (i,j,0)
for (int i=0; i<boardSize.height; i++) {
  for (int j=0; j<boardSize.width; j++) {
    objectCorners.push_back(cv::Point3f(i, j, 0.0f));
  }
}

// 2D Image points:
cv::Mat image; //to contain chessboard image
int successes = 0;
// for all viewpoints
for (int i=0; i<filelist.size(); i++) {

  // Open the image
  image = cv::imread(filelist[i],0);

  // Get the chessboard corners
  bool found = cv::findChessboardCorners(
                image,          // image of chessboard pattern
                boardSize,      // size of pattern
                imageCorners);  // list of detected corners

  // Get subpixel accuracy on the corners
  if (found) {
    cv::cornerSubPix(image, imageCorners,
        cv::Size(5, 5), // half size of serach window
        cv::Size(-1, -1),
        cv::TermCriteria( cv::TermCriteria::MAX_ITER +
            cv::TermCriteria::EPS, 30, // max number of iterations
            0.1));                     // min accuracy

    // If we have a good board, add it to our data
    if (imageCorners.size() == boardSize.area()) {
      //Add image and scene points from one view
      addPoints(imageCorners, objectCorners);
      successes++;
    }
  }

  // If we have a good board, add it to our data
  if (imageCorners.size() == boardSize.area()) {
    //Add image and scene points from one view
    addPoints(imageCorners, objectCorners);
```

```
              successes++;
          }
      }
      return successes;
  }
```

The first loop inputs the 3D coordinates of the chessboard, and the corresponding image points are the ones provided by the `cv::findChessboardCorners` function. This is done for all the available viewpoints. Moreover, in order to obtain a more accurate image point location, the `cv::cornerSubPix` function can be used; and as the name suggests, the image points will then be localized with subpixel accuracy. The termination criterion that is specified by the `cv::TermCriteria` object defines the maximum number of iterations and the minimum accuracy in subpixel coordinates. The first of these two conditions that is reached will stop the corner refinement process.

When a set of chessboard corners have been successfully detected, these points are added to our vectors of image and scene points using our `addPoints` method. Once a sufficient number of chessboard images have been processed (and consequently, a large number of 3D scene point/2D image point correspondences are available), we can initiate the computation of the calibration parameters as follows:

```
// Calibrate the camera
// returns the re-projection error
double CameraCalibrator::calibrate(cv::Size &imageSize) {
  // Output rotations and translations
  std::vector<cv::Mat> rvecs, tvecs;

  // start calibration
  return
    calibrateCamera(objectPoints,  // the 3D points
                    imagePoints,   // the image points
                    imageSize,     // image size
                    cameraMatrix,  // output camera matrix
                    distCoeffs,    // output distortion matrix
                    rvecs, tvecs,  // Rs, Ts
                    flag);         // set options
}
```

In practice, 10 to 20 chessboard images are sufficient, but these must be taken from different viewpoints at different depths. The two important outputs of this function are the camera matrix and the distortion parameters. These will be described in the next section.

How it works...

In order to explain the result of the calibration, we need to go back to the projective equation presented in the introduction of this chapter. This equation describes the transformation of a 3D point into a 2D point through the successive application of two matrices. The first matrix includes all of the camera parameters, which are called the intrinsic parameters of the camera. This 3×3 matrix is one of the output matrices returned by the `cv::calibrateCamera` function. There is also a function called `cv::calibrationMatrixValues` that explicitly returns the value of the intrinsic parameters given by a calibration matrix.

The second matrix is there to have the input points expressed into camera-centric coordinates. It is composed of a rotation vector (a 3×3 matrix) and a translation vector (a 3×1 matrix). Remember that in our calibration example, the reference frame was placed on the chessboard. Therefore, there is a rigid transformation (made of a rotation component represented by the matrix entries `r1` to `r9` and a translation represented by `t1`, `t2`, and `t3`) that must be computed for each view. These are in the output parameter list of the `cv::calibrateCamera` function. The rotation and translation components are often called the **extrinsic parameters** of the calibration, and they are different for each view. The intrinsic parameters remain constant for a given camera/lens system.

The calibration results provided by the `cv::calibrateCamera` are obtained through an optimization process. This process aims to find the intrinsic and extrinsic parameters that minimize the difference between the predicted image point position, as computed from the projection of the 3D scene points, and the actual image point position, as observed on the image. The sum of this difference for all the points specified during the calibration is called the **re-projection error**.

The intrinsic parameters of our test camera obtained from a calibration based on 27 chessboard images are `fx=409` pixels, `fy=408` pixels, `u0=237` pixels, and `v0=171`pixels. Our calibration images have a size of 536×356 pixels. From the calibration results, you can see that, as expected, the principal point is close to the center of the image, but yet off by few pixels. The calibration images were taken using a Nikon D500 camera with a 18mm lens. Looking at the manufacturer specifications, we find that the sensor size of this camera is 23.5mm x 15.7mm, which gives us a pixel size of 0.0438mm. The estimated focal length is expressed in pixels, so multiplying the result by the pixel size gives us an estimated focal length of 17.8mm, which is consistent with the actual lens we used.

Let's now turn our attention to the distortion parameters. So far, we have mentioned that under the pin-hole camera model, we can neglect the effect of the lens. However, this is only possible if the lens that is used to capture an image does not introduce important optical distortions. Unfortunately, this is not the case with lower quality lenses or with lenses that have a very short focal length. Even the lens we used in this experiment introduced some distortion: the edges of the rectangular board are curved in the image. Note that this distortion becomes more important as we move away from the center of the image. This is a typical distortion observed with a fish-eye lens, and it is called **radial distortion**.

It is possible to compensate for these deformations by introducing an appropriate distortion model. The idea is to represent the distortions induced by a lens by a set of mathematical equations. Once established, these equations can then be reverted in order to undo the distortions visible on the image. Fortunately, the exact parameters of the transformation that will correct the distortions can be obtained together with the other camera parameters during the calibration phase. Once this is done, any image from the newly calibrated camera will be undistorted. Therefore, we have added an additional method to our calibration class:

```cpp
// remove distortion in an image (after calibration)
cv::Mat CameraCalibrator::remap(const cv::Mat &image) {

    cv::Mat undistorted;

    if (mustInitUndistort) { // called once per calibration

        cv::initUndistortRectifyMap(
                    cameraMatrix,  // computed camera matrix
                    distCoeffs,    // computed distortion matrix
                    cv::Mat(),     // optional rectification (none)
                    cv::Mat(),     // camera matrix to generate undistorted
                    image.size(),  // size of undistorted
                    CV_32FC1,      // type of output map
                    map1, map2);   // the x and y mapping functions

        mustInitUndistort= false;
    }

    // Apply mapping functions
    cv::remap(image, undistorted, map1, map2,
            cv::INTER_LINEAR);     // interpolation type

    return undistorted;
}
```

Running this code on one of our calibration image results in the following undistorted image:

To correct the distortion, OpenCV uses a polynomial function that is applied to the image points in order to move them to their undistorted position. By default, five coefficients are used; a model made of eight coefficients is also available. Once these coefficients are obtained, it is possible to compute two `cv::Mat` mapping functions (one for the x coordinate and one for the y coordinate) that will give the new undistorted position of an image point on a distorted image. This is computed by the `cv::initUndistortRectifyMap` function, and the `cv::remap` function remaps all the points of an input image to a new image. Note that because of the nonlinear transformation, some pixels of the input image now fall outside the boundary of the output image. You can expand the size of the output image to compensate for this loss of pixels, but you now obtain output pixels that have no values in the input image (they will then be displayed as black pixels).

There's more...

More options are available when it comes to camera calibration.

Calibration with known intrinsic parameters

When a good estimate of the camera's intrinsic parameters is known, it could be advantageous to input them in the cv::calibrateCamera function. They will then be used as initial values in the optimization process. To do so, you just need to add the cv::CALIB_USE_INTRINSIC_GUESS flag and input these values in the calibration matrix parameter. It is also possible to impose a fixed value for the principal point (cv::CALIB_FIX_PRINCIPAL_POINT), which can often be assumed to be the central pixel. You can also impose a fixed ratio for the focal lengths fx and fy (cv::CALIB_FIX_RATIO), in which case, you assume that the pixels are square.

Using a grid of circles for calibration

Instead of the usual chessboard pattern, OpenCV also offers the possibility to calibrate a camera by using a grid of circles. In this case, the centers of the circles are used as calibration points. The corresponding function is very similar to the function we used to locate the chessboard corners, for example:

```
cv::Size boardSize(7,7);
std::vector<cv::Point2f> centers;
bool found = cv:: findCirclesGrid(image, boardSize, centers);
```

See also

- The *A flexible new technique for camera calibration* article by *Z. Zhang* in *IEEE Transactions on Pattern Analysis and Machine Intelligence, vol. 22*, no 11, 2000, is a classic paper on the problem of camera calibration

Recovering camera pose

When a camera is calibrated, it becomes possible to relate the captured images with the outside world. We previously explained that if the 3D structure of an object is known, then one can predict how the object will be imaged on the sensor of the camera. The process of image formation is indeed completely described by the projective equation that was presented at the beginning of this chapter. When most of the terms of this equation are known, then it becomes possible to infer the value of the other elements (2D or 3D) through the observation of some images. In this recipe, we will look at the camera pose recovery problem when a known 3D structure is observed.

How to do it...

Let's consider a simple object, a bench in a park. We took an image of this one using the camera/lens system calibrated in the previous recipe. We also have manually identified eight distinct image points on the bench that we will use for our camera pose estimation:

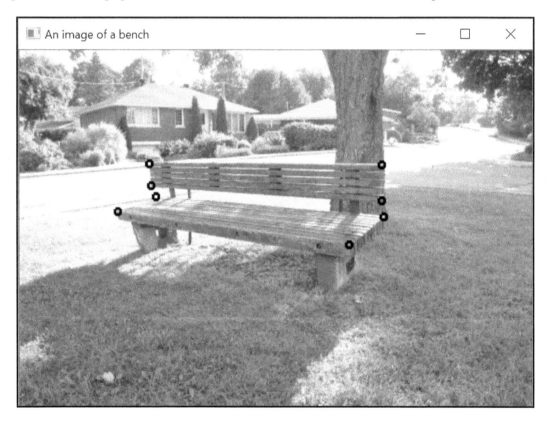

Having access to this object, it is possible to make some physical measurements. The bench is composed of a seat that is 242.5cm x 53.5cm x 9cm and a back that is 242.5cm x 24cm x 9cm fixed 12cm over the seat. Using this information, we can then easily derive the 3D coordinates of the eight identified points in some object-centric reference frame (here, we fixed the origin at the left extremity of the intersection between the two planes). We can then create a `cv::Point3f` vector containing these coordinates:

```
// Input object points
std::vector<cv::Point3f> objectPoints;
objectPoints.push_back(cv::Point3f(0, 45, 0));
objectPoints.push_back(cv::Point3f(242.5, 45, 0));
objectPoints.push_back(cv::Point3f(242.5, 21, 0));
objectPoints.push_back(cv::Point3f(0, 21, 0));
objectPoints.push_back(cv::Point3f(0, 9, -9));
objectPoints.push_back(cv::Point3f(242.5, 9, -9));
objectPoints.push_back(cv::Point3f(242.5, 9, 44.5));
objectPoints.push_back(cv::Point3f(0, 9, 44.5));
```

The question now is where the camera was with respect to these points when the shown picture was taken. Since the coordinates of the image of these known points on the 2D image plane are also known, then it becomes easy to answer this question by using the `cv::solvePnP` function. Here, the correspondence between the 3D and the 2D points has been established manually, but one should be able to come up with some methods that would allow you to obtain this information automatically:

```
// Input image points
std::vector<cv::Point2f> imagePoints;
imagePoints.push_back(cv::Point2f(136, 113));
imagePoints.push_back(cv::Point2f(379, 114));
imagePoints.push_back(cv::Point2f(379, 150));
imagePoints.push_back(cv::Point2f(138, 135));
imagePoints.push_back(cv::Point2f(143, 146));
imagePoints.push_back(cv::Point2f(381, 166));
imagePoints.push_back(cv::Point2f(345, 194));
imagePoints.push_back(cv::Point2f(103, 161));

// Get the camera pose from 3D/2D points
cv::Mat rvec, tvec;
cv::solvePnP(
            objectPoints, imagePoints,       // corresponding 3D/2D pts
            cameraMatrix, cameraDistCoeffs, // calibration
            rvec, tvec);                     // output pose

//Convert to 3D rotation matrix
cv::Mat rotation;
cv::Rodrigues(rvec, rotation);
```

This function in fact, computes the rigid transformation (rotation and translation) that brings the object coordinates in the camera-centric reference frame (that is, the one that has its origin at the focal point). It is also important to note that the rotation computed by this function is given in the form of a 3D vector. This is a compact representation in which the rotation to apply is described by a unit vector (an axis of rotation) around which the object is rotated by a certain angle. This axis-angle representation is also called the **Rodrigues' rotation formula**. In OpenCV, the angle of the rotation corresponds to the norm of the output rotation vector, the latter being aligned with the axis of rotation. This is why the `cv::Rodrigues` function is used to obtain the 3D matrix of rotation that appears in our projective equation.

The pose recovery procedure described here is simple, but how do we know we obtained the right camera/object pose information? We can visually assess the quality of the results by using the `cv::viz` module that gives us the ability to visualize 3D information. The use of this module is explained in the last section of this recipe, but let's display a simple 3D representation of our object and the camera that captured it:

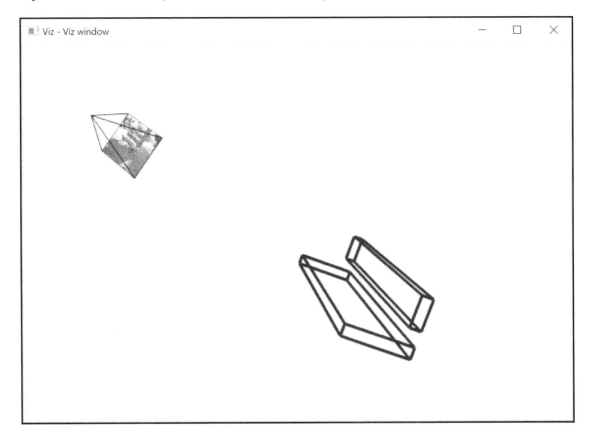

It might be difficult to judge of the quality of the pose recovery just by looking at this image but if you test the example of this recipe on your computer, you will have the possibility to move this representation in 3D using your mouse, which should give you a better sense of the solution obtained.

How it works...

In this recipe, we assumed that the 3D structure of the object was known, as well as the correspondence between sets of object points and image points. The camera's intrinsic parameters were also known through calibration. If you look at our projective equation presented at the end of the *Digital image formation* section of the introduction of this chapter, this means that we have points for which coordinates (X, Y, Z) and (x, y) are known. We also have the elements of the first matrix known (the intrinsic parameters). Only the second matrix is unknown; this is the one that contains the extrinsic parameters of the camera that is the camera/object pose information. Our objective is then to recover these unknown parameters from the observation of 3D scene points. This problem is known as the **Perspective-n-Point** (**PnP**) problem.

Rotation has three degrees of freedom (for example, angle of rotation around the three axes) and translation also has three degrees of freedom. We therefore have a total of six unknowns. For each object point/image point correspondence, the projective equation gives us three algebraic equations, but since the projective equation is up to a scale factor, we only have two independent equations. A minimum of three points is therefore required to solve this system of equations. Obviously, more points provide a more reliable estimate.

In practice, many different algorithms have been proposed to solve this problem and OpenCV proposes a number of different implementation in its `cv::solvePnP` function. The default method consists in optimizing what is called the reprojection error. Minimizing this type of error is considered to be the best strategy to get accurate 3D information from camera images. In our problem, it corresponds to finding the optimal camera position that minimizes the 2D distance between the projected 3D points (as obtained by applying the projective equation) and the observed image points given as input.

Note that OpenCV also has a `cv::solvePnPRansac` function. As the name suggests, this function uses the **RANSAC** algorithm in order to solve the PnP problem. This means that some of the object point/image point correspondences may be wrong and the function will return the ones that have been identified as outliers. This is very useful when these correspondences have been obtained through an automatic process that can fail for some points.

There's more...

When working with 3D information, it often difficult to validate the solutions obtained. To this end, OpenCV offers a simple yet powerful visualization module that facilitates the development and debugging of 3D vision algorithms. It allows inserting points, lines, cameras and other objects in a virtual 3D environment that you can interactively visualize from various points of views.

cv::Viz, a 3D Visualizer module

`cv::Viz` is an extra module of the OpenCV library that is built on top of the **Visualization Toolkit** (**VTK**) open source library. This is a powerful framework used for 3D computer graphics. With `cv::viz`, you create a 3D virtual environment to which you can add a variety of objects. A visualization window is created that displays the environment from a given point of view. You saw in this recipe an example of what can be displayed in a `cv::viz` window. This window responds to mouse events that are used to navigate inside the environment (through rotations and translations). This section describes the basic use of the `cv::viz` module.

The first thing to do is to create the visualization window. Here, we use a white background:

```
// Create a viz window
cv::viz::Viz3d visualizer("Viz window");
visualizer.setBackgroundColor(cv::viz::Color::white());
```

Next, you create your virtual objects and insert them into the scene. There is a variety of predefined objects. One of them is particularly useful for us; it is the one that creates a virtual pin-hole camera:

```
// Create a virtual camera
cv::viz::WCameraPosition cam(
            cMatrix,     // matrix of intrinsics
            image,       // image displayed on the plane
            30.0,        // scale factor
            cv::viz::Color::black());
// Add the virtual camera to the environment
visualizer.showWidget("Camera", cam);
```

The `cMatrix` variable is a `cv::Matx33d` (that is, a `cv::Matx<double,3,3>`) instance containing the intrinsic camera parameters as obtained from calibration. By default, this camera is inserted at the origin of the coordinate system. To represent the bench, we used two rectangular cuboid objects:

```
// Create a virtual bench from cuboids
cv::viz::WCube plane1(cv::Point3f(0.0, 45.0, 0.0),
                      cv::Point3f(242.5, 21.0, -9.0),
                      true,      // show wire frame
                      cv::viz::Color::blue());
plane1.setRenderingProperty(cv::viz::LINE_WIDTH, 4.0);
cv::viz::WCube plane2(cv::Point3f(0.0, 9.0, -9.0),
                      cv::Point3f(242.5, 0.0, 44.5),
                      true,      // show wire frame
                      cv::viz::Color::blue());
plane2.setRenderingProperty(cv::viz::LINE_WIDTH, 4.0);
// Add the virtual objects to the environment
visualizer.showWidget("top", plane1);
visualizer.showWidget("bottom", plane2);
```

This virtual bench is also added at the origin; it then needs to be moved at its camera-centric position as found from our `cv::solvePnP` function. It is the responsibility of the `setWidgetPose` method to perform this operation. This one simply applies the rotation and translation components of the estimated motion:

```
cv::Mat rotation;
// convert vector-3 rotation
// to a 3x3 rotation matrix
cv::Rodrigues(rvec, rotation);

// Move the bench
cv::Affine3d pose(rotation, tvec);
visualizer.setWidgetPose("top", pose);
visualizer.setWidgetPose("bottom", pose);
```

The final step is to create a loop that keeps displaying the visualization window. The `1ms` pause is there to listen to mouse events:

```
// visualization loop
while(cv::waitKey(100)==-1 && !visualizer.wasStopped()) {

    visualizer.spinOnce(1,      // pause 1ms
                        true);  // redraw
}
```

This loop will stop when the visualization window is closed or when a key is pressed over an OpenCV image window. Try to apply inside this loop some motion on an object (using `setWidgetPose`); this is how animation can be created.

See also

- *Model-based object pose in 25 lines of code* by *D. DeMenthon* and *L. S. Davis*, in the *European Conference on Computer Vision*, 1992, pp.335-343 is a famous method for recovering camera pose from scene points
- The *Matching images using random sample consensus* recipe in `Chapter 10`, *Estimating Projective Relations in Images* describes the RANSAC algorithm
- The *Installing the OpenCV library* recipe in `Chapter 1`, *Playing with Images* explains how to install the RANSAC `cv::viz` extra module

Reconstructing a 3D scene from calibrated cameras

We saw in the previous recipe that it is possible to recover the position of a camera observing a 3D scene, when this one is calibrated. The approach described took advantage of the fact that, sometimes, the coordinates of some 3D points visible in the scene might be known. We will now learn that if a scene is observed from more than one point of view, 3D pose and structure can be reconstructed even if no information about the 3D scene is available. This time, we will use correspondences between image points in the different views in order to infer 3D information. We will introduce a new mathematical entity encompassing the relation between two views of a calibrated camera, and we will discuss the principle of triangulation in order to reconstruct 3D points from 2D images.

How to do it...

Let's again use the camera we calibrated in the first recipe of this chapter and take two pictures of some scene. We can match feature points between these two views using, for example, the SIFT detector and descriptor presented in `Chapter 8`, *Detecting Interest Points* and `Chapter 9`, *Describing and Matching interest points*.

The fact that the calibration parameters of the camera are available, allows us to work in world coordinates; and therefore establish a physical constraint between the camera poses and the position of the corresponding points. Basically, we introduce a new mathematical entity called the **Essential matrix**, which is the calibrated version of the fundamental matrix introduced in the previous chapter. Therefore, there is a `cv::findEssentialMat` function that's identical to the `cv::findFundametalMat` that was used in the *Computing the fundamental matrix of an image pair* recipe in `Chapter 10`, *Estimating Projective Relations in Images*. We can call this function with the established point correspondences and through a RANSAC scheme, filter out the outlier points to retain only the matches that comply with the found geometry:

```cpp
// vector of keypoints and descriptors
std::vector<cv::KeyPoint> keypoints1;
std::vector<cv::KeyPoint> keypoints2;
cv::Mat descriptors1, descriptors2;

// Construction of the SIFT feature detector
cv::Ptr<cv::Feature2D> ptrFeature2D =
                    cv::xfeatures2d::SIFT::create(500);

// Detection of the SIFT features and associated descriptors
ptrFeature2D->detectAndCompute(image1, cv::noArray(),
                        keypoints1, descriptors1);
ptrFeature2D->detectAndCompute(image2, cv::noArray(),
                        keypoints2, descriptors2);

// Match the two image descriptors
// Construction of the matcher with crosscheck
cv::BFMatcher matcher(cv::NORM_L2, true);
std::vector<cv::DMatch> matches;
matcher.match(descriptors1, descriptors2, matches);

// Convert keypoints into Point2f
std::vector<cv::Point2f> points1, points2;
for (std::vector<cv::DMatch>::const_iterator it =
        matches.begin(); it != matches.end(); ++it) {

  // Get the position of left keypoints
  float x = keypoints1[it->queryIdx].pt.x;
  float y = keypoints1[it->queryIdx].pt.y;
  points1.push_back(cv::Point2f(x, y));
  // Get the position of right keypoints
  x = keypoints2[it->trainIdx].pt.x;
  y = keypoints2[it->trainIdx].pt.y;
  points2.push_back(cv::Point2f(x, y));
}
```

```
// Find the essential between image 1 and image 2
cv::Mat inliers;
cv::Mat essential = cv::findEssentialMat(points1, points2,
                        Matrix,         // intrinsic parameters
                        cv::RANSAC,
                        0.9, 1.0,       // RANSAC method
                        inliers);       // extracted inliers
```

The resulting set of inliers matches is then as follows:

As it will be explained in the next section, the essential matrix encapsulates the rotation and translation components that separate the two views. It is therefore possible to recover the relative pose between our two views directly from this matrix. OpenCV has a function that performs this operation, it is the `cv::recoverPose` function. This one is used as follows:

```
// recover relative camera pose from essential matrix
cv::Mat rotation, translation;
cv::recoverPose(essential,             // the essential matrix
                points1, points2,      // the matched keypoints
                cameraMatrix,          // matrix of intrinsics
                rotation, translation, // estimated motion
                inliers);              // inliers matches
```

Now that we have the relative pose between the two cameras, it becomes possible to estimate the location of points for which we have established correspondence between the two views. The following screenshot illustrates how this is possible. It shows the two cameras at their estimated position (the left one is placed at the origin). We also have selected a pair of corresponding points and, for these image points, we traced a ray that, according to the projective geometry model, corresponds to all possible locations of the associated 3D point:

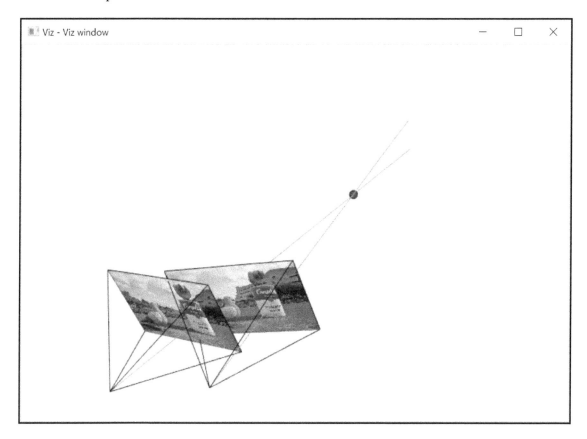

Clearly, since these two image points have been generated by the same 3D point, the two rays must intersect at one location, the location of the 3D point. The method that consists of intersecting the lines of projection of two corresponding image points, when the relative position of two cameras is known, is called **triangulation**. This process first requires the two projection matrices and can be repeated for all matches. Remember, however, that these ones must be expressed in world coordinates; this is done here by using the cv::undistortPoints function.

Finally, we call our triangulate function, which computes the position of the triangulated point, and that will be described in the next section:

```cpp
// compose projection matrix from R,T
cv::Mat projection2(3, 4, CV_64F); // the 3x4 projection matrix
rotation.copyTo(projection2(cv::Rect(0, 0, 3, 3)));
translation.copyTo(projection2.colRange(3, 4));
// compose generic projection matrix
cv::Mat projection1(3, 4, CV_64F, 0.); // the 3x4 projection matrix
cv::Mat diag(cv::Mat::eye(3, 3, CV_64F));
diag.copyTo(projection1(cv::Rect(0, 0, 3, 3)));

// to contain the inliers
std::vector<cv::Vec2d> inlierPts1;
std::vector<cv::Vec2d> inlierPts2;

// create inliers input point vector for triangulation
int j(0);
for (int i = 0; i < inliers.rows; i++) {
  if (inliers.at<uchar>(i)) {
    inlierPts1.push_back(cv::Vec2d(points1[i].x, points1[i].y));
    inlierPts2.push_back(cv::Vec2d(points2[i].x, points2[i].y));
  }
}

// undistort and normalize the image points
std::vector<cv::Vec2d> points1u;
cv::undistortPoints(inlierPts1, points1u,
                    cameraMatrix, cameraDistCoeffs);
std::vector<cv::Vec2d> points2u;
cv::undistortPoints(inlierPts2, points2u,
                    cameraMatrix, cameraDistCoeffs);

// triangulation
std::vector<cv::Vec3d> points3D;
triangulate(projection1, projection2,
            points1u, points2u, points3D);
```

A cloud of 3D points located on the surface of the scene elements is thus found:

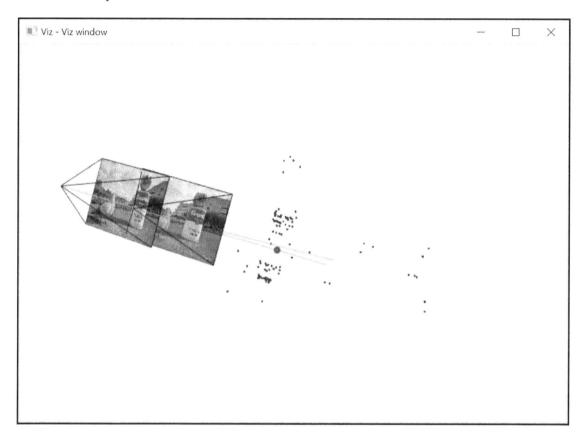

Note that from this new point of view, we can see that the two rays we drew do not intersect as they were supposed to. This fact will be discussed in the next section.

How it works...

The calibration matrix is the entity allowing us to transform pixel coordinates into world coordinates. We can then more easily relate image points to the 3D points that have produced them. This is demonstrated in the following figure, which we will now use to demonstrate a simple relationship between a world point and its images:

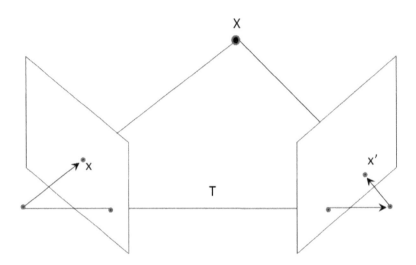

The figure shows two cameras separated by a rotation R and a translation T. It is interesting to note that the translation vector T joins the centers of projection of the two cameras. We also have a vector x joining the first camera center to an image point and a vector x' joining the second camera center to the corresponding image point. Since we have the relative motion between the two cameras, we can express the orientation of x in terms of the second camera reference as Rx. Now, if you carefully observe the geometry of the image points shown, you will observe that vectors T, Rx, and x' are all coplanar. This fact can be expressed by the following mathematical relation:

$$x'.(T \times Rx) = x'Ex = 0$$

It was possible to reduce the first relation to a single 3x3 matrix E because a cross-product can also be expressed by a matrix operation. This matrix E is called the essential matrix and the associated equation is the calibrated equivalent of the epipolar constraint presented in the *Computing the fundamental matrix of an image pair* recipe in Chapter 10, *Estimating Projective Relations in Images*. We can then estimate this one from image correspondences, as we did for the fundamental matrix, but this time expressing these ones in world coordinates. Also, as demonstrated, the essential matrix is built from the rotation and translation components of the motion between the two cameras. This means that once this one has been estimated, it can be decomposed to obtain the relative pose between the cameras. This is what we did by using the cv::recoverPose function. This function calls the cv::decomposeEssentialMat function, which produces four possible solutions for the relative pose. The right one is identified by looking at the set of provided matches to determine the solution that is physically possible.

Once the relative pose between the cameras has been obtained, the position of any point corresponding to a match pair is recovered through triangulation. Different methods have been proposed to solve the triangulation problem. Probably the simplest solution consists of considering the two projection matrices, P and P'. The seek 3D point in homogenous coordinates can be expressed as X=[X,Y,Z,1]^T, and we know that x=PX and x'=P'X. Each of these two homogenous equations brings two independent equations, which is sufficient to solve the three unknowns of the 3D point position. This over determined system of equation can be solved using a least-square approach, which can be accomplished using a convenient OpenCV utility function called cv::solve. The complete function is as follows:

```
// triangulate using Linear LS-Method
cv::Vec3d triangulate(const cv::Mat &p1,
                      const cv::Mat &p2,
                      const cv::Vec2d &u1,
                      const cv::Vec2d &u2) {

    // system of equations assuming image=[u,v] and X=[x,y,z,1]
    // from u(p3.X)= p1.X and v(p3.X)=p2.X
    cv::Matx43d A(u1(0)*p1.at<double>(2, 0) - p1.at<double>(0, 0),
                  u1(0)*p1.at<double>(2, 1) - p1.at<double>(0, 1),
                  u1(0)*p1.at<double>(2, 2) - p1.at<double>(0, 2),
                  u1(1)*p1.at<double>(2, 0) - p1.at<double>(1, 0),
                  u1(1)*p1.at<double>(2, 1) - p1.at<double>(1, 1),
                  u1(1)*p1.at<double>(2, 2) - p1.at<double>(1, 2),
                  u2(0)*p2.at<double>(2, 0) - p2.at<double>(0, 0),
                  u2(0)*p2.at<double>(2, 1) - p2.at<double>(0, 1),
                  u2(0)*p2.at<double>(2, 2) - p2.at<double>(0, 2),
                  u2(1)*p2.at<double>(2, 0) - p2.at<double>(1, 0),
                  u2(1)*p2.at<double>(2, 1) - p2.at<double>(1, 1),
                  u2(1)*p2.at<double>(2, 2) - p2.at<double>(1, 2));
```

```
        cv::Matx41d B(p1.at<double>(0, 3) - u1(0)*p1.at<double>(2, 3),
                      p1.at<double>(1, 3) - u1(1)*p1.at<double>(2, 3),
                      p2.at<double>(0, 3) - u2(0)*p2.at<double>(2, 3),
                      p2.at<double>(1, 3) - u2(1)*p2.at<double>(2, 3));

        // X contains the 3D coordinate of the reconstructed point
        cv::Vec3d X;
        // solve AX=B
        cv::solve(A, B, X, cv::DECOMP_SVD);
        return X;
    }
```

We have noted in the previous section that very often, because of noise and digitization, the projection lines that should normally intersect do not intersect in practice. The least-square solution will therefore find a solution somewhere around the point of intersection. Also, this method will not work if you try to reconstruct a point at infinity. This is because, for such a point, the fourth element of the homogenous coordinates should be at 0 not at 1 as assumed.

Finally, it is important to understand that this 3D reconstruction is done up to a scale factor only. If you need to make real measurements, you need to know at least one physical distance, for example, the real distance between the two cameras or the height of one of the visible objects.

There's more...

The 3D reconstruction is a rich field of research in computer vision, and there is much more to explore in the OpenCV library on the subject.

Decomposing a homography

We learned in this recipe that an essential matrix can be decomposed in order to recover the rotation and translation between two cameras. We also learned in the previous chapter that a homography exists between two views of a plane. In this case, this homography contains also the rotational and translational components. In addition, it contains information about the plane, namely its normal with respect to each camera. The function cv::decomposeHomographyMat can be used to decompose this matrix; the condition, however, is to have a calibrated camera.

Bundle adjustment

In this recipe, we first estimate the camera position from matches and then reconstruct the associated 3D points through triangulation. It is possible to generalize this process by using any number of views. For each of these views, feature points are detected and are matched with the other views. Using this information, it is possible to write equations that relate the rotations and translations between the views, the set of 3D points and the calibration information. All these unknowns can be optimized together through a large optimization process that aims at minimizing the reprojection errors of all points in each view where they are visible. This combined optimization procedure is called **bundle adjustment**. Have a look at the `cv::detail::BundleAdjusterReproj` class, which implements a camera parameters refinement algorithm that minimizes the sum of the reprojection error squares.

See also

- *Triangulation* by *R. Hartley* and *P. Sturm* in *Computer Vision and Image Understanding vol. 68*, no. 2, 1997 presents a formal analysis of different triangulation methods
- *Modeling the World from Internet Photo Collections* by *N. Snavely, S.M. Seitz*, and *R. Szeliski* in *International Journal of Computer Vision,* vol. 80, no 2, 2008 describes a large-scale application of 3D reconstruction through bundle adjustment

Computing depth from stereo image

Humans view the world in three dimensions using their two eyes. Robots can do the same when they are equipped with two cameras. This is called **stereovision**. A stereo rig is a pair of cameras mounted on a device, looking at the same scene and separated by a fixed baseline (distance between the two cameras). This recipe will show you how a depth map can be computed from two stereo images by computing dense correspondence between the two views.

Getting ready

A stereovision system is generally made of two side-by-side cameras looking at the same direction. The following figure illustrates such a stereo system in a perfectly aligned configuration:

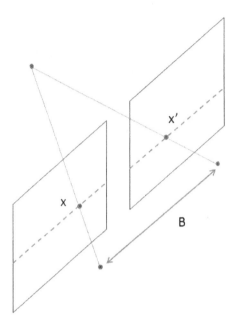

Under this ideal configuration the cameras are only separated by a horizontal translation and therefore all epipolar lines are horizontal. This means that corresponding points have the same y coordinates, which reduces the search for matches to a 1D line. The difference in their x coordinates depends on the depth of the points. Points at infinity have image points at the same (x, y) coordinates and the closer the points are to the stereo rig the greater will be the difference of their x coordinates. This fact can be demonstrated formally by looking at the projective equation. When cameras are separated by a pure horizontal translation, then the projective equation of the second camera (the one on the right) becomes this:

$$
s \begin{bmatrix} x' \\ y' \\ 1 \end{bmatrix} = \begin{bmatrix} f & 0 & u_0 \\ 0 & f & v_0 \\ 0 & 0 & 1 \end{bmatrix} \begin{bmatrix} 1 & 0 & 0 & -B \\ 0 & 1 & 0 & 0 \\ 0 & 0 & 1 & 0 \end{bmatrix} \begin{bmatrix} X \\ Y \\ Z \\ 1 \end{bmatrix}
$$

Here, for simplicity, we assume square pixels and same calibration parameters for both cameras. Now if you compute the difference of x–x' (do not forget to divide by s to normalize the homogenous coordinates) and isolate the z coordinate, you obtain the following:

$$Z = f\frac{\left(x - x'\right)}{B}$$

The term (x–x') is called the **disparity**. To compute the depth map of a stereovision system, the disparity of each pixel must be estimated. This recipe will show you how to do it.

How to do it...

The ideal configuration shown in the previous section is, in practice, very difficult to realize. Even if they are accurately positioned, the cameras of the stereo rig will unavoidably include some extra translational and rotational components. But, fortunately, the images can be rectified such to produce horizontal epilines. This can be achieved by computing the fundamental matrix of the stereo system using, for example, the robust matching algorithm of the previous chapter. This is what we did for the following stereo pair (with some epipolar lines drawn on it):

OpenCV offers a rectifying function that uses a homographic transformation to project the image plane of each camera onto perfectly aligned virtual plane. This transformation is computed from a set of matched points and a fundamental matrix. Once computed, these homographies are then used to wrap the images:

```
// Compute homographic rectification
cv::Mat h1, h2;
cv::stereoRectifyUncalibrated(points1, points2,
                              fundamental,
                              image1.size(), h1, h2);

// Rectify the images through warping
cv::Mat rectified1;
cv::warpPerspective(image1, rectified1, h1, image1.size());
cv::Mat rectified2;
cv::warpPerspective(image2, rectified2, h2, image1.size());
```

For our example, the rectified image pair is as follows:

Computing the disparity map can then be accomplished using methods that assume parallelism of the cameras (and consequently horizontal epipolar lines):

```
// Compute disparity
cv::Mat disparity;
cv::Ptr<cv::StereoMatcher> pStereo =
    cv::StereoSGBM::create(0,    // minimum disparity
                           32,   // maximum disparity
                           5);   // block size
pStereo->compute(rectified1, rectified2, disparity);
```

The obtained disparity map can then be displayed as an image. Bright values correspond to high disparities and, from what we learned earlier in this recipe, those high disparity values correspond to proximal objects:

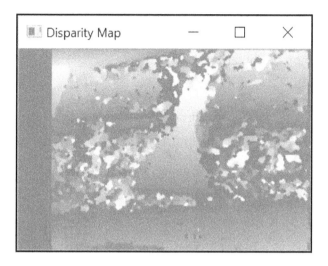

The quality of the computed disparity mainly depends on the appearance of the different objects that compose the scene. Highly-textured regions tend to produce more accurate disparity estimates since they can be non-ambiguously matched. Also, a larger baseline increases the range of detectable depth values. However, enlarging the baseline also makes disparity computation more complex and less reliable.

How it works...

Computing disparities is a pixel matching exercise. We already mentioned that when the images are properly rectified, the search space is conveniently aligned with the image rows. The difficulty, however, is that, in stereovision, we are generally seeking a dense disparity map, that is, we want to match every pixel of one image with the pixels of the other image.

This can be more challenging than selecting a few distinctive points in an image and finding their corresponding points in the other image. Disparity computation is therefore a complex process that is generally composed of four steps:

1. Matching cost calculation.
2. Cost aggregation.
3. Disparity computation and optimization.
4. Disparity refinement.

These steps are detailed in the next paragraph.

Assigning a disparity to one pixel, is putting a pair of points in correspondence in a stereo set. Finding the best disparity map is often posed as an optimization problem. With this perspective, matching two points has a cost that must be computed following a defined metric. This can be, for example, a simple absolute or squared difference of intensities, colors or gradients. In the search for an optimal solution, the matching cost is generally aggregated over a region in order to cope with noise local ambiguity. The global disparity map can then be estimated by evaluating an energy function that includes terms to smooth the disparity map, take into account any possible occlusion, and enforce a uniqueness constraint. Finally, a post-processing step is often applied in order to refine the disparity estimates during which, for example, planar regions are detected or depth discontinuities are detected.

OpenCV implements a number of disparity computation methods. Here, we used the `cv::StereoSGBM` approach. The simplest method is `cv::StereoBM`, which is based on block matching.

Finally, it should be noted that a more accurate rectification can be performed if you are ready to undergo a full calibration process. The `cv::stereoCalibrate` and `cv::stereoRectify` functions are in this case used in conjunction with a calibration pattern. The rectification mapping then computes new projection matrices for the cameras instead of simple homographies.

See also

- The article *A Taxonomy and Evaluation of Dense two-Frame Stereo Correspondence Algorithms* by *D. Scharstein* and *R. Szeliski* in *International Journal of Computer Vision,* vol. 47, 2002 is a classic reference on disparity computation methods
- The article *Stereo processing by semiglobal matching and mutual information* by *H. Hirschmuller* in *IEEE Transactions on Pattern Analysis and Machine Intelligence,* vol. 30, no 2, pp. 328-341, 2008 describes the approach used for computing the disparity in this recipe

12
Processing Video Sequences

In this chapter, we will cover the following recipes:

- Reading video sequences
- Processing the video frames
- Writing video sequences
- Extracting the foreground objects in a video

Introduction

Video signals constitute a rich source of visual information. They are made of a sequence of images, called **frames**, that are taken at regular time intervals (specified as the **frame rate**, generally expressed in frames per second) and show a scene in motion. With the advent of powerful computers, it is now possible to perform advanced visual analysis on video sequences-sometimes at rates close to, or even faster than, the actual video frame rate. This chapter will show you how to read, process, and store video sequences.

We will see that once the individual frames of a video sequence have been extracted, the different image processing functions presented in this book can be applied to each of them. In addition, we will also look at algorithms that perform a temporal analysis of the video sequence, comparing adjacent frames and accumulating image statistics over time in order to extract foreground objects.

Reading video sequences

In order to process a video sequence, we need to be able to read each of its frames. OpenCV has put in place an easy-to-use framework that can help us perform frame extraction from video files or even from USB or IP cameras. This recipe shows you how to use it.

How to do it...

Basically, all you need to do in order to read the frames of a video sequence is create an instance of the cv::VideoCapture class. You then create a loop that will extract and read each video frame. Here is a basic main function that displays the frames of a video sequence:

```cpp
int main()
{
  // Open the video file
  cv::VideoCapture capture("bike.avi");
  // check if video successfully opened
  if (!capture.isOpened())
    return 1;

  // Get the frame rate
  double rate= capture.get(CV_CAP_PROP_FPS);

  bool stop(false);
  cv::Mat frame;    // current video frame
  cv::namedWindow("Extracted Frame");

  // Delay between each frame in ms
  // corresponds to video frame rate
  int delay= 1000/rate;

  // for all frames in video
  while (!stop) {

    // read next frame if any
    if (!capture.read(frame))
      break;

    cv::imshow("Extracted Frame",frame);

    // introduce a delay
    // or press key to stop
    if (cv::waitKey(delay)>=0)
      stop= true;
```

```
    }

    // Close the video file.
    // Not required since called by destructor
    capture.release();
    return 0;
}
```

A window will appear on which the video will play as shown in the following screenshot:

How it works...

To open a video, you simply need to specify the video filename. This can be done by providing the name of the file in the constructor of the cv::VideoCapture object. It is also possible to use the open method if the cv::VideoCapture object has already been created. Once the video is successfully opened (this can be verified through the isOpened method), it is possible to start frame extraction. It is also possible to query the cv::VideoCapture object for information associated with the video file by using its get method with the appropriate flag. In the preceding example, we obtained the frame rate using the CV_CAP_PROP_FPS flag. Since it is a generic function, it always returns a double even if another type would be expected in some cases. For example, the total number of frames in the video file would be obtained (as an integer) as follows:

```
long t= static_cast<long>( capture.get(CV_CAP_PROP_FRAME_COUNT));
```

Have a look at the different flags that are available in the OpenCV documentation in order to find out what information can be obtained from the video.

There is also a `set` method that allows you to input parameters into the `cv::VideoCapture` instance. For example, you can request to move to a specific frame using the `CV_CAP_PROP_POS_FRAMES` flag:

```
// goto frame 100
double position= 100.0;
capture.set(CV_CAP_PROP_POS_FRAMES, position);
```

You can also specify the position in milliseconds using `CV_CAP_PROP_POS_MSEC`, or you can specify the relative position inside the video using `CV_CAP_PROP_POS_AVI_RATIO` (with `0.0` corresponding to the beginning of the video and `1.0` to the end). The method returns `true` if the requested parameter setting is successful. Note that the possibility to get or set a particular video parameter largely depends on the codec that is used to compress and store the video sequence. If you are unsuccessful with some parameters, that could be simply due to the specific codec you are using.

Once the captured video is successfully opened, the frames can be sequentially obtained by repetitively calling the `read` method, as we did in the example of the previous section. One can equivalently call the overloaded reading operator:

```
capture >> frame;
```

It is also possible to call the two basic methods:

```
capture.grab();
capture.retrieve(frame);
```

Also note how, in our example, we introduced a delay in displaying each frame. This is done using the `cv::waitKey` function. Here, we set the delay at a value that corresponds to the input video frame rate (if `fps` is the number of frames per second, then `1/fps` is the delay between two frames in milliseconds). You can obviously change this value to display the video at a slower or faster speed. However, if you are going to display the video frames, it is important that you insert such a delay if you want to make sure that the window has sufficient time to refresh (since it is a process of low priority, it will never refresh if the CPU is too busy). The `cv::waitKey` function also allows us to interrupt the reading process by pressing any key. In this case, the function returns the ASCII code of the key that is pressed. Note that, if the delay specified to the `cv::waitKey` function is 0, then it will wait indefinitely for the user to press a key. This is very useful if someone wants to trace a process by examining the results frame by frame.

The final statement calls the `release` method, which will close the video file. However, this call is not required since `release` is also called by the `cv::VideoCapture` destructor.

It is important to note that in order to open the specified video file, your computer must have the corresponding codec installed; otherwise, `cv::VideoCapture` will not be able to decode the input file. Normally, if you are able to open your video file with a video player on your machine (such as Windows Media Player), then OpenCV should also be able to read this file.

There's more...

You can also read the video stream produced by a camera that is connected to your computer (a USB camera, for example). In this case, you simply specify an ID number (an integer) instead of a filename to the `open` function. Specifying `0` for the ID will open the default installed camera. In this case, the role of the `cv::waitKey` function that stops the processing becomes essential, since the video stream from the camera will be infinitely read.

Finally, it is also possible to load a video from the Web. In this case, all you have to do is provide the correct address, for example:

```
cv::VideoCapture capture("http://www.laganiere.name/bike.avi");
```

See also

- The *Writing video sequences* recipe in this chapter has more information on video codecs.
- The `http://ffmpeg.org/` website presents a complete open source and cross-platform solution for audio/video reading, recording, converting, and streaming. The OpenCV classes that manipulate video files are built on top of this library.

Processing the video frames

In this recipe, our objective is to apply some processing functions to each of the frames of a video sequence. We will do this by encapsulating the OpenCV video capture framework into our own class. Among other things, this class will allow us to specify a function that will be called each time a new frame is extracted.

How to do it...

What we want is to be able to specify a processing function (a **callback function**) that will be called for each frame of a video sequence. This function can be defined as receiving a `cv::Mat` instance and outputting a processed frame. Therefore, in our framework, the processing function must have the following signature to be a valid callback:

```
void processFrame(cv::Mat& img, cv::Mat& out);
```

As an example of such a processing function, consider the following simple function that computes the Canny edges of an input image:

```
void canny(cv::Mat& img, cv::Mat& out) {
  // Convert to gray
  if (img.channels()==3)
    cv::cvtColor(img,out, cv::COLOR_BGR2GRAY);
  // Compute Canny edges
  cv::Canny(out,out,100,200);
  // Invert the image
  cv::threshold(out,out,128,255,cv::THRESH_BINARY_INV);
}
```

Our `VideoProcessor` class encapsulates all aspects of a video-processing task. Using this class, the procedure will be to create a class instance, specify an input video file, attach the callback function to it, and then start the process. Programmatically, these steps are accomplished using our proposed class, as follows:

```
// Create instance
VideoProcessor processor;
// Open video file
processor.setInput("bike.avi");
// Declare a window to display the video
processor.displayInput("Current Frame");
processor.displayOutput("Output Frame");
// Play the video at the original frame rate
processor.setDelay(1000./processor.getFrameRate());
// Set the frame processor callback function
processor.setFrameProcessor(canny);
// Start the process
processor.run();
```

If this code is run, then two windows will play the input video and the output result at the original frame rate (a consequence of the delay introduced by the `setDelay` method). For example, considering the input video for which a frame is shown in the previous recipe, the output window will look as follows:

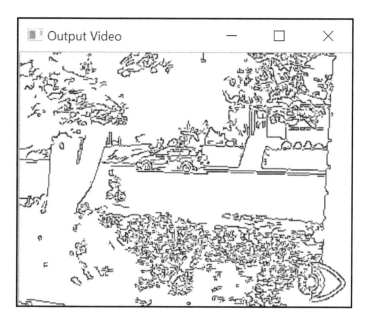

How it works...

As we did in other recipes, our objective was to create a class that encapsulates the common functionalities of a video-processing algorithm. As one might expect, the class includes several member variables that control the different aspects of the video frame processing:

```
class VideoProcessor {

  private:

    // the OpenCV video capture object
    cv::VideoCapture capture;
    // the callback function to be called
    // for the processing of each frame
    void (*process)(cv::Mat&, cv::Mat&);
    // a bool to determine if the
    // process callback will be called
    bool callIt;
    // Input display window name
```

```
std::string windowNameInput;
// Output display window name
std::string windowNameOutput;
// delay between each frame processing
int delay;
// number of processed frames
long fnumber;
// stop at this frame number
long frameToStop;
// to stop the processing
bool stop;
```

The first member variable is the cv::VideoCapture object. The second attribute is the process function pointer that will point to the callback function. This function can be specified using the corresponding setter method:

```
// set the callback function that
// will be called for each frame
void setFrameProcessor(void (*frameProcessingCallback)
                            (cv::Mat&, cv::Mat&)) {

  process= frameProcessingCallback;
}
```

The following method opens the video file:

```
//set the name of the video file
bool setInput(std::string filename) {

  fnumber= 0;
  // In case a resource was already
  // associated with the VideoCapture instance
  capture.release();
  // Open the video file
  return capture.open(filename);
}
```

It is generally interesting to display the frames as they are processed. Therefore, two methods are used to create the display windows:

```
// to display the input frames
void displayInput(std::string wn) {

  windowNameInput= wn;
  cv::namedWindow(windowNameInput);
}
// to display the processed frames
void displayOutput(std::string wn) {
```

```
      windowNameOutput= wn;
      cv::namedWindow(windowNameOutput);
   }
```

The main method, called `run`, is the one that contains the frame extraction loop:

```
// to grab (and process) the frames of the sequence
void run() {
  // current frame
  cv::Mat frame;
  //output frame
  cv::Mat output;

  // if no capture device has been set
  if (!isOpened())
    return;

    stop= false;
  while (!isStopped()) {
    // read next frame if any
    if (!readNextFrame(frame))
      break;
    // display input frame
    if (windowNameInput.length()!=0)
      cv::imshow(windowNameInput,frame);

     // calling the process function
    if (callIt) {

      //process the frame
      process(frame, output);
      //increment frame number
      fnumber++;

    }
    else {
      // no processing
      output= frame;
    }

    // display output frame
    if (windowNameOutput.length()!=0)
      cv::imshow(windowNameOutput,output);
      // introduce a delay
      if (delay>=0 && cv::waitKey(delay)>=0)
        stopIt();

      // check if we should stop
```

```
        if (frameToStop>=0 && getFrameNumber()==frameToStop)
          stopIt();
      }
  }

  // Stop the processing
  void stopIt() {
    stop= true;
  }

  // Is the process stopped?
  bool isStopped() {
    return stop;
  }

  // Is a capture device opened?
  bool isOpened() {
    capture.isOpened();
  }

  // set a delay between each frame
  // 0 means wait at each frame
  // negative means no delay
  void setDelay(int d) {
    delay= d;
  }
```

This method uses a `private` method that reads the frames:

```
  // to get the next frame
  // could be: video file or camera
  bool readNextFrame(cv::Mat& frame) {
    return capture.read(frame);
  }
```

The `run` method proceeds by first calling the read method of the `cv::VideoCapture` class. There is then a series of operations that are executed, but before each of them is invoked, a check is made to determine whether it has been requested. The input window is displayed only if an input window name has been specified (using the `displayInput` method); the callback function is called only if one has been specified (using the `setFrameProcessor` method). The output window is displayed only if an output window name has been defined (using `displayOutput`); a delay is introduced only if one has been specified (using the `setDelay` method). Finally, the current frame number is checked if a stop frame has been defined (using the `stopAtFrameNo` method).

One might also wish to simply open and play the video file (without calling the callback function). Therefore, we have two methods that specify whether or not we want the callback function to be called:

```
// process callback to be called
void callProcess() {
  callIt= true;
}

// do not call process callback
void dontCallProcess() {
  callIt= false;
}
```

Finally, the class also offers the possibility to stop at a certain frame number:

```
void stopAtFrameNo(long frame) {
  frameToStop= frame;
}

// return the frame number of the next frame
long getFrameNumber() {
  // get info of from the capture device
  long fnumber= static_cast<long>(capture.get(CV_CAP_PROP_POS_FRAMES));
  return fnumber;
}
```

The class also contains a number of getter and setter methods that are basically just a wrapper over the general `set` and `get` methods of the `cv::VideoCapture` framework.

There's more...

Our `VideoProcessor` class is there to facilitate the deployment of a video-processing module. A few additional refinements can be made to it.

Processing a sequence of images

Sometimes, the input sequence is made of a series of images that are individually stored in distinct files. Our class can be easily modified to accommodate such input. You just need to add a member variable that will hold a vector of image filenames and its corresponding iterator:

```
// vector of image filename to be used as input
std::vector<std::string> images;
```

```
// image vector iterator
std::vector<std::string>::const_iterator itImg;
```

A new `setInput` method is used to specify the filenames to be read:

```
// set the vector of input images
bool setInput(const std::vector<std::string>& imgs) {
  fnumber= 0;
  // In case a resource was already
  // associated with the VideoCapture instance
  capture.release();

  // the input will be this vector of images
  images= imgs;
  itImg= images.begin();
  return true;
}
```

The `isOpened` method becomes as follows:

```
// Is a capture device opened?
bool isOpened() {
  return capture.isOpened() || !images.empty();
}
```

The last method that needs to be modified is the private `readNextFrame` method that will read from the video or from the vector of filenames, depending on the input that has been specified. The test is that if the vector of image filenames is not empty, then that is because the input is an image sequence. The call to `setInput` with a video filename clears this vector:

```
// to get the next frame
// could be: video file; camera; vector of images
bool readNextFrame(cv::Mat& frame) {

  if (images.size()==0)
    return capture.read(frame);

  else {
    if (itImg != images.end()) {
      frame= cv::imread(*itImg);
      itImg++;
      return frame.data != 0;
    } else

      return false;
  }
}
```

Using a frame processor class

In an object-oriented context, it might make more sense to use a frame processing class instead of a frame processing function. Indeed, a class would give the programmer much more flexibility in the definition of a video-processing algorithm. We can, therefore, define an interface that any class that wishes to be used inside the `VideoProcessor` will need to implement:

```
// The frame processor interface
class FrameProcessor {
  public:
  // processing method
  virtual void process(cv:: Mat &input, cv:: Mat &output)= 0;
};
```

A setter method allows you to input a `FrameProcessor` instance to the `VideoProcessor` framework and assign it to the added `FrameProcessor` member variable that is defined as a pointer to a `FrameProcessor` object:

```
// set the instance of the class that
// implements the FrameProcessor interface
void setFrameProcessor(FrameProcessor* frameProcessorPtr) {
  // invalidate callback function
  process= 0;
  // this is the frame processor instance
  // that will be called
  frameProcessor= frameProcessorPtr;
  callProcess();
}
```

When a frame `processor` class instance is specified, it invalidates any frame processing function that could have been set previously. The same obviously applies if a frame processing function is specified instead. The `while` loop of the `run` method is modified to take into account this modification:

```
while (!isStopped()) {

  // read next frame if any
  if (!readNextFrame(frame))
    break;

  // display input frame
  if (windowNameInput.length()!=0)
    cv::imshow(windowNameInput,frame);

  //** calling the process function or method **
```

```
      if (callIt) {

        // process the frame
        if (process) // if call back function
          process(frame, output);
        else if (frameProcessor)
          // if class interface instance
          frameProcessor->process(frame,output);
        // increment frame number
        fnumber++;
      }
      else {
        output= frame;
      }
      // display output frame
      if (windowNameOutput.length()!=0)
        cv::imshow(windowNameOutput,output);
      // introduce a delay
      if (delay>=0 && cv::waitKey(delay)>=0)
        stopIt();
      // check if we should stop
      if (frameToStop>=0 && getFrameNumber()==frameToStop)
        stopIt();
  }
```

See also

- The *Tracking feature points in a video* recipe of `Chapter 13`, *Tracking Visual Motion*, gives you an example of how to use the `FrameProcessor` class interface
- The GitHub project at `https://github.com/asolis/vivaVideo` presents a more sophisticated framework for processing video with multithreading in OpenCV

Writing video sequences

In the previous recipes, we learned how to read a video file and extract its frames. This recipe will show you how to write frames and, therefore, create a video file. This will allow us to complete the typical video-processing chain: reading an input video stream, processing its frames, and then storing the results in a new video file.

How to do it...

Writing video files in OpenCV is done using the `cv::VideoWriter` class. An instance is constructed by specifying the filename, the frame rate at which the generated video should play, the size of each frame, and whether or not the video will be created in color:

```
writer.open(outputFile,    // filename
            codec,         // codec to be used
            framerate,     // frame rate of the video
            frameSize,     // frame size
            isColor);      // color video?
```

In addition, you must specify the way you want the video data to be saved. This is the `codec` argument; this will be discussed at the end of this recipe.

Once the video file is opened, frames can be added to it by repetitively calling the `write` method:

```
writer.write(frame);   // add the frame to the video file
```

Using the `cv::VideoWriter` class, our `VideoProcessor` class introduced in the previous recipe can easily be expanded in order to give it the ability to write video files. A simple program that will read a video, process it, and write the result to a video file would then be written as follows:

```
// Create instance
VideoProcessor processor;

// Open video file
processor.setInput("bike.avi");
processor.setFrameProcessor(canny);
processor.setOutput("bikeOut.avi");
// Start the process
processor.run();
```

Proceeding as we did in the preceding recipe, we also want to give the user the possibility to write the frames as individual images. In our framework, we adopt a naming convention that consists of a prefix name followed by a number made of a given number of digits. This number is automatically incremented as frames are saved. Then, to save the output result as a series of images, you would swap the preceding statement with this one:

```
processor.setOutput("bikeOut",  //prefix
                    ".jpg",     // extension
                    3,          // number of digits
                    0);         // starting index
```

Using the specified number of digits, this call will create the `bikeOut000.jpg`, `bikeOut001.jpg`, and `bikeOut002.jpg` files, and so on.

How it works...

Let's now describe how to modify our `VideoProcessor` class in order to give it the ability to write video files. First, a `cv::VideoWriter` variable member must be added to our class (plus a few other attributes):

```cpp
class VideoProcessor {

  private:

    // the OpenCV video writer object
    cv::VideoWriter writer;
    // output filename
    std::string outputFile;
    // current index for output images
    int currentIndex;
    // number of digits in output image filename
    int digits;
    // extension of output images
    std::string extension;
```

An extra method is used to specify (and open) the output video file:

```cpp
    // set the output video file
    // by default the same parameters than
    // input video will be used
    bool setOutput(const std::string &filename, int codec=0,
                   double framerate=0.0, bool isColor=true) {

      outputFile= filename;
      extension.clear();
      if (framerate==0.0)
        framerate= getFrameRate(); // same as input

      char c[4];
      // use same codec as input
      if (codec==0) {
        codec= getCodec(c);
      }

      // Open output video
      return writer.open(outputFile,      // filename
                         codec,           // codec to be used
```

```
                framerate,        // frame rate of the video
                getFrameSize(),   // frame size
                isColor);         // color video?
}
```

A private method, called the `writeNextFrame` method, handles the frame writing procedure (in a video file or as a series of images):

```
// to write the output frame
// could be: video file or images
void writeNextFrame(cv::Mat& frame) {
  if (extension.length()) { // then we write images

    std::stringstream ss;
    // compose the output filename
    ss << outputFile << std::setfill('0')
       << std::setw(digits) << currentIndex++ << extension;
    cv::imwrite(ss.str(),frame);
  } else {
    // then write to video file
    writer.write(frame);
  }
}
```

For the case where the output is made of individual image files, we need an additional setter method:

```
// set the output as a series of image files
// extension must be ".jpg", ".bmp"
bool setOutput(const std::string &filename, // prefix
               const std::string &ext,      // image file extension
               int numberOfDigits=3,        // number of digits
               int startIndex=0) {          // start index

  // number of digits must be positive
  if (numberOfDigits<0)
    return false;

  // filenames and their common extension
  outputFile= filename;
  extension= ext;

  // number of digits in the file numbering scheme
  digits= numberOfDigits;
  // start numbering at this index
  currentIndex= startIndex;

  return true;
```

```
        }
```

Finally, a new step is then added to the video capture loop of the `run` method:

```
while (!isStopped()) {

  // read next frame if any
  if (!readNextFrame(frame))
    break;

  // display input frame
  if (windowNameInput.length()!=0)
    cv::imshow(windowNameInput,frame);

  // calling the process function or method
  if (callIt) {

    // process the frame
    if (process)
      process(frame, output);
    else if (frameProcessor)
      frameProcessor->process(frame,output);
    // increment frame number
    fnumber++;
  } else {
    output= frame;
  }

  //** write output sequence **
  if (outputFile.length()!=0)
    writeNextFrame(output);
  // display output frame
  if (windowNameOutput.length()!=0)
    cv::imshow(windowNameOutput,output);
  // introduce a delay
  if (delay>=0 && cv::waitKey(delay)>=0)
    stopIt();

  // check if we should stop
  if (frameToStop>=0 && getFrameNumber()==frameToStop)
    stopIt();
  }
}
```

There's more...

When a video is written to a file, it is saved using a codec. A **codec** is a software module that is capable of encoding and decoding video streams. The codec defines both the format of the file and the compression scheme that is used to store the information. Obviously, a video that has been encoded using a given codec must be decoded with the same codec. For this reason, four-character codes have been introduced to uniquely identify codecs. This way, when a software tool needs to write a video file, it determines the codec to be used by reading the specified four-character code.

The codec four-character code

As the name suggests, the four-character code is made up of four ASCII characters that can also be converted into an integer by appending them together. Using the cv::CAP_PROP_FOURCC flag of the get method of an opened cv::VideoCapture instance, you can obtain the code of an opened video file. We can define a method in our VideoProcessor class to return the four-character code of an input video:

```
// get the codec of input video
int getCodec(char codec[4]) {
  // undefined for vector of images
  if (images.size()!=0) return -1;
  union { // data structure for the 4-char code
    nt value;
    char code[4];
  } returned;

  // get the code
  returned.value= static_cast<int>(capture.get(cv::CAP_PROP_FOURCC));
  // get the 4 characters
  codec[0]= returned.code[0];
  codec[1]= returned.code[1];
  codec[2]= returned.code[2];
  codec[3]= returned.code[3];

  // return the int value corresponding to the code
  return returned.value;
}
```

The `get` method always returns a `double` value that is then casted into an `integer`. This integer represents the code from which the four characters can be extracted using a `union` data structure. If we open our test video sequence, then we have the following statements:

```
char codec[4];
processor.getCodec(codec);
std::cout << "Codec: " << codec[0] << codec[1]
          << codec[2] << codec[3] << std::endl;
```

From the preceding statements, we obtain, for our example, the following:

```
Codec : XVID
```

When a video file is written, the codec must be specified using its four-character code. This is the second parameter in the `open` method of the `cv::VideoWriter` class. You can use, for example, the same one as the input video (this is the default option in our `setOutput` method). You can also pass the value `-1` and the method will pop up a window that will ask you to select one codec from the list of available codecs. The list you will see in this window corresponds to the list of installed codecs on your machine. The code of the selected codec is then automatically sent to the `open` method.

See also

- The `https://www.xvid.com/` website offers you an open source video codec library based on the MPEG-4 standard for video compression. **Xvid** also has a competitor called **DivX**, which offers proprietary but free codec and software tools.

Extracting the foreground objects in a video

This chapter is about reading, writing, and processing video sequences. The objective is to be able to analyze a complete video sequence. As an example, in this recipe, you will learn how to perform temporal analysis of a sequence in order to extract the moving foreground objects. Indeed, when a fixed camera observes a scene, the background remains mostly unchanged. In this case, the interesting elements are the moving objects that evolve inside this scene. In order to extract these foreground objects, we need to build a model of the background, and then compare this model with a current frame in order to detect any foreground objects. This is what we will do in this recipe. Foreground extraction is a fundamental step in intelligent surveillance applications.

If we had an image of the background of the scene (that is, a frame that contains no foreground objects) at our disposal, then it would be easy to extract the foreground of a current frame through a simple image difference:

```
// compute difference between current image and background
cv::absdiff(backgroundImage,currentImage,foreground);
```

Each pixel for which this difference is high enough would then be declared as a foreground pixel. However, most of the time, this background image is not readily available. Indeed, it could be difficult to guarantee that no foreground objects are present in a given image, and in busy scenes, such situations might rarely occur. Moreover, the background scene often evolves over time because, for instance, the lighting condition changes (for example, from sunrise to sunset) or because new objects are added or removed from the background.

Therefore, it is necessary to dynamically build a model of the background scene. This can be done by observing the scene for a period of time. If we assume that most often, the background is visible at each pixel location, then it could be a good strategy to simply compute the average of all of the observations. However, this is not feasible for a number of reasons. First, this would require a large number of images to be stored before computing the background. Second, while we are accumulating images to compute our average image, no foreground extraction is done. This solution also raises the problem of when and how many images should be accumulated to compute an acceptable background model. In addition, the images where a given pixel is observing a foreground object would have an impact on the computation of the average background.

A better strategy is to dynamically build the background model by regularly updating it. This can be accomplished by computing what is called a **running average** (also called **moving average**). This is a way to compute the average value of a temporal signal that takes into account the latest received values. If p_t is the pixel value at a given time t and μ_{t-1} is the current average value, then this average is updated using the following formula:

$$\mu_t = \left(1 - \alpha\right)\mu_{t-1} + \alpha p_t$$

The α parameter is called the **learning rate**, and it defines the influence of the current value over the currently estimated average. The larger this value is, the faster the running average will adapt to changes in the observed values but, at the same time, slowly moving objects will tend to disappear in the background when the learning rate is set too high. In fact, the appropriate learning rate largely depends on the dynamic of the scene. To build a background model, one just has to compute a running average for every pixel of the incoming frames. The decision to declare a foreground pixel is then simply based on the difference between the current image and the background model.

How to do it...

Let's build a class that will learn a background model using a moving average and that will extract foreground objects by subtraction. The required attributes are as follows:

```
class BGFGSegmentor : public FrameProcessor {
  cv::Mat gray;           // current gray-level image
  cv::Mat background;     // accumulated background
  cv::Mat backImage;      // current background image
  cv::Mat foreground;     // foreground image
  // learning rate in background accumulation
  double learningRate;
  int threshold;          // threshold for foreground extraction
```

The main process consists of comparing the current frame with the background model and then updating this model:

```
// processing method
void process(cv:: Mat &frame, cv:: Mat &output) {
  // convert to gray-level image
  cv::cvtColor(frame, gray, cv::COLOR_BGR2GRAY);
  // initialize background to 1st frame
  if (background.empty())
    gray.convertTo(background, CV_32F);
  // convert background to 8U
  background.convertTo(backImage,CV_8U);

  // compute difference between image and background
  cv::absdiff(backImage,gray,foreground);
  // apply threshold to foreground image
  cv::threshold(foreground,output,threshold,
                255,cv::THRESH_BINARY_INV);

  // accumulate background
  cv::accumulateWeighted(gray, background,
                // alpha*gray + (1-alpha)*background
                learningRate,  // alpha
                output);       // mask
}
```

Using our video-processing framework, the foreground extraction program will be built as follows:

```
int main() {
  // Create video procesor instance
  VideoProcessor processor;
  // Create background/foreground segmentor
  BGFGSegmentor segmentor;
```

```
    segmentor.setThreshold(25);

    // Open video file
    processor.setInput("bike.avi");

    // Set frame processor
    processor.setFrameProcessor(&segmentor);

    // Declare a window to display the video
    processor.displayOutput("Extracted Foreground");

    // Play the video at the original frame rate
    processor.setDelay(1000./processor.getFrameRate());

    // Start the process
    processor.run();
}
```

One of the resulting binary foreground images that will be displayed is as follows:

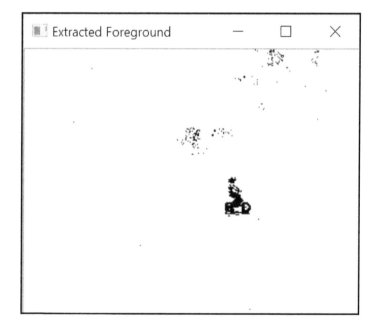

How it works...

Computing the running average of an image is easily accomplished through the `cv::accumulateWeighted` function that applies the running average formula to each pixel of the image. Note that the resulting image must be a floating point image. This is why we had to convert the background model into a background image before comparing it with the current frame. A simple thresholded absolute difference (computed by `cv::absdiff` followed by `cv::threshold`) extracts the foreground image. Note that we then used the foreground image as a mask to `cv::accumulateWeighted` in order to avoid updating pixels declared as foreground. This works because our foreground image is defined as being `false` (that is, `0`) at foreground pixels (which also explains why the foreground objects are displayed as black pixels in the resulting image).

Finally, it should be noted that, for simplicity, the background model that is built by our program is based on the gray-level version of the extracted frames. Maintaining a color background would require the computation of a running average in some color space. As it is often the case with parametric vision algorithms, the main difficulty in the presented approach is to determine the appropriate value for the threshold that would give good results for a given video.

There's more...

The preceding, simple method to extract foreground objects in a scene works well for simple scenes that show a relatively stable background. However, in many situations, the background scene might fluctuate in certain areas between different values, thus causing frequent false foreground detections. These might be due to, for example, a moving background object (for example, tree leaves) or a glaring effect (for example, on the surface of water). Casted shadows also pose a problem since they are often detected as part of a moving object. In order to cope with these problems, more sophisticated background modeling methods have been introduced.

The Mixture of Gaussian method

One of these algorithms is the **Mixture of Gaussian** method. It proceeds in a way that is similar to the method presented in this recipe, but adds a number of improvements.

First, the method maintains more than one model per pixel (that is, more than one running average). This way, if a background pixel fluctuates between, let's say, two values, two running averages are then stored. A new pixel value will be declared as the foreground only if it does not belong to any of the most frequently observed models. The number of models used is a parameter of the method, and a typical value is 5.

Second, not only is the running average maintained for each model, but also for the running variance. This is computed as follows:

$$\sigma_t^2 = (1-\alpha)\sigma_{t-1}^2 + \alpha(p_t - \mu_t)^2$$

These computed averages and variances are used to build a Gaussian model from which the probability of a given pixel value belonging to the background can be estimated. This makes it easier to determine an appropriate threshold since it is now expressed as a probability rather than an absolute difference. Consequently, in areas where the background values have larger fluctuations, a greater difference will be required to declare a foreground object.

Finally, this is an adaptive model, that is when a given Gaussian model is not hit sufficiently often, it is excluded from being part of the background model. Reciprocally, when a pixel value is found to be outside the currently maintained background models (that is, it is a foreground pixel), a new Gaussian model is created. If, in the future, this new model frequently receives pixels, then it becomes associated with the background.

This more sophisticated algorithm is obviously more complex to implement than our simple background/foreground segmentor. Fortunately, an OpenCV implementation exists, called `cv::bgsegm::createBackgroundSubtractorMOG`, and is defined as a subclass of the more general `cv::BackgroundSubtractor` class. When used with its default parameter, this class is very easy to use:

```
int main(){
  // Open the video file
  cv::VideoCapture capture("bike.avi");
  // check if video successfully opened
  if (!capture.isOpened())
    return 0;

  // current video frame
  cv::Mat frame;
  // foreground binary image
  cv::Mat foreground;
  // background image
  cv::Mat background;
  cv::namedWindow("Extracted Foreground");
```

```
// The Mixture of Gaussian object
// used with all default parameters
cv::Ptr<cv::BackgroundSubtractor> ptrMOG =
                cv::bgsegm::createBackgroundSubtractorMOG();
bool stop(false);
// for all frames in video
while (!stop) {
  // read next frame if any
  if (!capture.read(frame))
    break;

  // update the background
  // and return the foreground
   ptrMOG->apply(frame,foreground,0.01);

  // Complement the image
  cv::threshold(foreground,foreground,128,
                255,cv::THRESH_BINARY_INV);
  //show foreground and background
  cv::imshow("Extracted Foreground",foreground);

  // introduce a delay
  // or press key to stop
  if (cv::waitKey(10)>=0)
    stop= true;
  }
}
```

As you can see, it is just a matter of creating the class instance and calling the method that simultaneously updates the background and returns the foreground image (the extra parameter being the learning rate). Also note that the background model is computed in color here. The method implemented in OpenCV also includes a mechanism to reject shadows by checking whether the observed pixel variation is simply caused by a local change in brightness (if so, then it is probably due to a shadow) or whether it also includes some change in chromaticity.

A second implementation is also available and is simply called cv::BackgroundSubtractorMOG2. One of the improvements is that the number of appropriate Gaussian models per pixel to be used is now determined dynamically. You can use this in place of the previous one in the preceding example. You should run these different methods on a number of videos in order to appreciate their respective performances. In general, you will observe that cv::BackgroundSubtractorMOG2 is much faster.

See also

- The article by *C. Stauffer* and *W.E.L. Grimso*n, *Adaptive Background Mixture Models for Real-Time Tracking*, in *Conf. on Computer Vision and Pattern Recognition*, 1999, gives you a more complete description of the Mixture of Gaussian algorithm

13
Tracking Visual Motion

In this chapter, we will cover the following recipes:

- Tracing feature points in a video
- Estimating the optical flow
- Tracking an object in a video

Introduction

Video sequences are interesting because they show scenes and objects in motion. The preceding chapter introduced the tools for reading, processing, and saving videos. In this chapter, we will look at different algorithms that track the visible motion in a sequence of images. This visible or **apparent motion** can be caused by objects that move in different directions and at various speeds or by the motion of the camera (or a combination of both).

Tracking apparent motion is of utmost importance in many applications. It allows you to follow specific objects while they are moving in order to estimate their speed and determine where they are going. It also permits you to stabilize videos taken from handheld cameras by removing or reducing the amplitude of camera jitters. Motion estimation is also used in video coding to compress a video sequence in order to facilitate its transmission or storage. This chapter will present a few algorithms that track the motion in an image sequence, and as we will see, this tracking can be achieved either sparsely (that is, at few image locations, this is **sparse motion**) or densely (at every pixel of an image, this is **dense motion**).

Tracing feature points in a video

We learned in previous chapters that analyzing an image through some of its most distinctive points can lead to effective and efficient computer vision algorithms. This is also true for image sequences in which the motion of some interest points can be used to understand how the different elements of a captured scene move. In this recipe, you will learn how to perform a temporal analysis of a sequence by tracking feature points as they move from frame to frame.

How to do it...

To start the tracking process, the first thing to do is to detect the feature points in an initial frame. You then try to track these points in the next frame. Obviously, since we are dealing with a video sequence, there is a good chance that the object, on which the feature points are found, has moved (this motion can also be due to camera movement). Therefore, you must search around a point's previous location in order to find its new location in the next frame. This is what accomplishes the cv::calcOpticalFlowPyrLK function. You input two consecutive frames and a vector of feature points in the first image; the function then returns a vector of new point locations. To track the points over a complete sequence, you repeat this process from frame to frame. Note that as you follow the points across the sequence, you will unavoidably lose track of some of them such that the number of tracked feature points will gradually reduce. Therefore, it could be a good idea to detect new features from time to time.

We will now take advantage of the video-processing framework we defined in Chapter 12, *Processing Video Sequences*, and we will define a class that implements the FrameProcessor interface introduced in the *Processing the video frames* recipe of this chapter. The data attributes of this class include the variables that are required to perform both the detection of feature points and their tracking:

```
class FeatureTracker : public FrameProcessor {

  cv::Mat gray;       // current gray-level image
  cv::Mat gray_prev; // previous gray-level image
  // tracked features from 0->1
  std::vector<cv::Point2f> points[2];
  // initial position of tracked points
  std::vector<cv::Point2f> initial;
  std::vector<cv::Point2f> features;  // detected features
  int max_count;                // maximum number of features to detect
  double qlevel;                // quality level for feature detection
  double minDist;               // min distance between two points
```

```
std::vector<uchar> status;    // status of tracked features
std::vector<float> err;       // error in tracking

public:

    FeatureTracker() : max_count(500), qlevel(0.01), minDist(10.) {}
```

Next, we define the `process` method that will be called for each frame of the sequence. Basically, we need to proceed as follows. First, the feature points are detected if necessary. Next, these points are tracked. You reject the points that you cannot track or you no longer want to track. You are now ready to handle the successfully tracked points. Finally, the current frame and its points become the previous frame and points for the next iteration. Here is how to do this:

```
void process(cv:: Mat &frame, cv:: Mat &output) {

    // convert to gray-level image
    cv::cvtColor(frame, gray, CV_BGR2GRAY);
    frame.copyTo(output);

    // 1. if new feature points must be added
    if(addNewPoints()){
        // detect feature points
        detectFeaturePoints();
        // add the detected features to
        // the currently tracked features
        points[0].insert(points[0].end(),
                    features.begin(), features.end());
        initial.insert(initial.end(),
                    features.begin(), features.end());
    }

    // for first image of the sequence
    if(gray_prev.empty())
        gray.copyTo(gray_prev);

    // 2. track features
    cv::calcOpticalFlowPyrLK(
            gray_prev, gray,   // 2 consecutive images
            points[0],         // input point positions in first image
            points[1],         // output point positions in the 2nd image
            status,            // tracking success
            err);              // tracking error

    // 3. loop over the tracked points to reject some
    int k=0;
    for( int i= 0; i < points[1].size(); i++ ) {
```

```
    // do we keep this point?
    if (acceptTrackedPoint(i)) {
      // keep this point in vector
      initial[k]= initial[i];
      points[1][k++] = points[1][i];
    }
  }

  // eliminate unsuccesful points
  points[1].resize(k);
  initial.resize(k);

  // 4. handle the accepted tracked points
  handleTrackedPoints(frame, output);

  // 5. current points and image become previous ones
  std::swap(points[1], points[0]);
  cv::swap(gray_prev, gray);
}
```

This method makes use of four utility methods. It should be easy for you to change any of these methods in order to define a new behavior for your own tracker. The first of these methods detects the feature points. Note that we have already discussed the cv::goodFeatureToTrack function in the first recipe of Chapter 8, *Detecting Interest Points*:

```
// feature point detection
void detectFeaturePoints() {

  // detect the features
  cv::goodFeaturesToTrack(gray,      // the image
                          features,   // the output detected features
                          max_count,  // the maximum number of features
                          qlevel,     // quality level
                          minDist);   // min distance between two features
}
```

The second method determines whether new feature points should be detected. This will happen when a negligible number of tracked points remain:

```
// determine if new points should be added
bool addNewPoints() {

  // if too few points
  return points[0].size()<=10;
}
```

The third method rejects some of the tracked points based on a criteria defined by the application. Here, we decided to reject the points that do not move (in addition to those that cannot be tracked by the `cv::calcOpticalFlowPyrLK` function). We consider that non-moving points belong to the background scene and are therefore uninteresting:

```
//determine which tracked point should be accepted
bool acceptTrackedPoint(int i) {

  return status[i] &&  //status is false if unable to track point i
    // if point has moved
    (abs(points[0][i].x-points[1][i].x)+
      (abs(points[0][i].y-points[1][i].y))>2);
}
```

Finally, the fourth method handles the tracked feature points by drawing all the tracked points with a line that joins them to their initial position (that is, the position where they were detected the first time) on the current frame:

```
// handle the currently tracked points
void handleTrackedPoints(cv:: Mat &frame, cv:: Mat &output) {

  // for all tracked points
  for (int i= 0; i < points[1].size(); i++ ) {

    // draw line and circle
    cv::line(output, initial[i],  // initial position
            points[1][i],          // new position
            cv::Scalar(255,255,255));
    cv::circle(output, points[1][i], 3,
            cv::Scalar(255,255,255),-1);

  }
}
```

A simple main function to track the feature points in a video sequence would then be written as follows:

```
int main() {
  // Create video procesor instance
  VideoProcessor processor;
  // Create feature tracker instance
  FeatureTracker tracker;
  // Open video file
  processor.setInput("bike.avi");

  // set frame processor
  processor.setFrameProcessor(&tracker);
```

```
// Declare a window to display the video
processor.displayOutput("Tracked Features");

// Play the video at the original frame rate
processor.setDelay(1000./processor.getFrameRate());

// Start the process
processor.run();
}
```

The resulting program will show you the evolution of the moving tracked features over time. Here are, for example, two such frames at two different instants. In this video, the camera is fixed. The young cyclist is therefore the only moving object. Here is the result that is obtained after a few frames have been processed:

A few seconds later, we obtain the following frame:

How it works...

To track the feature points from frame to frame, we must locate the new position of a feature point in the subsequent frame. If we assume that the intensity of the feature point does not change from one frame to the next one, we are looking for a displacement (u, v) as follows:

$$I_t\left(x, y\right) = I_{t+1}\left(x+u, y+v\right)$$

Here, I_t and I_{t+1} are the current frame and the one at the next instant, respectively. This constant intensity assumption generally holds for small displacement in images that are taken at two nearby instants. We can then use the Taylor expansion in order to approximate this equation by an equation that involves the image derivatives:

$$I_{t+1}\left(x+u, y+v\right) \approx I_t\left(x, y\right) + \frac{\partial I}{\partial x}u + \frac{\partial I}{\partial y}v + \frac{\partial I}{\partial t}$$

This latter equation leads us to another equation (as a consequence of the constant intensity assumption that cancels the two intensity terms):

$$\frac{\partial I}{\partial x}u + \frac{\partial I}{\partial y}v = -\frac{\partial I}{\partial t}$$

This constraint is the fundamental **optical flow** constraint equation and is known as the **brightness constancy equation**.

This constraint is exploited by the so-called **Lukas-Kanade feature tracking** algorithm. In addition to using this constraint, the Lukas-Kanade algorithm also makes an assumption that the displacement of all the points in the neighborhood of the feature point is the same. We can therefore impose the optical flow constraint on all these points with a unique (u, v) unknown displacement. This gives us more equations than the number of unknowns (two), and therefore, we can solve this system of equations in a mean-square sense. In practice, it is solved iteratively, and the OpenCV implementation also offers us the possibility to perform this estimation at a different resolution in order to make the search more efficient and more tolerant to a larger displacement. By default, the number of image levels is 3 and the window size is 15. These parameters can obviously be changed. You can also specify the termination criteria, which define the conditions that stop the iterative search. The sixth parameter of `cv::calcOpticalFlowPyrLK` contains the residual mean-square error that can be used to assess the quality of the tracking. The fifth parameter contains binary flags that tell us whether tracking the corresponding point was considered successful or not.

The preceding description represents the basic principles behind the Lukas-Kanade tracker. The current implementation contains other optimizations and improvements that make the algorithm more efficient in the computation of the displacement of a large number of feature points.

See also

- `Chapter 8`, *Detecting Interest Points*, where there is a discussion on feature point detection
- The *Tracking an object in a video* recipe of this chapter uses feature point tracking in order to track objects
- The classic article by *B. Lucas* and *T. Kanade, An Iterative Image Registration Technique with an Application to Stereo Vision*, at the *Int. Joint Conference in Artificial Intelligence*, pp. 674-679, 1981, describes the original feature point tracking algorithm

- The article by J. Shi and C. Tomasi, *Good Features to Track*, at the *IEEE Conference on Computer Vision and Pattern Recognition*, pp. 593-600, 1994, describes an improved version of the original feature point tracking algorithm

Estimating the optical flow

When a scene is observed by a camera, the observed brightness pattern is projected on the image sensor and thus forms an image. In a video sequence, we are often interested in capturing the motion pattern, that is the projection of the 3D motion of the different scene elements on an image plane. This image of projected 3D motion vectors is called the **motion field**. However, it is not possible to directly measure the 3D motion of scene points from a camera sensor. All we observe is a brightness pattern that is in motion from frame to frame. This apparent motion of the brightness pattern is called the **optical flow**. One might think that the motion field and optical flow should be equal, but this is not always true. An obvious case would be the observation of a uniform object; for example, if a camera moves in front of a white wall, then no optical flow is generated.

Another classical example is the illusion produced by a rotating barber pole:

In this case, the motion field should show motion vectors in the horizontal direction as the vertical cylinder rotates around its main axis. However, observers perceive this motion as red and blue strips moving up and this is what the optical flow will show. In spite of these differences, the optical flow is considered to be a valid approximation of the motion field. This recipe will explain how the optical flow of an image sequence can be estimated.

Getting ready

Estimating the optical flow means quantifying the apparent motion of the brightness pattern in an image sequence. So let's consider one frame of the video at one given instant. If we look at one particular pixel (x,y) on the current frame, we would like to know where this point is moving in the subsequent frames. That is to say that the coordinates of this point are moving over time-a fact that can be expressed as $(x(t),y(t))$-and our goal is to estimate the velocity of this point $(dx/dt, dy/dt)$. The brightness of this particular point at time t can be obtained by looking at the corresponding frame of the sequence, that is, $I(x(t),y(t),t)$.

From our **image brightness constancy** assumption, we can write that the brightness of this point does not vary with respect to time:

$$\frac{dI\left(x(t),y(t),t\right)}{dt} = 0$$

The chain rule allows us to write the following:

$$\frac{dI}{dx}\frac{dx}{dt} + \frac{dI}{dy}\frac{dy}{dt} + \frac{dI}{dt} = 0$$

This equation is known as the **brightness constancy equation** and it relates the optical flow components (the derivatives of x and y with respect to time) with the image derivatives. This is exactly the equation we derived in the previous recipe; we simply demonstrated it differently.

This single equation (composed of two unknowns) is however insufficient to compute the optical flow at a pixel location. We therefore need to add an additional constraint. A common choice is to assume the smoothness of the optical flow, which means that the neighboring optical flow vectors should be similar. Any departure from this assumption should therefore be penalized. One particular formulation for this constraint is based on the Laplacian of the optical flow:

$$\frac{\partial^2}{\partial x^2}(\frac{dx}{dt}) + \frac{\partial^2}{\partial y^2}(\frac{dy}{dt})$$

The objective is therefore to find the optical flow field that minimizes both the deviations from the brightness constancy equation and the Laplacian of the flow vectors.

How to do it...

Several approaches have been proposed to solve the dense optical flow estimation problem, and OpenCV implements a few of them. Let's use the `cv::DualTVL1OpticalFlow` class that is built as a subclass of the generic `cv::Algorithm` base class. Following the implemented pattern, the first thing to do is to create an instance of this class and obtain a pointer to it:

```
//Create the optical flow algorithm
cv::Ptr<cv::DualTVL1OpticalFlow> tvl1 = cv::createOptFlow_DualTVL1();
```

Since the object we just created is in a ready-to-use state, we simply call the method that calculates an optical flow field between the two frames:

```
cv::Mat oflow;    // image of 2D flow vectors
//compute optical flow between frame1 and frame2
tvl1->calc(frame1, frame2, oflow);
```

The result is an image of 2D vectors (`cv::Point`) that represents the displacement of each pixel between the two frames. In order to display the result, we must therefore show these vectors. This is why we created a function that generates an image map for an optical flow field. To control the visibility of the vectors, we used two parameters. The first one is a stride value that is defined such that only one vector over a certain number of pixels will be displayed. This stride makes space for the display of the vectors. The second parameter is a scale factor that extends the vector length to make it more apparent. Each drawn optical flow vector is then a simple line that ends with a plain circle to symbolize the tip of an arrow. Our mapping function is therefore as follows:

```
// Drawing optical flow vectors on an image
void drawOpticalFlow(const cv::Mat& oflow,   // the optical flow
      cv::Mat& flowImage,       // the produced image
      int stride,               // the stride for displaying the vectors
      float scale,              // multiplying factor for the vectors
      const cv::Scalar& color)  // the color of the vectors
{
  // create the image if required
  if (flowImage.size() != oflow.size()) {
    flowImage.create(oflow.size(), CV_8UC3);
    flowImage = cv::Vec3i(255,255,255);
  }

  //for all vectors using stride as a step
  for (int y = 0; y < oflow.rows; y += stride)
    for (int x = 0; x < oflow.cols; x += stride) {
      //gets the vector
      cv::Point2f vector = oflow.at< cv::Point2f>(y, x);
```

```
            // draw the line
            cv::line(flowImage, cv::Point(x,y),
                    cv::Point(static_cast<int>(x + scale*vector.x + 0.5),
                            static_cast<int>(y + scale*vector.y + 0.5)),
                    color);
            // draw the arrow tip
            cv::circle(flowImage,
                    cv::Point(static_cast<int>(x + scale*vector.x + 0.5),
                            static_cast<int>(y + scale*vector.y + 0.5)),
                    1, color, -1);
        }
    }
```

Consider the following two frames:

If these frames are used, then the estimated optical flow field can be visualized by calling our drawing function:

```
    // Draw the optical flow image
    cv::Mat flowImage;
    drawOpticalFlow(oflow,                   // input flow vectors
                    flowImage,               // image to be generated
                    8,                       // display vectors every 8 pixels
                    2,                       // multiply size of vectors by 2
                    cv::Scalar(0, 0, 0));    // vector color
```

The result is as follows:

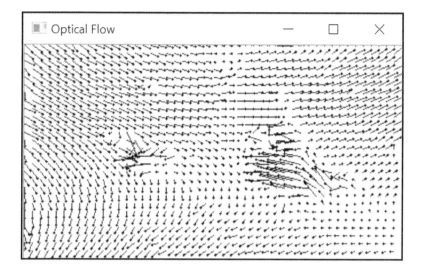

How it works...

We explained in the first section of this recipe that an optical flow field can be estimated by minimizing a function that combines the brightness constancy constraint and a smoothness function. The equations we presented then constitute the classical formulation of the problem, and this one has been improved in many ways.

The method we used in the previous section is known as the **Dual TV L1** method. It has two main ingredients. The first one is the use of a smoothing constraint that aims at minimizing the absolute value of the optical flow gradient (instead of the square of it). This choice reduces the impact of the smoothing term, especially at regions of discontinuity where, for example, the optical flow vectors of a moving object are quite different from the ones of its background. The second ingredient is the use of a **first-order Taylor approximation**; this linearizes the formulation of the brightness constancy constraint. We will not enter into the details of this formulation here; it is suffice to say that this linearization facilitates the iterative estimation of the optical flow field. However, since the linear approximation is only valid for small displacements, the method requires a coarse-to-fine estimation scheme.

In this recipe, we used this method with its default parameters. A number of setters and getters methods allow you to modify the ones which can have an impact on the quality of the solution and on the speed of the computation. For example, one can modify the number of scales used in the pyramidal estimation or specify a more or less strict stopping criterion to be adopted during each iterative estimation step. Another important parameter is the weight associated with the brightness constancy constraint versus the smoothness constraint. For example, if we reduce the importance given to brightness constancy by two, we then obtain a smoother optical flow field:

```
// compute a smoother optical flow between 2 frames
tvl1->setLambda(0.075);
tvl1->calc(frame1, frame2, oflow);
```

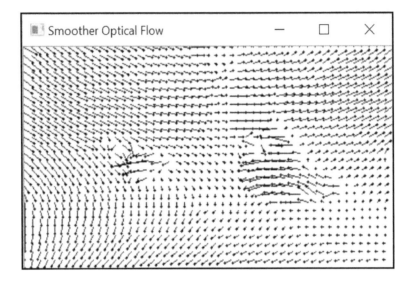

See also

- The article by *B.K.P. Horn* and *B.G. Schunck, Determining optical flow, in Artificial Intelligence*, 1981, is the classical reference on optical flow estimation
- The article by *C. Zach, T. Pock,* and *H. Bischof, A duality based approach for real time tv-l 1 optical flow,* at *IEEE conference on Computer Vision and Pattern Recognition* 2007, describes the details of the `Dual TV-L1` method

Tracking an object in a video

In the previous two recipes, we learned how to track the motion of points and pixels in an image sequence. In many applications, however, the requirement is rather to track a specific moving object in a video. An object of interest is first identified and then it must be followed over a long sequence. This is challenging because as it evolves in the scene, the image of this object will undergo many changes in appearance due to viewpoint and illumination variations, non-rigid motion, occlusion, and so on.

This recipe presents some of the object-tracking algorithms implemented in the OpenCV library. These implementations are based on a common framework, which facilitates the substitution of one method by another. Contributors have also made available a number of new methods. Note that, we have already presented a solution to the object-tracking problem in the *Counting pixels with integral images* recipe in Chapter 4, *Counting the Pixels with Histograms*; this one was based on the use of histograms computed through integral images.

How to do it...

The visual object-tracking problem generally assumes that no prior knowledge about the objects to be tracked is available. Tracking is therefore initiated by identifying the object in a frame, and tracking must start at this point. The initial identification of the object is achieved by specifying a bounding box inside which the target is inscribed. The objective of the tracker module is then to reidentify this object in a subsequent frame.

The cv::Tracker class of OpenCV that defines the object-tracking framework has therefore, two main methods. The first one is the init method used to define the initial target bounding box. The second one is the update method that outputs a new bounding box, given a new frame. Both the methods accept a frame (a cv::Mat instance) and a bounding box (a cv::Rect2D instance) as arguments; in one case, the bounding box is an input, while for the second method, the bounding box is an output parameter.

In order to test one of the proposed object tracker algorithms, we use the video-processing framework that has been presented in the previous chapter. In particular, we define a frame-processing subclass that will be called by our `VideoProcessor` class when each frame of the image sequence is received. This subclass has the following attributes:

```
class VisualTracker : public FrameProcessor {

   cv::Ptr<cv::Tracker> tracker;
   cv::Rect2d box;
   bool reset;

   public:
   // constructor specifying the tracker to be used
   VisualTracker(cv::Ptr<cv::Tracker> tracker) :
                   reset(true), tracker(tracker) {}
```

The `reset` attribute is set to `true` whenever the tracker has been reinitiated through the specification of a new target's bounding box. It is the `setBoundingBox` method that is used to store a new object position:

```
// set the bounding box to initiate tracking
void setBoundingBox(const cv::Rect2d& bb) {
   box = bb;
   reset = true;
}
```

The callback method used to process each frame then simply calls the appropriate method of the tracker and draws the new computed bounding box on the frame to be displayed:

```
// callback processing method
void process(cv:: Mat &frame, cv:: Mat &output) {

  if (reset) { // new tracking session
     reset = false;
     tracker->init(frame, box);

  } else {
     // update the target's position
     tracker->update(frame, box);
  }

  // draw bounding box on current frame
  frame.copyTo(output);
  cv::rectangle(output, box, cv::Scalar(255, 255, 255), 2);
}
```

To demonstrate how an object can be tracked using the `VideoProcessor` and `FrameProcessor` instances, we use the **Median Flow tracker** defined in OpenCV:

```cpp
int main(){
  // Create video procesor instance
  VideoProcessor processor;

  // generate the filename
  std::vector<std::string> imgs;
  std::string prefix = "goose/goose";
  std::string ext = ".bmp";

  // Add the image names to be used for tracking
  for (long i = 130; i < 317; i++) {

    std::string name(prefix);
    std::ostringstream ss; ss << std::setfill('0') <<
            std::setw(3) << i; name += ss.str();
    name += ext;
    imgs.push_back(name);
  }

  // Create feature tracker instance
  VisualTracker tracker(cv::TrackerMedianFlow::createTracker());

  // Open video file
  processor.setInput(imgs);

  // set frame processor
  processor.setFrameProcessor(&tracker);

  // Declare a window to display the video
  processor.displayOutput("Tracked object");

  // Define the frame rate for display
  processor.setDelay(50);

  // Specify the original target position
  tracker.setBoundingBox(cv::Rect(290,100,65,40));

  // Start the tracking
  processor.run();
}
```

The first bounding box identifies one goose in our test image sequence. This one is then automatically tracked in the subsequent frames:

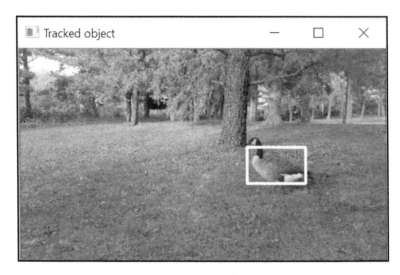

Unfortunately, as the sequence progresses, the tracker will unavoidably make errors. The accumulation of these small errors will cause the tracker to slowly drift from the real target position. Here is, for example, the estimated position of our target after 130 frames have been processed:

Eventually, the tracker will lose track of the object. The ability of a tracker to follow an object over a long period of time is the most important criteria that characterizes the performance of an object tracker.

How it works...

In this recipe, we showed how the generic `cv::Tracker` class can be used to track an object in an image sequence. We selected the Median Flow tracker algorithm to illustrate the tracking result. This is a simple but effective method to track a textured object as long as its motion is not too rapid and it is not too severely occluded.

The Median Flow tracker is based on feature point tracking. It first starts by defining a grid of points over the object to be tracked. One could have instead detected interest points on the object using, for instance, the `FAST` operator presented in `Chapter 8`, *Detecting Interest Points*. However, using points at predefined locations presents a number of advantages. It saves time by avoiding the computation of interest points. It guarantees that a sufficient number of points will be available for tracking. It also makes sure that these points will be well distributed over the whole object. The Median Flow implementation uses, by default, a grid of `10x10` points:

The next step is to use the Lukas-Kanade feature-tracking algorithm presented in the first recipe of this chapter, *Tracing feature points in a video*. Each point of the grid is then tracked over the next frame:

The Median Flow algorithm then estimates the errors made when tracking these points. These errors can be estimated, for example, by computing the sum of absolute pixel difference in a window around the point at its initial and tracked position. This is the type of error that is conveniently computed and returned by the `cv::calcOpticalFlowPyrLK` function. Another error measure proposed by the Median Flow algorithm is to use the so-called forward-backward error. After the points have been tracked between a frame and the next one, these points at their new position are backward-tracked to check whether they will return to their original position in the initial image. The difference between the thus obtained forward-backward position and the initial one is the error in tracking.

Once the tracking error of each point has been computed, only 50 percent of the points having the smallest error are considered. This group is used to compute the new position of the bounding box in the next image. Each of these points votes for a displacement value, and the median of these possible displacements is retained. For the change in scale, the points are considered in pairs. The ratio of the distance between the two points in the initial frame and the next one is estimated. Again, it is the median of these scales that is finally applied.

The Median Tracker is one of many other visual object trackers based on feature point tracking. Another family of solutions is the one that is based on template matching, a concept we discussed in the *Matching local templates* recipe in `Chapter 9`, *Describing and Matching Interest Points*. A good representative of these kinds of approaches is the **Kernelized Correlation Filter** (**KCF**) algorithm, implemented as the `cv::TrackerKCF` class in OpenCV:

```
VisualTracker tracker(cv::TrackerKCF::createTracker());
```

Basically, this one uses the target's bounding box as a template to search for the new object position in the next view. This is normally computed through a simple correlation, but KCF uses a special trick based on the Fourier transform that we briefly mentioned in the introduction of `Chapter 6`, *Filtering the Images*. Without entering into any details, the signal-processing theory tells us that correlating a template over an image corresponds to simple image multiplication in the frequency domain. This considerably speeds up the identification of the matching window in the next frame and makes KCF one of the fastest and robust trackers. As an example, here is the position of the bounding box after a tracking of `130` frames using KCF:

See also

- The article by *Z. Kalal, K. Mikolajczyk,* and *J. Matas, Forward-backward error: Automatic detection of tracking failures*, in *Int. Conf. on Pattern Recognition*, 2010, describes the Median Flow algorithm
- The article by *Z. Kalal, K. Mikolajczyk,* and *J. Matas, Tracking-learning-detection*, in *IEEE Transactions on Pattern Analysis and Machine Intelligence*, vol 34, no 7, 2012, is an advanced tracking method that uses the Median Flow algorithm
- The article by *J.F. Henriques, R. Caseiro, P. Martins, J. Batista, High-Speed Tracking with Kernelized Correlation Filters*, in *IEEE Transactions on Pattern Analysis and Machine Intelligence*, vol 37, no 3, 2014, describes the KCF tracker algorithm

14
Learning from Examples

In this chapter, we will cover the following recipes:

- Recognizing faces using nearest neighbors of local binary patterns
- Finding objects and faces with a cascade of Haar features
- Detecting objects and people with Support Vector Machines and histograms of oriented gradients

Introduction

Machine learning is nowadays, very often used to solve difficult machine vision problems. In fact, it is a rich field of research encompassing many important concepts that would deserve a complete cookbook by itself. This chapter surveys some of the main machine learning techniques and explains how these can be deployed in computer vision systems using OpenCV.

At the core of machine learning is the development of computer systems that can learn how to react to data inputs by themselves. Instead of being explicitly programmed, machine learning systems automatically adapt and evolve when examples of desired behaviors are presented to them. Once a successful training phase is completed, it is expected that the trained system will output the correct response to new unseen queries.

Machine learning can solve many types of problems; our focus here will be on classification problems. Formally, in order to build a classifier that can recognize instances of a specific class of concepts, this one must be trained with a large set of annotated samples. In a 2-class problem, this set will be made of **positive samples** representing instances of the class to be learned, and of **negative samples** made of counter-examples of instances not belonging to the class of interest. From these observations, a **decision function** predicting the correct class of any input instances has to be learned.

In computer vision, those samples are images (or video segments). The first thing to do is therefore find a representation that will ideally describe the content of each image in a compact and distinctive way. One simplistic representation could be to use a fixed-size thumbnail image. The row-by-row succession of the pixels of this thumbnail image forms a vector that can then be used as a training sample presented to a machine learning algorithm. Other alternative and probably more effective representations can also be used. The recipes of this chapter describe different image representations and introduce some well-known machine learning algorithms. We should emphasize that we will not be able to cover in detail, all the theoretical aspects of the different machine learning techniques discussed in the recipes; our objective is rather to present the main principles governing their functioning.

Recognizing faces using nearest neighbors of local binary patterns

Our first exploration of machine learning techniques will start with what is probably the simplest approach, namely **nearest neighbor classification**. We will also present the local binary pattern feature, a popular representation encoding the textural patterns and contours of an image in a contrast independent way.

Our illustrative example will concern the face recognition problem. This is a very challenging problem that has been the object of numerous researches over the past 20 years. The basic solution we present here is one of the face recognition methods implemented in OpenCV. You will quickly realize that this solution is not very robust and works only under very favorable conditions. Nevertheless, this approach constitutes an excellent introduction to machine learning and to the face recognition problem.

How to do it...

The OpenCV library proposes a number of face recognition methods implemented as a subclass of the generic `cv::face::FaceRecognizer`. In this recipe, we will have a look at the `cv::face::LBPHFaceRecognizer` class, which is interesting to us because it is based on a simple but often very effective classification approach, the nearest neighbor classifier. Moreover, the image representation it uses is built from the **local binary pattern** feature (**LBP**) which is a very popular way of describing image patterns.

In order to create an instance of the cv::face::LBPHFaceRecognizer, its static create method is called:

```
cv::Ptr<cv::face::FaceRecognizer> recognizer =
        cv::face::createLBPHFaceRecognizer(1, // radius of LBP pattern
                8,        // the number of neighboring pixels to consider
                8, 8,    // grid size
                200.8);  // minimum distance to nearest neighbor
```

As will be explained in the next section, the first two arguments provided serve to describe the characteristic of the LBP feature to be used. The next step is to feed the recognizer with a number of reference face images. This is done by providing two vectors, one containing the face images and the other one containing the associated labels. Each label is an arbitrary integer value identifying a particular individual. The idea is to train the recognizer by showing it different images of each of the people to be recognized. As you may imagine, the more representative images you provide, the better the chances that the correct person will be identified. In our very simplistic example, we simply provide two images of two reference persons. The train method is the one to call:

```
// vectors of reference image and their labels
std::vector<cv::Mat> referenceImages;
std::vector<int> labels;
// open the reference images
referenceImages.push_back(cv::imread("face0_1.png",
                        cv::IMREAD_GRAYSCALE));
labels.push_back(0); // person 0
referenceImages.push_back(cv::imread("face0_2.png",
                        cv::IMREAD_GRAYSCALE));
labels.push_back(0); // person 0
referenceImages.push_back(cv::imread("face1_1.png",
                        cv::IMREAD_GRAYSCALE));
labels.push_back(1); // person 1
referenceImages.push_back(cv::imread("face1_2.png",
                        cv::IMREAD_GRAYSCALE));
labels.push_back(1); // person 1

// train the recognizer by computing the LBPHs
recognizer->train(referenceImages, labels);
```

The images used are below, with the top row being images of person 0 and the second row images of person 1:

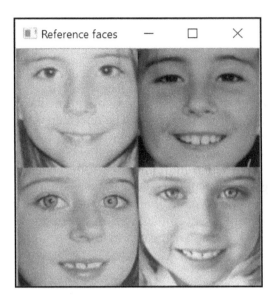

The quality of these reference images is also very important. In addition, it would be a good idea to have them normalized such as to have the main facial features at standardized locations. For example, having the tip of the nose located in the middle of the image, and the two eyes horizontally aligned at a specific image row. Facial feature detection methods exist that can be used to automatically normalize face images this way. This was not done in our example, and the robustness of the recognizer will suffer from this. Nevertheless, this one is ready to be used, an input image can be provided, and it will try to predict the label to which this face image corresponds:

```
// predict the label of this image
recognizer->predict(inputImage,       // face image
                    predictedLabel,   // predicted label of this image
                    confidence);      // confidence of the prediction
```

Our input image is the following:

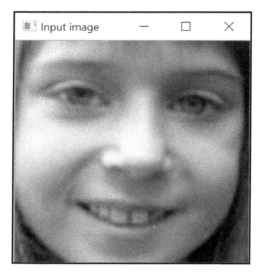

Not only does the recognizer return the predicted label, but it also returns a confidence score. In the case of the `cv::face::LBPHFaceRecognizer`, the lower this confidence value is, the more confident is the recognizer of its prediction. Here, we obtain a correct label prediction (1) with a confidence value of 90.3.

How it works...

In order to understand the functioning of the face recognition approach presented in this recipe, we need to explain its two main components: the image representation used and the classification method that is applied.

As its name indicates, the `cv::face::LBPHFaceRecognizer` algorithm makes use of the LBP feature. This is a contrast independent way of describing image patterns present in an image. It is a local representation that transforms every pixel into a binary representation encoding the pattern of image intensities found in a neighborhood. To achieve this goal, a simple rule is applied; a local pixel is compared to each of its selected neighbors; if its value is greater than that of its neighbor, then a `0` is assigned to the corresponding bit position, if not, then a `1` is assigned. In its simplest and most common form, each pixel is compared to its `8` immediate neighbors, which generates an 8-bit pattern. For example, let's consider the following local pattern:

87	98	17
21	26	89
19	24	90

Applying the described rule generates the following binary values:

1	1	0
0		1
0	0	1

Taking as initial position, the top left pixel and moving clockwise, the central pixel will be replaced by the binary sequence `11011000`. Generating a complete 8-bit LBP image is then easily achieved by looping over all pixels of an image to produce all corresponding LBP bytes. This is accomplished by the following function:

```
//compute the Local Binary Patterns of a gray-level image
void lbp(const cv::Mat &image, cv::Mat &result) {

    result.create(image.size(), CV_8U); // allocate if necessary

    for (int j = 1; j<image.rows - 1; j++) {
        //for all rows (except first and last)

        // pointers to the input rows
        const uchar* previous = image.ptr<const uchar>(j - 1);
        const uchar* current  = image.ptr<const uchar>(j);
        const uchar* next     = image.ptr<const uchar>(j + 1);
```

```
    uchar* output = result.ptr<uchar>(j);          //output row

    for (int i = 1; i<image.cols - 1; i++) {

      // compose local binary pattern
      *output =  previous[i - 1] > current[i] ? 1 : 0;
      *output |= previous[i] > current[i] ?       2 : 0;
      *output |= previous[i + 1] > current[i] ? 4 : 0;
      *output |= current[i - 1] > current[i] ?  8 : 0;
      *output |= current[i + 1] > current[i] ? 16 : 0;
      *output |= next[i - 1] > current[i] ?      32 : 0;
      *output |= next[i] > current[i] ?          64 : 0;
      *output |= next[i + 1] > current[i] ?    128 : 0;
      output++; // next pixel
    }
  }
  // Set the unprocess pixels to 0
  result.row(0).setTo(cv::Scalar(0));
  result.row(result.rows - 1).setTo(cv::Scalar(0));
  result.col(0).setTo(cv::Scalar(0));
  result.col(result.cols - 1).setTo(cv::Scalar(0));
}
```

The body of the loop compares each pixel with its 8 neighbors and the bit values are
assigned through simple bit shifts. With the following image:

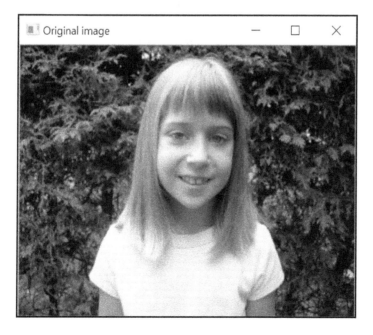

An LBP image is obtained and can be displayed as a gray-level image:

This gray-level representation is not really interpretable, but it simply illustrates the encoding process that occurred.

Returning to our `cv::face::LBPHFaceRecognizer` class, it can be seen that the first two parameters of its `create` method specify the size (radius in pixels) and dimension (number of pixels along the circle, possibly applying interpolation) of the neighborhood to be considered. Once the LBP image is generated, the image is divided into a grid. The size of this grid is specified as the third parameter of the `create` method. For each block of this grid, a histogram of LBP values is constructed. A global image representation is finally obtained by concatenating the bin counts of all these histograms into one large vector. With an 8×8 grid, the set of computed 256-bin histograms then forms a 16384-dimensional vector.

The `train` method of the `cv::face::LBPHFaceRecognizer` class therefore generates this long vector for each of the provided reference images. Each face image can then be seen as a point in a very high dimensional space. When a new image is submitted to the recognizer through its `predict` method, the closest reference point to this image is found. The label associated with this point is therefore the predicted label and the confidence value will be the computed distance. This is the principle that defines a nearest neighbor classifier. One more ingredient is generally added. If the nearest neighbor of the input point is too far from it, then this could mean that this point in fact does not belong to any of the reference classes. How far away must this point be to be considered as an outlier? This is specified by the fourth parameter of the `create` method of the `cv::face::LBPHFaceRecognizer` class.

As you can see, this is a very simple idea and it turns out to be very effective when the different classes generate distinct clouds of points in the representational space. Another benefit of this approach is that the method implicitly handles multiple classes, as it simply reads the predicted class from its nearest neighbors. The main drawback is its computational cost. Finding the nearest neighbor in such a large space, possibly composed of many reference points, can take time. Storing all these reference points is also costly in memory.

See also

- The article by *T. Ahonen, A. Hadid* and *M. Pietikainen, Face description with Local Binary Patterns: Application to Face Recognition* in IEEE transaction on *Pattern Analysis and Machine Intelligence*, 2006 describes the use of LBP for face recognition
- The article by *B. Froba* and *A. Ernst, Face detection with the modified census transform* in IEEE conference on *Automatic Face and Gesture Recognition*, 2004 proposes a variant of the LBP features
- The article by *M. Uricar, V. Franc* and *V. Hlavac, Detector of Facial Landmarks Learned by the Structured Output SVM* in International Conference on *Computer Vision Theory and Applications*, 2012 describes a facial feature detector based on the SVMs discussed in the last recipe of this chapter

Finding objects and faces with a cascade of Haar features

We learned in the previous recipe, some of the basic concepts of machine learning. We showed how a classifier can be built by collecting samples of the different classes of interest. However, for the approach that was considered in this previous recipe, training a classifier simply consists of storing all the samples' representations. From there, the label of any new instance can be predicted by looking at the closest (nearest neighbor) labeled point. For most machine learning methods, training is rather an iterative process during which machinery is built by looping over the samples. Performance of the classifier thus produced gradually improves as more samples are presented. Learning eventually stops when a certain performance criterion is reached or when no more improvements can be obtained by considering the current training dataset. This recipe will present a machine learning algorithm that follows this procedure, the **cascade of boosted classifiers**.

But before we look at this classifier, we will first turn our attention to the Haar feature image representation. We indeed learned that a good representation is an essential ingredient in the production of a robust classifier. LBPs, as described in the previous recipe, *Recognizing faces using nearest neighbors of local binary patterns*, constitute one possible choice; the next section describes another popular representation.

Getting ready

The first step in the generation of a classifier is to assemble a (preferably) large collection of image samples showing different instances of the classes of objects to be identified. The way these samples are represented has been shown to have an important impact on the performance of the classifier that is to be built from them. Pixel-level representations are generally considered to be too low-level to robustly describe the intrinsic characteristics of each class of objects. Representations that can describe, at various scales, the distinctive patterns present in an image are preferable. This is the objective of the **Haar features** also sometimes called Haar-like features because they derive from the Haar transform basis functions.

The Haar features define small rectangular areas of pixels, these later being compared through simple subtractions. Three different configurations are generally considered, namely the 2-rectangle, 3-rectangle, and 4-rectangle features

These features can be of any size and applied on any area of the image to be represented. For example, here are two Haar features applied on a face image:

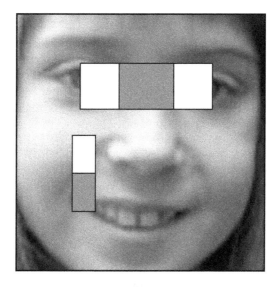

Building a Haar representation consists of selecting a number of Haar features of given types, sizes, and locations and applying them on images. The specific set of values obtained from the chosen set of Haar features constitutes the image representation. The challenge is then to determine which set of features to select. Indeed, to distinguish one class of objects from another, some Haar features must be more relevant than others. For example, in the case of the class of face images, applying a 3-rectangle Haar feature between the eyes (as shown in the figure above) could be a good idea as we expect all face images to consistently produce a high value in this case. Obviously, since there exist hundreds of thousands of possible Haar features, it would certainly be difficult to manually make a good selection. We are then looking for a machine learning method that would select the most relevant features for a given class of objects.

How to do it...

In this recipe, we will learn how we can build, using OpenCV, a **boosted cascade of features** to produce a 2-class classifier. But before we do, let's explain the terminology that is used here. A 2-class classifier is one that can identify the instances of one class (for example, face images) from the rest (for example, images that do not contain faces). We therefore have in this case the **positive samples** (that is, face images) and the **negative samples** (that is, non-face images), these latter are also called the background images. The classifier of this recipe will be made of a cascade of simple classifiers that will be sequentially applied. Each stage of the cascade will make a quick decision about rejecting or not rejecting the object shown based on the values obtained for a small subset of features. This cascade is boosted in the sense that each stage improves (boosts) the performance of the previous ones by making more accurate decisions. The main advantage of this approach is that the early stages of the cascade are composed of simple tests that can then quickly reject instances that certainly do not belong to the class of interest. These early rejections make the cascade classifier quick, because when searching for a class of objects by scanning an image, most sub-windows to be tested will not belong to the class of interest. This way, only few windows will have to pass through all stages before being accepted or rejected.

In order to train a boosted classifier cascade for a specific class, OpenCV offers a software tool that will perform all the required operations. When you install the library, you should have two executable modules created and located in the appropriate `bin` directory, these are `opencv_createsamples.exe` and `opencv_traincascade.exe`. Make sure your system `PATH` points to this directory so that you can execute these tools from anywhere.

When training a classifier, the first thing to do is to collect the samples. The positive ones are made of images showing instances of the target class. In our simple example, we decided to train a classifier to recognize stop signs. Here are the few positive samples we have collected:

The list of the positive samples to be used must be specified in a text file that we have, here, named `stop.txt`. It contains image filenames and bounding box coordinates:

```
stop00.png 1 0 0 64 64
stop01.png 1 0 0 64 64
stop02.png 1 0 0 64 64
stop03.png 1 0 0 64 64
stop04.png 1 0 0 64 64
stop05.png 1 0 0 64 64
stop06.png 1 0 0 64 64
stop07.png 1 0 0 64 64
```

The first number after the filename is the number of positive samples visible in the image. Next is the upper left coordinate of the bounding box containing this positive sample and finally its width and height. In our case, the positive samples have already been extracted from their original images, this is why we have always one sample per file and upper-left coordinates at (0,0). Once this file is available, you can then create the positive sample file by running the extractor tool.

```
opencv_createsamples -info stop.txt -vec stop.vec -w 24 -h 24 -num 8
```

This will create an output file `stop.vec` that will contain all the positive samples specified in the input text file. Note that we made the sample size smaller (24×24) than the original size (64×64). The extractor tool resizes all samples to the specified size. Usually, Haar features work better with smaller templates, but this is something that has to be validated on a case-by-case basis.

The negative samples are simply background images containing no instances of the class of interest (no stop signs in our case). But these images should show a good variety of what the classifier is expected to see. These negative images could be of any size, the training tool will extract random negative samples from them. Here is one example of a background image we wish to use.

Once the positive and negative sample sets are in place, the classifier cascade is ready to be trained. Calling the tool is done as follows:

```
opencv_traincascade  -data classifier -vec stop.vec
              -bg neg.txt -numPos 9  -numNeg 20
              -numStages 20 -minHitRate 0.95
              -maxFalseAlarmRate 0.5 -w 24 -h 24
```

The parameters used here will be explained in the next section. Note that this training process can take a very long time; in some complex cases with thousands of samples, it can even take days to execute. As it runs, the cascade trainer will print out performance reports each time the training of a stage is completed. In particular, the classifier will tell you what the current **hit rate** (**HR**) is; this is the percentage of positive samples that are currently accepted by the cascade (that is, correctly recognized as positive instances, they are also called the **true positives**). You want this number to be as close as possible to 1.0. It will also give you the current **false alarm rate** (**FA**) which is the number of tested negative samples that are wrongly classified as positive instances (also called the **false positives**). You want this number to be as close as possible to 0.0. These numbers are reported for each of the features introduced in each stage.

Our simple example took only few seconds. The structure of the classifier produced is described in an XML file that results from the training phase. The classifier is then ready to be used! You can submit any sample to it and it will tell you if it thinks that it is a positive or a negative one.

In our example, we trained our classifier with 24×24 images but in general, what you want is to find out if there are any instances of your class of objects somewhere in an image (of any size). To achieve this objective, you simply have to scan the input image and extract all possible windows of the sample size. If your classifier is accurate enough, only the windows that contain the seek objects will return a positive detection. But this works as long as the visible positive samples have the appropriate size. To detect instances at multiple scales, you then have to build a pyramid of images by reducing the size of the original image by a certain factor at each level of the pyramid. This way, bigger objects will eventually fit the trained sample size as we go down the pyramid. This is a long process, but the good news is that OpenCV provides a class that implements this process. Its use is pretty straightforward. First you construct the classifier by loading the appropriate XML file:

```
cv::CascadeClassifier cascade;
if (!cascade.load("stopSamples/classifier/cascade.xml")) {
  std::cout << "Error when loading the cascade classfier!"
          << std::endl;
  return -1;
}
```

Then, you call the detection method with an input image:

```
cascade.detectMultiScale(inputImage, // input image
    detections,              // detection results
    1.1,                     // scale reduction factor
    2,                       // number of required neighbor detections
    0,                       // flags (not used)
    cv::Size(48, 48),        // minimum object size to be detected
    cv::Size(128, 128));     // maximum object size to be detected
```

The result is provided as a vector of cv::Rect instances. To visualize the detection results, you just have to draw these rectangles on your input image:

```
for (int i = 0; i < detections.size(); i++)
  cv::rectangle(inputImage, detections[i],
            cv::Scalar(255, 255, 255), 2);
```

When our classifier is tested on an image, here is the result we obtained:

How it works...

In the previous section we explained how it is possible to build an OpenCV cascade of classifiers using positive and negative samples of a class of objects. We will now overview the basic steps of the learning algorithm used to train this cascade. Our cascade has been trained using the Haar features that were described in the introductory section of this recipe but, as we will see, any other simple feature can be used to build a boosted cascade. As the theory and principles of boosted learning are pretty complex, we will not cover all aspects in this recipe; interested readers should refer to the articles listed in the last section.

Let's first restate that there are two core ideas behind the cascade of boosted classifiers. The first one is that a strong classifier can be built by combining together several weak classifiers (that is, those based on simple features). Secondly, because in machine vision, negative instances are found much more frequently than the positive ones, effective classification can be performed in stages. The early stages make quick rejection of obvious negative instances, and more refined decisions can be made at later stages for more difficult samples. Based on these two ideas, we now describe the boosted cascade learning algorithm. Our explanations are based on the variant of boosting called **AdaBoost,** which is the one most often used. Our description will also allow us to explain some of the parameters used in the `opencv_traincascade` tool.

In this recipe, we use the Haar features in order to build our weak classifier. When one Haar feature is applied (of given type, size, and location), a value is obtained. A simple classifier is then obtained by finding the threshold value that would best classify the negative and positive class instances based on this feature value. To find this optimal threshold, we have at our disposal, a number of positive and negative samples (the number of positive and negative samples to be used at this step by `opencv_traincascade` is given by the – `numPos` and `–numNeg` parameters). Since we have a large number of possible Haar features, we examine all of them and select the one that best classifies our sample set. Obviously, this very basic classifier will make errors (that is, misclassify several samples); this is why we need to build several of these classifiers. These classifiers are added iteratively, each time searching for the new Haar feature giving the best classification. But since, at each iteration, we want to focus on the samples that are currently misclassified, the classification performance is measured by giving a higher weight to the misclassified samples. A set of simple classifiers is thus obtained and a strong classifier is then built from a weighted sum of these weak classifiers (classifiers with better performance being given a higher weight). Following this approach, a strong classifier with good performance can be obtained by combining a few hundred simple features.

But in order to build a cascade of classifiers in which early rejection is a central mechanism, we do not want a strong classifier made of a large number of weak classifiers. Instead, we need to find very small classifiers that will use only a handful of Haar features in order to quickly reject the obvious negative samples while keeping all positive ones. In its classical form, AdaBoost aims at minimizing the total classification error by counting the number of false negatives (a positive sample classified as a negative one) and false positives (a negative sample classified as a positive one). In the present case, we need to have most, if not all, the positive samples correctly classified while minimizing the false positive rate. Fortunately, it is possible to modify AdaBoost such that true positives are rewarded more strongly. Consequently, when training each stage of a cascade, two criteria must be set: the minimum hit rate and the maximum false alarm rate; in `opencv_traincascade` these are specified using the `-minHitRate` (`0.995` default value) and `-maxFalseAlarmRate` (`0.5` default value) parameters. Haar features are added to the stage until the two performance criteria are met. The minimum hit rate must be set pretty high to make sure the positive instances will go through the next stage; remember that if a positive instance is rejected by a stage, then this error cannot be recovered. Therefore, to facilitate the generation of a classifier of low complexity, you should set the maximum false alarm rate relatively high. Otherwise, your stage will need many Haar features in order to meet the performance criteria, which contradicts the idea of early rejection by simple and quick to compute classifier stages.

A good cascade will therefore be made of early stages with few features, the number of features per stage growing as you go up the cascade. In `opencv_traincascade`, the maximum number of features per stage is set using the `-maxWeakCount` (default is `100`) parameter and the number of stages is set using `-numStages` (default is `20`).

When the training of a new stage starts, then new negative samples must be collected. These are extracted from the provided background images. The difficulty here is to find negative samples that pass through all previous stages (that is, that are wrongly classified as positives). The more stages you have trained, the more difficult it will be to collect these negative samples. This is why it is important to provide the classifier with a large variety of background images. It will then be able to extract patches from these that are difficult to classify (because they resemble the positive samples). Note also that if at a given stage, the two performance criteria are met without adding any new features, then the cascade training is stopped at this point (you can use it as is, or re-train it by providing more difficult samples). Reciprocally, if the stage is unable to meet the performance criteria, the training will also be stopped; in this case you should retry a new training with easier performance criteria.

With a cascade made of n stages, it can easily be shown that the global performance of the classifier will be at least better than $minHitRate^n$ and $maxFalseAlarmRate^n$. This is the result of each stage being built on top of the results of the previous cascade of stages. For example, if we consider the default values of $opencv\_traincascade$, we expect our classifier to have an accuracy (hit rate) of 0.995^{20} and a false alarm rate of 0.5^{20}. This means that 90% of the positive instances will be correctly identified and 0.001% of negative samples will be wrongly classified as positive. Note that an important consequence of the fact that a fraction of the positive samples will be lost as we go up the cascade is that you always have to provide more positive samples than the specified number of samples to use in each stage. In the numerical example we just gave, we need $numPos$ to be set at 90% of the number of available positive samples.

One important question is how many samples should be used for training? This is difficult to answer but, obviously, your positive sample set must be large enough to cover a wide range of possible appearances of your class instances. Your background images should also be relevant. In the case of our stop sign detector, we included urban images as stop sign are expected to be seen in that context. A usual rule of thumb is to have $numNeg= 2*numPos$, but this has be validated on your own dataset.

Finally, we explained in this recipe how to build a cascade of classifiers using Haar features. Such features can also be built using other features such as the Local Binary Patterns discussed in the previous recipes or the histograms of oriented gradient that will be presented in the next recipe. The $opencv\_traincascade$ has a $-featureType$ parameter allowing selection of different feature types.

There's more...

The OpenCV library proposes a number of pre-trained cascades that you can use to detect faces, facial features, people, and other things. You will find these cascades in the form of XML files in the data directory of the library source directory.

Face detection with a Haar cascade

The pre-trained models are ready to be used. All you have to do is to create an instance of the `cv::CascadeClassifier` class using the appropriate XML file:

```
cv::CascadeClassifier faceCascade;
if (!faceCascade.load("haarcascade_frontalface_default.xml")) {
  std::cout << "Error when loading the face cascade classfier!"
          << std::endl;
  return -1;
}
```

Then to detect faces with Haar features, you proceed this way:

```
faceCascade.detectMultiScale(picture, // input image
        detections,              // detection results
        1.1,                     // scale reduction factor
        3,                       // number of required neighbor detections
        0,                       // flags (not used)
        cv::Size(48, 48),        // minimum object size to be detected
        cv::Size(128, 128));     // maximum object size to be detected
// draw detections on image
for (int i = 0; i < detections.size(); i++)
  cv::rectangle(picture, detections[i],
          cv::Scalar(255, 255, 255), 2);
```

The same process can be repeated for an eye detector, and the following image is obtained:

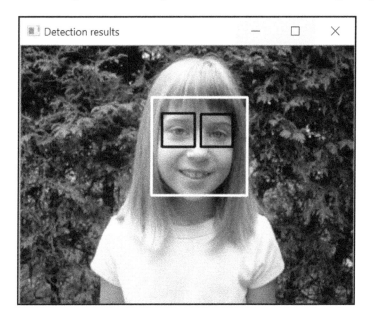

See also

- The *Describing and matching local intensity patterns* recipe in `Chapter 9`, *Describing and Matching Interest Points,* described the SURF descriptor which also uses Haar-like features

- The article *Rapid object detection using a boosted cascade of simple features* by *P. Viola* and *M. Jones* in *Computer Vision and Pattern Recognition* conference, 2001, is the classical paper that describes the cascade of boosted classifiers and the Haar features

- The article *A short introduction to boosting* by *Y. Freund* and *R.E. Schapire* in *Journal of Japanese Society for Artificial Intelligence,* 1999 describes the theoretical foundations of boosting

- The article *Filtered Channel Features for Pedestrian Detection* by *S. Zhang, R. Benenson* and *B. Schiele* in *IEEE Conference on Computer Vision and Pattern Recognition,* 2015 presents features similar to Haar and that can produce highly accurate detections

Detecting objects and people with Support Vector Machines and histograms of oriented gradients

This recipe presents another machine learning method, the **Support Vector Machines (SVM)**, which can produce accurate 2-class classifiers from training data. They have been largely used to solve many computer vision problems. This time, classification is solved by using a mathematical formulation that looks at the geometry of the problem in high-dimension spaces.

In addition, we will also present a new image representation that is often used in conjunction with SVMs to produce robust object detectors.

Getting ready

Images of objects are mainly characterized by their shape and textural content. This is the aspect that is captured by the **Histogram of Oriented Gradients** (**HOG**) representation. As its name indicates, this representation is based on building histograms from image gradients. In particular, because we are more interested by shapes and textures, it is the distribution of the gradient orientations that is analyzed. In addition, in order to take into consideration the spatial distribution of these gradients, multiple histograms are computed over a grid that divides the image into regions.

The first step in building a HOG representation is therefore to compute the gradient of an image. The image is then subdivided into small cells (for example, 8×8 pixels) and histograms of gradient orientations are built for each of these cells. The range of possible orientations must therefore be divided into bins. Most often, only the gradient orientations are considered but not their directions (these are called unsigned gradients). In this case, the range of possible orientations is from 0 to 180 degrees. A 9-bin histogram in this case would divide the possible orientations into intervals of 20 degrees. Each gradient vector in a cell contributes to a bin with a weight corresponding to the magnitude of this gradient.

The cells are then grouped into blocks. A block is then made of a certain number of cells. These blocks that cover the image can overlap each other (that is, they can share cells). For example, in the case where blocks are made of 2×2 cells, a new block can be defined every one cell; this would represent a block stride of 1 cell and each cell (except the last one in a row) would then contribute to 2 blocks. Conversely, with a block stride of 2 cells, the blocks would not overlap at all. A block contains a certain number of cell histograms (for example, 4 in the case of a block made of 2×2 cells). These histograms are simply concatenated together to form a long vector (for example, 4 histograms of 9 bins each then produce a vector of length 36). To make the representation invariant to changes in contrast, this vector is then normalized (for example, each element is divided by the magnitude of the vector). Finally you also concatenate together all the vectors associated with all blocks of the image (row order) into a very large one (for example, in a 64×64 image, you will have a total of seven 16×16 blocks when a stride of 1 is applied on cells of size 8×8; this represents a final vector of 49x36 = 1764 dimensions). This long vector is the HOG representation of the image.

As you can see, the HOG of an image leads to a vector of very high dimension (see the *There's more...* section of this recipe that proposes a way to visualize a HOG representation). This vector characterizes the image and can then be used to classify images of different classes of objects. To achieve this goal, we therefore need a machine learning method that can handle vectors of very high dimension.

How to do it...

In this recipe, we will build another stop sign classifier. This is obviously just a toy example that serves to illustrate the learning procedure. As we explained in the previous recipe, the first step is to collect samples for training. In our example, the set of positive samples that we will be using is the following:

And our (very small) set of negative samples is as follows:

We will now learn how to differentiate these two classes using SVM as implemented in the `cv::svm` class. To build a robust classifier, we will represent our class instances using HOG as described in the introductory section of this recipe. More precisely, we will use 8×8 blocks made of 2×2 cells with a block stride of 1 cell:

```
cv::HOGDescriptor hogDesc(positive.size(), // size of the window
                   cv::Size(8, 8),   // block size
                   cv::Size(4, 4),   // block stride
                   cv::Size(4, 4),   // cell size
                   9);               // number of bins
```

With 9-bin histograms and 64×64 samples, this configuration produces HOG vectors (made of 225 blocks) of size 8100. We compute this descriptor for each of our samples and transfer them into a single matrix (one HOG per row):

```
// compute first descriptor
std::vector<float> desc;
hogDesc.compute(positives[0], desc);

// the matrix of sample descriptors
int featureSize = desc.size();
int numberOfSamples = positives.size() + negatives.size();

// create the matrix that will contain the samples HOG
cv::Mat samples(numberOfSamples, featureSize, CV_32FC1);
// fill first row with first descriptor
for (int i = 0; i < featureSize; i++)
  samples.ptr<float>(0)[i] = desc[i];

// compute descriptor of the positive samples
for (int j = 1; j < positives.size(); j++) {
  hogDesc.compute(positives[j], desc);
  // fill the next row with current descriptor
  for (int i = 0; i < featureSize; i++)
    samples.ptr<float>(j)[i] = desc[i];
}
// compute descriptor of the negative samples
for (int j = 0; j < negatives.size(); j++) {
  hogDesc.compute(negatives[j], desc);
  // fill the next row with current descriptor
  for (int i = 0; i < featureSize; i++)
    samples.ptr<float>(j + positives.size())[i] = desc[i];
}
```

Note how we computed the first HOG in order to obtain the size of the descriptor and then created the matrix of descriptors. A second matrix is then created to contain the labels associated to each sample. In our case, the first rows are the positive samples (and must be assigned a label of 1), the reminder rows are the negative samples (labeled −1):

```
// Create the labels
cv::Mat labels(numberOfSamples, 1, CV_32SC1);
// labels of positive samples
labels.rowRange(0, positives.size()) = 1.0;
// labels of negative samples
labels.rowRange(positives.size(), numberOfSamples) = -1.0;
```

The next step is to build the SVM classifier that will be used for training; we also select the type of SVM and the kernel to be used (these parameters will be discussed in the next section):

```
// create SVM classifier
cv::Ptr<cv::ml::SVM> svm = cv::ml::SVM::create();
svm->setType(cv::ml::SVM::C_SVC);
svm->setKernel(cv::ml::SVM::LINEAR);
```

We are now ready for training. The labeled samples are first provided to the classifier and the train method is called:

```
// prepare the training data
cv::Ptr<cv::ml::TrainData> trainingData =
    cv::ml::TrainData::create(samples,
                    cv::ml::SampleTypes::ROW_SAMPLE, labels);
// SVM training
svm->train(trainingData);
```

Once the training phase completes, any sample of unknown class can be submitted to the classifier, which will try to predict the class to which it belongs (here we test four samples):

```
cv::Mat queries(4, featureSize, CV_32FC1);

// fill the rows with query descriptors
hogDesc.compute(cv::imread("stop08.png",
                    cv::IMREAD_GRAYSCALE), desc);
for (int i = 0; i < featureSize; i++)
  queries.ptr<float>(0)[i] = desc[i];
hogDesc.compute(cv::imread("stop09.png",
                    cv::IMREAD_GRAYSCALE), desc);
for (int i = 0; i < featureSize; i++)
  queries.ptr<float>(1)[i] = desc[i];
hogDesc.compute(cv::imread("neg08.png",
                    cv::IMREAD_GRAYSCALE), desc);
```

```
    for (int i = 0; i < featureSize; i++)
      queries.ptr<float>(2)[i] = desc[i];
    hogDesc.compute(cv::imread("neg09.png",
                         cv::IMREAD_GRAYSCALE), desc);
    for (int i = 0; i < featureSize; i++)
      queries.ptr<float>(3)[i] = desc[i];
    cv::Mat predictions;

    // Test the classifier
    svm->predict(queries, predictions);
    for (int i = 0; i < 4; i++)
      std::cout << "query: " << i << ": " <<
             ((predictions.at<float>(i,) < 0.0)?
                "Negative" : "Positive") << std::endl;
```

If the classifier has been trained with representative samples, then it should be able to correctly predict the label of a new instance.

How it works...

In our stop sign recognition example, each instance of our class is represented by a point in an 8100-dimensional HOG space. It is obviously impossible to visualize such a large space but the idea behind support vector machines is to trace a boundary in that space that will segregate points that belongs to one class from points belonging to the other class. More specifically, this boundary will in fact be just a simple hyperplane. This idea is better explained considering a 2D space where each instance is represented as a 2D point. The hyperplane is, in this case, a simple line.

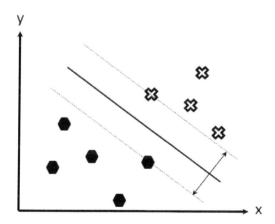

This is obviously a trivial example but, conceptually, working in a two-dimensional space or in a 8100-dimensional space is the same thing. The preceding figure shows then, how a simple line can separate the points of the two classes well. In the case illustrated here, it can also be seen that many other lines could also achieve this perfect class separation. One question is therefore; which exact line one should choose. To answer this question, you must first realize that the samples we used to build our classifier constitute just a small snapshot of all possible instances that will need to be classified when the classifier is used in a target application. This means that we would like our classifier, not only to be able to correctly separate the provided sample sets but we also would like this one to make the best decision on the future instances shown to it. This concept is often referred to as the **generalization** power of a classifier. Intuitively, it would be reasonable to believe that our separating hyperplane should be located in between the two classes, not closer to one class than the other. More formally, SVMs propose setting the hyperplane at a position that maximizes the margin around the defined boundary. This **margin** is defined as the minimum distance between the separating hyperplane and the closest point in the positive sample set plus the distance between the hyperplane and the closest negative sample. The closest points (the ones that define the margin) are called the **support vectors**. The mathematics behind SVM defines an optimization function aiming at identifying these support vectors.

But the proposed solution to the classification problem cannot be that simple. What happens if the distribution of the sample points is as follows?

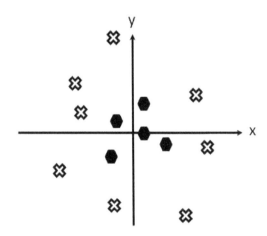

In this case, a simple hyperplane (a line here) cannot achieve a proper separation. SVM solves this problem by introducing artificial variables that bring the problem into a higher dimensional space through some non-linear transformations. For example, in the example above, one might propose to add the distance to the origin as an additional variable, that is to compute $r = sqrt(x^2+y^2)$ for each point. We now have a three-dimensional space; for simplicity, let's just draw the points on the (r,x) plane:

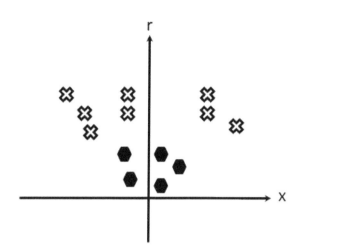

As you can see, our set of sample points can now be separated by a simple hyperplane. This implies that you now have to find the support vectors in this new space. In fact, in the SVM formulation, you do not have to bring all the points into that new space, you just have to define a way to measure point-to-hyperplane distance in that augmented space. SVM therefore defines **kernel functions** that allow you to measure this distance in higher space without having to explicitly compute the point coordinates in that space. This is just a mathematical trick that explains why support vectors producing the maximal margin can be efficiently computed in very high (artificial) dimensional space. This also explains why, when you want to use support vector machines, you need to specify which kernel you want to use. This is by applying these kernels that you will make non-linearly separable to become separable in the kernel space.

One important remark here however. Since with Support Vector Machines we often work with features of very high dimension (for example, `8100` dimension in our HOG example), then it may very well happen that our samples will be separable with a simple hyperplane. This is why it still make sense to not use non-linear kernels (or more precisely to use a linear kernel, that is, `cv::ml::SVM::LINEAR`) and work in the original feature space. The resulting classifier will then be computationally simpler. But for more challenging classification problems, kernels remain a very effective tool. OpenCV offers you a number of standard kernels (for example, radial basis functions, sigmoid functions, and so on); the objective of these is to send the samples into a larger non-linear space that will make the classes separable by a hyperplane. SVM has a number of variants; the most common is the C-SVM, which adds a penalty for each outlier sample that does not lie on the right side of the hyperplane.

Finally, we insist on the fact that, because of their strong mathematical foundations, SVMs work very well with features of very high dimension. In fact, they have been shown to operate best when the number of dimensions of the feature space is larger than the number of samples. They are also memory efficient, as they just have to store the support vectors (in contrast to a method like nearest-neighbor that requires keeping in memory all sample points).

There's more...

Histograms of oriented gradients and SVM form a good combination for the construction of good classifiers. One of the reasons for this success is the fact that HOG can be viewed as a robust high-dimensional descriptor that captures the essential aspects of an object class. HOG-SVM classifiers have been used successfully in many applications; pedestrian detection is one of them.

Finally, since this is the last recipe of this book, we will therefore end it with a perspective on a recent trend in machine learning that is revolutionizing computer vision and artificial intelligence.

HOG visualization

HOGs are built from cells combined in overlapping blocks. It is therefore difficult to visualize this descriptor. Nevertheless, they are often represented by displaying the histograms associated to each cell. In this case, instead of aligning the orientation bins in a regular bar graph, a histogram of orientation can be more intuitively drawn in a star-shape where each line has the orientation associated to the bin it represents and the length of the line is proportional to that bin count. These HOGs representations can then be displayed over an image:

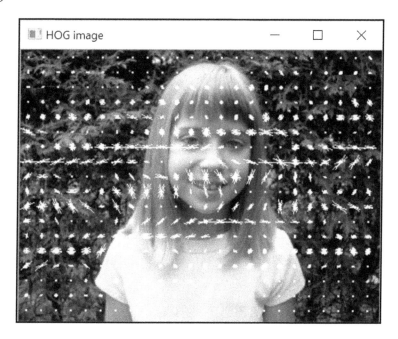

Each cell HOG representation can be produced by a simple function that accepts an iterator pointing to a histogram. Lines of proper orientation and length are then drawn for each bin:

```
//draw one HOG over one cell
void drawHOG(std::vector<float>::const_iterator hog,
                        // iterator to the HOG
             int numberOfBins,        // number of bins inHOG
             cv::Mat &image,          // image of the cell
             float scale=1.0) {       // length multiplier

    const float PI = 3.1415927;
    float binStep = PI / numberOfBins;
    float maxLength = image.rows;
```

```
float cx = image.cols / 2.;
float cy = image.rows / 2.;

// for each bin
for (int bin = 0; bin < numberOfBins; bin++) {

  // bin orientation
  float angle = bin*binStep;
  float dirX = cos(angle);
  float dirY = sin(angle);
  // length of line proportion to bin size
  float length = 0.5*maxLength* *(hog+bin);

  // drawing the line
  float x1 = cx - dirX * length * scale;
  float y1 = cy - dirY * length * scale;
  float x2 = cx + dirX * length * scale;
  float y2 = cy + dirY * length * scale;
  cv::line(image, cv::Point(x1, y1), cv::Point(x2, y2),
           CV_RGB(255, 255, 255), 1);
  }
}
```

A HOG visualization function will then call this preceding function for each cell:

```
// Draw HOG over an image
void drawHOGDescriptors(const cv::Mat &image,  // the input image
       cv::Mat &hogImage, // the resulting HOG image
       cv::Size cellSize, // size of each cell (blocks are ignored)
       int nBins) {       // number of bins

  // block size is image size
  cv::HOGDescriptor hog(
       cv::Size((image.cols / cellSize.width) * cellSize.width,
              (image.rows / cellSize.height) * cellSize.height),
       cv::Size((image.cols / cellSize.width) * cellSize.width,
              (image.rows / cellSize.height) * cellSize.height),
       cellSize,     // block stride (ony 1 block here)
       cellSize,     // cell size
       nBins);       // number of bins
  //compute HOG
  std::vector<float> descriptors;
  hog.compute(image, descriptors);
  ...
  float scale= 2.0 / *
              std::max_element(descriptors.begin(),descriptors.end());
  hogImage.create(image.rows, image.cols, CV_8U);
  std::vector<float>::const_iterator itDesc= descriptors.begin();
```

```
for (int i = 0; i < image.rows / cellSize.height; i++) {
  for (int j = 0; j < image.cols / cellSize.width; j++) {
    //draw each cell
      hogImage(cv::Rect(j*cellSize.width, i*cellSize.height,
                cellSize.width, cellSize.height));
     drawHOG(itDesc, nBins,
             hogImage(cv::Rect(j*cellSize.width,
                               i*cellSize.height,
                               cellSize.width, cellSize.height)),
             scale);
     itDesc += nBins;
  }
 }
}
```

This function computes a HOG descriptor having the specified cell size but made of only one large block (that is, a block having the size of the image). This representation therefore ignores the effect of normalization that occurs at each block level.

People detection

OpenCV offers a pre-trained people detector based on HOG and SVM. As for the classifier cascades of the previous recipe, this SVM classifier can be used to detect instances in a full image by scanning a window across the image, at multiple scales. You then just have to construct the classifier and perform the detection on an image:

```
// create the detector
std::vector<cv::Rect> peoples;
cv::HOGDescriptor peopleHog;
peopleHog.setSVMDetector(
cv::HOGDescriptor::getDefaultPeopleDetector());
// detect peoples oin an image
peopleHog.detectMultiScale(myImage, // input image
        peoples,            // ouput list of bounding boxes
        0,         // threshold to consider a detection to be positive
        cv::Size(4, 4),    // window stride
        cv::Size(32, 32),  // image padding
        1.1,               // scale factor
        2);                // grouping threshold
```

The window stride defines how the 128×64 template is moved over the image (every 4 pixels horizontally and vertically in our example). Longer strides make the detection faster (because less windows are evaluated) but you may then miss some people falling in between tested windows. The image padding parameter simply adds pixels on the border of the image such that people at the edge of the image can be detected. The standard threshold for an SVM classifier is 0 (since 1 is the value assigned to positive instances and −1 to the negative ones). But if you really want to be certain that what you detect is a person, then you can raise this threshold value (this means that you want **high precision** at the price of missing some people in the image). Reciprocally, if you want to be certain of detecting all people (that is you want a **high recall** rate), then you can lower the threshold; more false detections will occur in that case.

Here is an example of the detection results obtained:

It is important to note that when a classifier is applied to a full image, the multiple windows applied at successive locations will often lead to multiple detections around a positive sample. The best thing to do when two or more bounding boxes overlap at about the same location is to retain only one of them. There is a function called `cv::groupRectangles` that simply combines rectangles of similar size at similar locations (this function is automatically called by `detectMultiScale`). In fact, obtaining a group of detections at a particular location can even be seen as an indicator confirming that we indeed have a positive instance at this location. This is why the `cv::groupRectangles` function allows us to specify the minimum size for a detection cluster to be accepted as a positive detection (that is, isolated detection should be discarded). This is the last parameter of the `detectMultiScale` method. Setting this one at `0` will keep all detections (no grouping done) which, in our example, leads to the following result:

Deep learning and Convolutional Neural Networks

We cannot conclude this chapter on machine learning without mentioning deep convolutional neural networks. The application of these to computer vision classification problems has led to impressive results. In fact, their outstanding performance when applied to real-world problems is such that they now open the door to a new family of applications that could not be envisioned before.

Deep learning is based on the theory of neural networks that was introduced in the late 1950s. So why are they generating such great interest today? Basically for two reasons: first, the computational power that is available nowadays allows deploying neural networks of a size that makes them able to solve challenging problems. While the first neural network (the perceptron) has only one layer and few weight parameters to tune, today's networks can have hundreds of layers and millions of parameters to be optimized (hence the name deep networks). Second, the large amount of data available today makes their training possible. In order to perform well, deep networks, indeed, required thousands, if not millions, of annotated samples (this is required because of the very large number of parameters that need to be optimized).

The most popular deep networks are the **Convolutional Neural Networks** (**CNN**). As the name suggests, they are based on convolution operations (see `Chapter 6`, *Filtering the Images*). The parameters to learn, in this case, are therefore the values inside the kernel of all filters that compose the network. These filters are organized into layers, in which the early layers extract the fundamental shapes such as lines and corners while the higher layers progressively detect more complex patterns (such as, for example, the presence of eyes, mouth, hair, in a human detector).

OpenCV3 has a **Deep Neural Network** module, but this one is mainly for importing deep networks trained using other tools such as TensorFlow, Caffe, or Torch. When building your future computer vision applications, you will certainly have to have a look at the deep learning theory and its related tools.

See also

- The *Describing and matching local intensity patterns* recipe in `Chapter 9`, *Describing and Matching Interest Points*, described the SIFT descriptor which is similar to the HOG descriptor
- The article *Histograms of Oriented Gradients for Human Detection* by N. Dalal and B. Triggs in *Computer Vision and Pattern Recognition* conference, 2005 is the classical paper that introduces histograms of oriented gradients for people detection
- The article *Deep Learning* by Y. LeCun, Y. Bengio and G. Hinton in *Nature, no 521*, 2015, is a good starting point for exploring the world of deep learning

Index